The Right to Speak

The Right to Speak
Working with the Voice

PATSY RODENBURG

with a Foreword
by Ian McKellen

Methuen Drama

To John Roberts
for his love, constancy and clarity
and to the memory of
Edith Winifred Moody,
my Nanna and very own storyteller

First published in Great Britain in 1992
in simultaneous hardback and paperback editions
by Methuen Drama, Michelin House,
81 Fulham Road, London SW3 6RB
and distributed in the United States of America
by HEB Inc, 361 Hanover Street,
Portsmouth, New Hampshire, NH 03801 3959

Copyright © 1992 by Patsy Rodenburg

The author has asserted her moral rights

Foreword copyright © 1992 by Ian McKellen

The poem *Everyone Sang* on p. 111
is reprinted by kind permission
of the Estate of Siegfried Sassoon

A CIP catalogue record for this book
is available from the British Library
ISBN 0 413 66140 7 (hardback)
ISBN 0 413 66130 X (paperback)

Typeset in Linotron Plantin
by Hewer Text Composition Services, Edinburgh
Printed in Great Britain
by Clays Ltd, St Ives plc

Contents

Foreword

Growing up in the North of England in the 1940s, we had no television. Our family enjoyed going out to the theatre but most of our entertainment came along the airwaves, through the bakelite wireless set which dominated the lounge. One of my favourites, although I didn't get the absurdity of it, was the ventriloquist Peter Brough, whose invisible lips never moved on radio. Prime Minister Churchill enthralled the nation with his wartime broadcasts and each year we dutifully tuned in for the monarch's Christmas speech to the nation. King George VI stammered and dreaded the ordeal. Lesser public figures were recognised by their voices rather than by their faces and when we did see them in the flesh, acting, singing or on the hustings at election time, entertainers and politicians rarely used microphones. In musicals, singers projected to the back of the gods, unaided by amplification.

These days, every singer (grand opera excepted) has a mike hidden in his hairline and a transmitter taped to the small of the back. That's because modern audiences expect to hear in the theatre the same balance between soloist and loud orchestrations that they get from their record-players. This has led some performers to the ultimate deception, miming in the theatre to a pre-recorded tape. Others, more robust, like Liza Minnelli and Tony Bennett, now introduce at least one song with the mike turned off. How their audiences love their bravado.

Amplification is everywhere – in churches, lecture theatres, trains, tour buses and in Parliament. The call-boy and page-boy have been made redundant by the Tannoy and the Palm

Court Trio sacked by Muzak. In politics, the change has been for the worse. The thrill of the open-air orator and the wit of the hecklers have given way to the television photo opportunity. Rhetoric has been drowned out by the sound bite: public relations instead of public speaking.

It is not all loss. A television close-up, particularly if it contains his nervous fingers, can be wonderfully revealing of a politician's performance. And, even on the box, the voice remains pre-eminent. Think of Ronald Reagan's confiding whisper or Margaret Thatcher's wider range through harangue to smarm. Any impressionist will tell you – get the voice right and the audience will recognise your victim. Isn't it odd how easy it is to be confused by an acquaintance's new hairdo and yet how invariably we can identify even a disguised voice on the telephone?

So perhaps it shouldn't surprise us that politicians, clerics, rock singers as well as actors queue up to train their voices under the supervision of Patsy Rodenburg. This book will explain her popularity amongst her pupils.

I know very little of her practical work because, although we meet often in the National Theatre corridors, only a couple of times have we worked together in the rehearsal room. That's been enough to realise that her expertise as a teacher lies in her unstoppable enthusiasm. As she coaxes the class to lie down, to relax, to feel and to think, she never seems to stop talking: 'There, did you feel the difference? Are you sure? Try it again. Or what about this way.' It's appropriate that her book is written in the rhythms of her urgent speaking voice and that you can detect Patsy's individual intonation in its conversational style. That should make it a great deal easier to use as a teaching aid than books by those theoreticians whose written instructions are impenetrably difficult to follow.

Back in Lancashire as a child, I spoke with a flat northern voice – two voices, actually – a broad, aggressive accent for school and the playground and a milder, more yielding tone at home. My would-be posher schoolmates went to 'Elocution'

viii   *The Right to Speak*

to have their native sounds taken out like the tonsils. Similar violations were perpetrated in drama schools of the time. At Cambridge, undergraduates from public school mocked my northern vowels and I taught myself to disguise them. But not entirely; and I now belong to that first generation of British actors who have been allowed to bring regional accents back to the classical drama.

In the professional theatre, I have been crucially helped by four voice teachers. Why they should all have been women was a mystery until I read this book. Its title is born of a feminist determination to realise a person's individuality. Instead of lecturing you on how to sound like everybody else and thereby keep your place, Patsy Rodenburg wants to free your voice so that you can express yourself fully and honestly in public. She'd be the first to agree that in the end what matters is what we say rather than how we say it. Her revelation is that, at best, the sounds, like the sense, can respond to the heart of our inner selves.

Ian McKellen
9 January 1992

Ian McKellen
London 1992

Introduction

Voice work is for everybody.

We all breathe and the vast majority of us speak. All of us would like to improve the sound of our voice and the way we speak. Doing voice and speech work can be, I think, as energising and liberating as any other kind of physical exercise. There is no mystique about it. It is powerful and also very simple. Easy exercises done for a few minutes a day can radically improve any speaker's voice within a matter of days and weeks.

Having said all that I have always found that most books on voice and speaking have been aimed at a narrow audience of actors, singers and public speakers who already have undergone some kind of initiation into the work. Many, too, thrust the reader immediately into the process through exercises without ever taking the time to explain why any of us need the work in the first place. Some books on voice also seem to me to be terribly clinical and strain too hard to be like medical texts. These are useful for practitioners and teachers but harder for the general reader. When my own students use them I always notice how they invariably get lost or lose interest.

The Right to Speak is meant to appeal both to the professional speaker and to anyone who breathes and communicates sound to the world. In it I have tried to simplify a process without being simplistic. I want you to understand the work and enjoy it without being put off it somewhere in the midst of the process. Mostly I want you to read the book from start to finish so you can discover how one thing connects to another.

What I have tried to do is concentrate on all the areas I focus on when I teach students in a two-year acting programme or work with professionals on a daily basis. There is a whole separate area that deals with language and text work which I have not included here but which will follow soon in a companion volume. At this point I only want to concentrate on the voice and how to work with it.

Throughout this book I refer a great deal to actors and singers because a large portion of my work centres on their needs. My experience is a result of their experiences. As a group they are useful models for all the voice and speech habits, constrictions and troubles that plague each of us. They use their voices so abundantly and regularly that every imaginable problem that any of us is likely to encounter bubbles to the surface in search of a cure. So for the average daily speaker they can be used as admirable models of how to work on your own voice.

This book not only gives basic exercises to physically work and improve the voice but explores primarily what I feel are the crucial factors that create problems in the first place. Time and again I have found that the wonders and colours of the natural voice are hidden beneath habits. We settle into habitual voices that can become ours forever. The single task I have set myself here is to release you from those habits.

When our breath, voice, speech and communication skills are effortless and free, we forget all about them and become blissfully liberated as we utter any sound or word. Too many of us speak frozen in fear, consumed by doubt about our vocal abilities and apparatus. We tend to blame and castigate ourselves rather than learn some useful, tested ways of exploring our voices and oiling our vocal mechanisms.

As we open our mouths to let sound and words pour forth, we frequently reveal the deepest parts of ourselves. Not only do we divulge class, background and education but also our perceived status in the world, our fears, our denials and in some crucial instances our very souls. No wonder it can be such a terrifying act to speak. No wonder it is a right attacked and repressed by those who think they are more powerful or articulate or have the right to control how and what we have to say.

'The right to speak' is a right we all have. The vast majority of us already possess superb vocal and speech instruments which we can wield better in order to assert that right. Our fundamental ease and enjoyment of conversation and making ourselves heard indicate that the right is fundamentally within us. All that remains is for us to release and employ the right fully.

At the outset I thought it might be helpful if you knew my own background and experience with voice and speech. Parts of my journey are similar to other people's.

When I was younger, I always thought of speaking as one of the most frightening and revealing of processes. Speaking never came to me naturally.

As a child I had a speech impediment, mumbled and was sent, most reluctantly, to speech classes in order to 'improve'. When I read out aloud in class I was so hesitant and incoherent that teachers eventually stopped asking me to contribute. And yet I loved reading. I especially loved poetry and language. At the age of nine I discovered Shakespeare and Coleridge. I fell in love with them both but this passion stayed locked inside me and couldn't find expression in my voice. Until the age of thirteen I would never speak to strangers, although my friends say I have made up for it since.

Maybe I felt myself smothering – unable to breathe, speak or commit – and that feeling is what drove me into voice work; an attempt to fathom the fear and anguish that lay behind my own fear of speaking. Sue Lefton, a dear friend and a brilliant movement teacher, talks in a similar way about a childhood fear of her body.

As a child my voice and speech training was traditional. Bone props stretched my mouth open and I lived in continual fear of swallowing these instruments of torture (there was even a string attached to the prop so it could be yanked out if it inadvertently slipped back into the throat). I recently experimented with one presented to me by a student. As I placed it in my mouth fear instantly gagged me, I travelled back twenty-eight years and broke out into a cold sweat. I instantly spat it out. I have never taught with a bone prop though there are some people who find them very useful aids to clear speech.

I learnt 'rib-reserve breathing' in order to extend my child's breath capacity to ridiculous lengths. This is the breathing you get from holding your ribcage up for unnaturally long periods of time. It can be physically deforming. All I remember was aching from my centre through to my shoulders and up to my ears as I strained to keep the ribcage hoisted.

I was encouraged to speak 'beautifully' (though I never achieved this) without understanding a thing I said. I still have vivid recollections of being detained after school when seven because I hadn't been able to memorise Rupert Brooke's poem 'If I Should Die Think Only This of Me'. I whined to the headmistress, 'But what does it mean?' She replied, 'Just speak it well.'

As I entered young adulthood I acquired a passion for theatre as the most interesting means of exploring life and I then trained as a teacher at London's Central School of Speech and Drama. The course was superb and has produced some of Britain's finest drama and voice teachers. I was finally given wonderful, sensitive and humane voice training by people like Joan Washington, Margo Braund and Helen Winter. I also met and developed a friendship with Gwynneth Thurburn, a legend who taught voice to all the great actors from the 1940s to the late 1960s. At Central we learnt how to understand both the voice and a text; how the voice should serve the writing and not smother it with well-resonating, articulated sound. That was a revelation.

As soon as I started my training I realised I wanted to specialise in voice and text work. I wanted finally to face the fear and reclaim what I have since called the right to speak. My first five years of teaching were spent in seven different schools. I dashed across London and throughout Britain – coaching, working, taking anyone for private classes, begging people to allow me to experiment with their voices, doing anything at all to learn my profession. Some weeks I was teaching voice for sixty hours to actors, singers, students, teachers, prisoners . . . anyone.

Ironically I was teaching mostly under very traditionally trained people who were asking me to teach exactly in the style of my childhood experiences. What I learned to do was to adapt my Central training by adding to it those 'rediscovered', useful aspects of so-called 'classical' voice training. There are, I learned, many enduring notions embedded in a 200-year-old tradition. Sheila Moriarity was most instrumental in getting me to see this.

Eventually I went to work with Cicely Berry at the Royal Shakespeare Company for nine years. No one in voice work today can deny the immense contribution that Cicely Berry has made. Almost single-handedly she has made the work both respectable and exciting for actors, theatre directors, educationalists and students alike. Her vigour and imagination have moved the voice coach from the periphery of the performance process to a place more central. Now all of us who work in companies, releasing actors' voices into the text, can not only help people transform themselves from production to production but also acquire those vocal rights which will change them forever. I thank Cis with much love and respect.

In May of 1990 Richard Eyre, the Director of Britain's Royal National Theatre, asked me to institute a Voice Department there and become its Head. Ever since I have been doing that along with everything else I still do. As I work here and abroad with actors, students and all sorts of speakers I still talk centrally about the same thing: your voice belongs to you, it is your responsibility and right to use it fully.

I will end by thanking a number of people who helped make this book possible. A very special thanks to Michael Earley – an inspiring editor. My gratitude also extends to Trish Baillie, Doris Cadney, David Carey, Ghita Cohen, Garfield Davies, Sabrina Dearborn, Sharon Duckworth, Ron Eyre, Robert and May Freeburn, Jane Gooderham, John Haynes, Elizabeth Himmelstein, John Hirsch (in memory), Ian Horsbrugh, Kelly McEvenue, Norma Miller, Tracey Mitchell, Cordelia Monsey, Caroline Noh, Cecil O'Neal, Kate Parker, Meera Popkin, Margaret and Max Rodenburgh, Robert Sataloff, Christina Shewell, Virginia Snyders, Gwynneth Thurburn and the students at the Guildhall School, past and present.

Patsy Rodenburg
London 1991

Part One
THE RIGHT TO SPEAK

In every cry of every Man,
In every Infant's cry of fear,
In every voice, in every ban,
The mind-forg'd manacles I hear

William Blake
Songs of Experience

1   Declaring Your Vocal Rights

The right to breathe, the right to be physically unashamed, to fully vocalise, to need, choose and make contact with a word, to release a word into space – the right to speak.

Every day I meet people in desperate need of voice and speech work who cannot adopt all, a few or even just one of these essential rights. Some outer or inner tension blocks their ability to communicate successfully. It is almost as if they have been forcibly gagged even though the muffle is an invisible one. The gag is usually one of an assortment of habits that undermine the potential of anyone's voice and speech. All these habits contribute to an acute fear that so many of us have in common: the fear of speaking out in public or even in private.

A recent opinion poll taken in America, asking people what single thing frightens them most, put speaking in public at the top of the list of fears above loneliness, financial worry . . . even death!

I am sure this is true wherever you go with anyone you meet.

My job, as a voice teacher, is to remove that dreaded fear and to hand back to any speaker the fun, joy and ultimately the liberating power that speaking well and forcefully can engender; power sadly taken away from most of us for a variety of reasons that will become abundantly clear as we go on.

So before we can adopt a right to speak – or even begin any practical work on the voice itself – we first have to begin to learn how we lost the right in the first place.

Snap Judgements

As soon as we open our mouths and speak we are judged. Instant assumptions are made about us by others; about our intelligence, our background, class, race, our education, abilities and ultimately our power. As listeners we do this to each other all the time.

What does our voice reveal about us? Quite a bit. Do we sound enfranchised or disenfranchised? Educated or uneducated? Hesitant or confident? Do we sound as if we should be in charge or just subordinate? Do we sound as though we should be heard and answered?

To the ears of others we are what we speak. For any new listener immediately tries to 'place us', instantly decides whether or not we are worth listening to, makes snap judgements about whether or not even to answer us.

I realise this blunt assertion is made most obviously about British society where we are still saddled by a fairly rigid and sharply attuned class system in which the voice immediately places us as upper, middle, lower or, probably worst of all, blandly suburban. But in all other countries in which I have worked, including the United States, Canada, India, Japan and throughout Europe, I have experienced the same brutally judgemental attitude based solely on the reaction to someone's voice and speech habits. Just like a fingerprint a voice-print is an almost infallible form of identification. Our voice marks us in certain ways. And it can mark us for life.

Whenever I work in the American South, for instance, I get telephone calls from businessmen and women who 'want to sound more northern' and not so rural. They believe they will earn more respect with a quick change of vocal identity. One of my students in Texas, with a particularly heavy and noticeable regional accent, was repeatedly mocked and mimicked by his classmates whenever he spoke. He believed he was stupid and took the role of class clown. When I challenged him about this he said: 'But I come from

Birmingham, Alabama, and anyone who talks the way I do has got to be *stupid!*'

A voice teacher in India I once worked with confided how she had to stop her southern Tamil dialect from seeping into her daily speech when speaking the more acceptable Hindi dialect. 'I won't be respected,' she said, 'if they hear that sound.' A famous Japanese film actor lamented to me once that his father's voice betrayed a lowly status. I shall never forget the uproar at a Canadian voice conference I attended in French-speaking Montreal when a Parisian voice coach bluntly asserted that 'no Canadian actor could speak the plays of Racine and Molière because they sounded too coarse.' So we are instantly known to others by our voice and dialect, and we are actually censored from having the right to speak certain things. You may not believe it is true but there is such a thing as 'vocal imperialism'.

It seems to me particularly demeaning and criminal, for instance, to tell anyone that their mother sound or accent is not good enough to speak the great texts. I think it is commonly agreed nowadays that Shakespeare's actors spoke in a variety of regional accents, many of them rough and broad and not the least bit elegant. So why is it that so many American actors, for example, in this day and age still mimic a so-called British voice and accent when they speak Shakespearean verse and prose? It only results in alienating both actor and audience further from the marvels of Shakespeare's text. Solid American accents, good British regional ones, are every bit as expressive as the refined ones we try to impose on any classical text. And the former two work extremely well when the text is given the right to return to its accentual roots.

Some older theatre audiences, however, still gasp in horror during intervals when they react to the way 'modern' actors speak the great dramatic texts in certain of these accents. When I worked with the English Shakespeare Company on their production of *The War of the Roses* many people who saw and heard those plays on a tour around Great Britain objected to the fact that the Northumberland lords spoke in heavy Northumberland accents!

If we are lucky enough to come from a socially advantaged and culturally dominant background, then snap judgements of this sort serve the speaker well. If not . . . well, that is a very different kind of story.

Whose Right Is It Anyway?

Spend some time wandering around the foyers of the Barbican Centre, the London home of the Royal Shakespeare Company, or that of the Royal National Theatre on London's South Bank (where I frequently do my rambling to sample voices) and you hear all around you the same upper class voices boring into your head. They sound demanding, belittling and frankly self-important. But listen carefully. They are actually saying very little, nor are they saying it very well. Only the sound is socially acceptable. Sit in any Mayfair restaurant or have tea in one of the grander London hotels and you can hear the same kind of voices zapping around the space as if all of us ought to be part of the conversation.

To me all these 'cultivated' voices are saying one thing: 'The right to speak is mine and mine alone.' They have overstepped the right and taken it as their prerogative. They were born, educated and live with the right and will not tolerate any voice that is different from theirs. In our society they have hegemony over the sound of us all.

I once happened to be teaching at Eton, one of the most privileged public schools in Britain, and I was stunned by the open vocal release and freedom, by the extravagant range and confidence which the boys used to address me and one another. This was in dire comparison to a comprehensive school in a depressed area of South London where I also taught. Here the voice and speech of students (all the same ages as the boys at Eton) were held, tight and pushed. Discussion was minimal. It was rare. What release and extravagance these less advantaged students had they kept to themselves and never dared to show a teacher. It was all just slightly short of vocal repression.

A whole set of negative assertions are probably being made by these comparisons and opinions. Assumptions that have to do with factors outside the scope of this book like race, culture and social mobility. I will not venture too far in this direction because I am not a sociologist. I teach voice and observe voices in action all day long. But I see and hear an awful lot.

What I have noticed as a teacher does support the notion, however unscientifically posited by me, that environment and social background leave us culturally possessed or dispossessed. The voice we have is a by-product of that background and an expression of it in every way. We are judged when we speak and we are also categorised. The voice, I think, can be likened to one of those 'identikits' that sketch artists use to draw an instant profile of someone. We speak and someone quickly takes our measure and has a picture. Through voice and speech we portray ourselves.

Making Sound *and* Sense

Many of us blithely will listen to a 'high status' sounding speaker, perhaps an eminent cabinet minister or a head of state, uttering complete nonsense and banal clichés but assume he – or she – must be making sense. You can hear it in the confident measured tones of his or her voice. It does sound awfully proper, after all. My, she sounds so good. We the listeners must be at fault for not understanding the nonsensical bits. This quick assumption on our part is based entirely on how the voice *sounds* and not at all on what *sense* is being made by the speaker.

I have found myself in many political discussions with people who vote for the Conservative Party even though that group's policies do not serve their needs. I have heard convictions expressed that simply boil down to: 'Well the

Labour or Liberal candidate doesn't *sound* as though he could govern. The Conservative fellow *sounds* more impressive.' What is usually swaying judgement is sound and fury not sense and issues. We all make choices like this based on something that ephemeral. But how many of us are aware of it?

We are all still haunted by the idea that upper-class accents are 'better'. Many of these so-called better voices are riddled with their own tensions and sound alarmingly unclear if you actually take the time to listen carefully. These voices, like our own, are riddled with tensions that block effective communication. Part of what I want to do in this book, along with helping you to work on your own voice, is also to educate your ear. I want to get you attuned to hearing the habits in your own voice and those of others.

A Quick Look at the Problem

Let's take a quick look at the problem and begin to explore all the forces that can conspire against our right to speak and which prevent us from working on our voices ourselves.

There is little real promise and point in jumping right into working with the voice, or in diagramming its anatomical functions as most books do, until we get to the root of the different kinds of problems so many of us share in common. Instead I shall ease you into the work we will be doing in the parts that follow by making you sensitive to all manner of obstructions that stand in your way. I believe that a lot of straight talk is a sensible place to start our work.

I want to look at how the voice gets blocked, the different kinds of strain and tensions we make our voices suffer and how the voice can be released from all this anxiety and extended in range and colour. Mostly I want you to see for yourself how the conspiracy against your right to speak evolves. How background, gender, injury or illness can all taint the sound we make. Maybe I can explode some of the nagging myths that awe, frighten and sometimes paralyse so many average speakers. You'll notice that among those myths is the daunting spectre of the Voice and Speech Teacher!

My job, as I see it, is to get you past a problem and to hand back to any speaker the fun, joy and ultimate power that each of us should experience though speaking and communicating easily; power sadly robbed from us for a variety of reasons.

Nothing is quite so freeing and enlarging as a liberated voice. So let's begin in a spirit of trust and see if it leads us to freedom. Let's start with a story.

2 'God Doesn't Mind A Bum Note'

I once met a Black American gospel singer on the London leg of a world tour. I imagine she was nearly eighty years old. During her concert I heard the most wonderful and exciting voice: liberated, clear and adventurous. She had the kind of voice any of us would love to possess. Sounds flowed freely from her. How did she do it? After her concert we met and talked.

'How long have you been singing?' I asked.

'Since I was seven,' she replied.

'How many times a week do you sing?'

'Oh, three or four times a day.'

'You mean one day once a week?'

'Oh, no, three or four times a day, *seven* days a week!'

'*Every* week?'

'Yes.'

At this point I began to sweat and stammer.

'Haven't you ever lost your voice or suffered acute strain and fatigue?'

'No.'

'That's amazing,' I said very weakly under my breath.

'Are you saying,' I went on, 'that in all your years of singing you've never had trouble with your voice, never had to see a doctor or throat specialist, never had special voice lessons?'

'Yes.'

'I am so astonished,' I continued, 'because most performers and public speakers, given such a punishing vocal chore, would be in serious trouble by now.'

At this reaction she threw back her head, laughed out loud

and through the hilarity said, 'Oh, my dear, but you see God doesn't mind a bum note!'

Any actor, singer or professional speaker – people who use their voices daily – will immediately see the relevance of this story. Performers particularly have a peculiar – if not down-right obsessive – need to sound right all the time, every time. 'Sounding right' haunts most speakers, not just professionals, and consequently freezes our ability and freedom both vocally and imaginatively. We resist taking our God-given right to speak and vocalise fully because all of us are afraid of sounding 'a bum note'. But like the lady says, if God doesn't mind why should we?

Self-Judgement

My encounter with that Black gospel singer (and my incredu-lous questions to her) stays with me even today because it relates, I have always felt, to any and all speakers: we all harbour a fundamental fear about our voices, we are all racked by severe self-judgements.

That fear is bound up with the way we *think* we sound to others. This self-judgement can and does prevent us from communicating fully to the world. This obstruction is so strong it will often create permanent vocal habits that physically and spiritually constrict our voices. It can actually turn some of us into vocal cripples.

Once coaxed into life these habits, or what I earlier called self-imposed gags, become afflictions that most of us are barely even aware of. They hide and nag us or even become comfortable and benign parts of us. They tend to be more subtle and even subliminal than overt and clinging. They become part of every speech transaction we make. The further we move away from our innate vocal freedom and hide behind habitual obstacles, the wider the gap becomes between us and our right to speak.

Each day I confront people who are handicapped with

self-judgements of all kinds. My task is to help them break what is usually a lifetime of habits or simply one bothersome tendency. Again and again I find myself saying: 'You have the right to speak. You have the right to breathe. Take your time. You have the right to be yourself.' And I always remember the simple straightforward message of that gospel singer: 'Oh, my dear . . . God doesn't mind a bum note!'

I usually deal with the end results of a chain of events and vocal recriminations that cut most of us off from these three rights: speaking, breathing and taking the time to do both. I deal with matters like posture, breath, speech, articulation, use of language, approaches to texts and more. Most of all I deal with voice. And to that end I usually have to confront what the habits of a lifetime have done to any individual's sense of self-esteem. Here is where habits do their most devious damage.

A Craving for Instant Results

Most of us live in such a fast, product-oriented world. We need and demand immediate results, instant gratification, sudden release from all pain. But a fully rounded and confident vocal capacity needs maturing.

Anybody in education or healthcare knows that quick fixes are simply not possible. Lasting work on the self and the body takes time. Vocal work often needs to be done at different stages of life for altogether different reasons. What a young voice student can do at eighteen is nowhere near what a great performer of fifty can achieve. But then few mature actors will ever realise the voice power that a vocally gifted actor had in his or her youthful prime. What politician today has the quirky and sly vocal resonances of a Winston Churchill? Vocal flexibility and daring take time to mature. Yet the craving to achieve instant results will often exert appalling pressure on our ability to communicate.

Just think for a moment about how many of us as children

were disciplined to 'stand up straight', told to 'stop mumbling' and commanded to 'speak up'. Sound familiar? I am sure it does. And to what lasting effect I wonder? Has it made us better speakers or just speakers filled with habits? And how long will it take us to chip away at a lifetime of built-up defences? It could take a while.

Some immediate vocal improvements are possible in a short space of time. With the right exercises improvements are possible within ten days. Lasting ones, however, do take longer. Maintaining them means starting a whole new lifetime of good habits.

From the start I must be clear about one thing: nothing in voice work happens instantaneously or through force. We should experiment, play and enjoy the work but never push, predict or judge it. You secure the right to speak by earning it. So consistent work is part of the process.

Yet before we start on the process of working with the voice, we first have to take a look at all those nasty habits I have been referring to obliquely without yet identifying. We'll start right off by exploding a few key myths having to do with voice work which in their own way have locked us into a habitual mind set and may have even convinced us that our own voices are not worth improving. For so many of us, I do believe, hate the sound of our own voices.

The Myth of the 'Bad Voice'

I have never heard a 'bad voice'.

Does that sound strange or unconvincing to you? If it does it is probably because you think you hear them daily. 'His voice is so overbearing.' 'Her voice is so shrill.' It might even be your own voice you are talking about.

Some voices have obviously suffered serious damage and are medically flawed. Others are susceptible to allergies and upper respiratory infection. There are croaky voices and squeaky voices. But if a voice is healthy and not the victim of chronic illness then it cannot be termed 'bad'. It may, of course, be grossly underdeveloped or overdeveloped, nervous or overconfident, untrained or very badly trained. Think of the muscles of the body as an analogy. Without some form of exercise and physical restraint we go either flabby or become muscle-bound. Sounding overbearing or shrill are simply vocal habits that have gone too far in either of two directions. Neither is 'bad' in itself. Both are easy to control. So it is not the voice that is bad but just the bad habits that suppress its freedom.

What I think worth remembering is that every human voice has thrilling potential waiting to be discovered and unleashed. And I do mean *every* human voice. As soon as any of us surrenders to a defeating habit and says, 'I have a bad voice', what happens? Our whole capacity to speak unashamedly and communicate expressively suffers a crisis of confidence. The whole vocal apparatus that physically allows us to speak in the first place shuts down. We begin to second-guess every statement we utter and each sound we make. A negative myth about a bad voice compromises our right to speak.

What I do meet most often in my work are constricted or 'held' voices that are often quite easily released and freed. Perhaps nine out of every ten speaker falls into this league of bad habit. Now that most of you know your so-called 'bad voice' is nothing other than a myth, wait a bit and we'll explore this phenomenon among others in greater detail below.

The Myth of the 'Beautiful Voice'

In Britain, especially, we have been dogged by the notion of the 'beautiful voice'.

The stage and screen actors we have grown used to seeing and hearing, the authoritative BBC-announcer voice that once filled the radio airwaves (now thankfully disappearing in favour of a more colloquial variety), the so-called 'posh accents' of the upper class and royalty have all conspired to create the myth of correct elegance in speaking. This is the sort of voice you *listen* to instead of *hearing* whatever statement or text it speaks. It lulls and enchants you like a gorgeous piece of swelling romantic music. You are overwhelmed by it, sometimes even envious of it. You are won over by it. You want to sound exactly like it. To you it is the civilised way of speaking. We describe such voices as 'sonorous'; that is, imposing and grand.

My image of the beautiful voice not only encompasses that of skilled legendary actors, but it also extends to wonderful bits of meaningful – and sometimes meaningless – rhetoric spoken in places like the House of Lords or the pulpits of the Church of England. When we listen to these beautiful voices are we more engaged with the issues and meanings of a play, commentary or sermon or are we merely swept away by the rhetorical dynamics of the speaker? I would say the latter is true.

Don't be fooled however. The beauty in some of these voices is only skin-deep and perhaps a mask for insincerity. Using another metaphor, these voices show the agility of a tumbler flipping across a stage. We are startled by one physical characteristic honed and practised to perform very well. But do we, as audiences, leave a theatre or public space talking about the message we have just heard or have we been captivated and lulled by the speaker? Aren't we seduced by beautiful voices just as we are repelled by bad ones? I think we should be able to hear any text first and forget about the speaker. But beauty bewitches us. And beautiful voices are like the mythical Sirens who lure us off course and onto the rocks.

In its own attractive way the 'beautiful voice', just as much as the 'bad voice', is a creature of habit. It can prove to be just as huge a barrier to the speaker as a shyly inaudible or aggressively pushed sound. In both instances, the voice fails the speaker in the essential goal to communicate a word and its sense; each is in some way disconnected from the voice's right to serve a message.

Please understand that this is not an attack on voices that are capable of speaking beautifully. I find a beautiful speaker as enchanting to listen to as you do. I am only arguing that each of us has the right to our own voice, and that the sound we make appropriately befits the ideas and emotions we express. Our voice, whenever we use it, should set out to match, organically and emotionally, whatever material we say and not be disconnected from it. The two must come into perfect alignment. The real beauty of speaking lies in attaining that perfection.

Proper voice work is neither a form of cosmetic surgery nor a version of old-fashioned elocution lessons but a path to speaking in your own way with your own God-given voice, bum notes and all.

We have all experienced listening to speakers who sound insincere, overbearing or just unsure of what they are saying. In effect, I think our voice becomes a sort of lie detector that instantly traps a speaker whenever he or she is being unauthentic. What we strive for, therefore, is not a 'beautiful' voice but a voice rid of doubt and insecurity, a voice perfectly in pitch with the honesty of any text or feeling, a voice that in essence is sincere. Sincerity gives any voice compelling beauty.

This sincerity can only emerge when a voice is completely free of any trace of lie or habit. In the quest for a beautiful voice most people would rather exchange sincerity for tricks. Usually they cut themselves off from their own individual sounds and impose on themselves some notion of a 'right way' to speak. In doing so, ironically, they cut themselves off further from the genuine right to speak by compounding old habits with new ones.

The Myth of the Voice Guru

There is no doubt that many areas of voice work are enormously potent. Working on the breath, for instance, can always expose and touch someone on the deepest level. It is penetrating work, both intimate and revealing. I will talk further about this later on when I explore the breath and then further on again I will demonstrate what I mean in the exercise section on deep breathing. Breath takes us to the core of voice work.

Exercises developed to open and free the voice can make anyone – female or male – suddenly vulnerable, tender and unguarded, rather like a snail without a shell. Work on this level can be intensely frank and personal. Human potential of any sort, once massaged and tapped, can be powerfully revealing.

Unfortunately there are some voice teachers, particularly in Britain and North America, who believe they, not the work itself, are the real sources of power. They provoke students to reveal secrets about themselves unwillingly. They dictate when and how to speak. They dangerously probe psyches, in some cases violating privacy and dignity. Like the 'beautiful voices' they sound good. I am sure that some of these teachers mean well but they approach voice work psychologically and not just physiologically which is where, I think, emphasis must always be anchored; they work without either anatomical training or licensing as therapists and healers.

I talked, for instance, to an actor in Canada a while ago whose voice teacher had told him 'to scream and scream until it hurt' as a prescribed method of releasing his voice. This, it turns out, is quite a common phenomenon and as unsound a bit of advice as you could possibly give someone. Did he follow that advice? Should he have followed it? No, of course not.

Every year at the Guildhall School's auditions in London I hear candidates who exhibit all the signs of vocal damage at the hands of unskilled voice teachers. This is no less true of people I have encountered auditioning for drama departments in America where the training and teaching of voice are not always carefully regulated. Abuse of this sort seems, in fact, to be most flagrant there. Even when actual damage of the vocal cords has not been the case, I have heard so many talented students made almost speechless and voiceless by the severe judgements and recommendations of voice teachers who have assumed the roles of gurus.

The role of the responsible voice teacher (and I say this for the benefit of teachers and students alike) is: a) to explain clearly the workings of a voice; b) to identify specific problems; c) to prescribe exercises to free the problem; and d) to offer choices that open up further options to vocal freedom. We are not out to make converts or acolytes. If we can pass on enough working knowledge to a student – show him or her the technical hows and whys of proper voice work – the voice teacher should become redundant in anyone's life. We should just be putting people on pathways towards personal goals. But leave the enlightenment up to them.

Anyone should be free to play and experiment with their voice without someone like me looking on in either judgement or approval. The right to speak involves you discovering your very own freedom to speak in ways that suit you best. There is no such thing as one 'method', no definitive vocal exercise has ever been devised to suit everyone's needs, there is no single way of attaining vocal release, no mumbo-jumbo to imbue strength and power, no 'mantras' and, because voice work is so very personal, no one teacher. There is simply no aura involved. Nobody working on their voice can learn to do so through fear, intimidation or charismatic pronouncements. I hope that everyone who follows me though this book remembers that. And if you begin encountering this attitude, the voice of the 'guru', then take heed. Especially if you should hear it from me!

3 The Roots of Habits

Throughout my work I refer a great deal to the 'natural' as opposed to the 'habitual'. The meanings are simple and clear enough.

The *natural voice* and its potential are what we came into the world with at birth. It is our basic vocal equipment that matures and flourishes (barring sickness) as we age. Our first experience of natural voice was in that initial gasping primal scream, that first chance we were given to 'catch our breath'. Life and our subsequent experiences should ideally enrich and broaden the natural voice, transforming it into a powerful instrument of self-expression.

But life batters and restricts us in such ways that most of us settle into what I term an *habitual voice*: a voice encrusted with restrictive tendencies that only awareness and exercise can undo and counteract. The natural voice (or what others term a 'free' or 'centred' voice) is quite simply an unblocked voice that is unhampered by debilitating habits.

Habits physically manifest themselves as holds or barriers to the sounds we make. They take many forms and shapes. We all have euphemistic sayings to describe this sensation: 'I had a lump in my throat', 'I was so petrified no sound came out' or 'I was lost for words'. Without habitual blocks, however, the natural voice rarely tires and is never damaged. Remember my gospel-singing friend? I think the key to her success was freedom from the tyranny of habits. The rest of us are not so lucky.

Habits are also something you can hear or actually feel if

you know what to listen for and where to probe. As we move along we shall be troubleshooting the voice for habits so that you can detect them on your own. There is nothing mysterious about this process. In fact once found or recognised, a habit of a lifetime can sometimes be eradicated quickly. It can be that easy. In many instances, however, the roots of habits run deep.

Physical Interrelations

Where do habits often begin? In the body.

Any voice, in order to make and project the appropriate sounds, requires the full use of a set of interrelated physical acts. The very sound we make is a result of physical exertion: sometimes it is as tender as in a barely voiced whisper, sometimes as strenuous as an alarming shout for help. Any useless tension, anywhere in the body, can constrict the freedom of the voice. The way we stand or sit, for instance, the ways our heads, necks or spines are correctly or incorrectly aligned, the carriage of our shoulders, upper chest and torso, the habitual set of our mouth and jaw – all of these influence the balance and functioning of our voice. Any one of these can be the land-mine sitting in the path of the voice's free passage. Breath, vocal release, range, 'placing' (or vocal focusing), resonance and speech are equally interrelated. So when I speak of the voice I am really speaking of an entire physical network. Everything is connected to everything else; everything works with everything else.

The voice is really like a physical jigsaw puzzle: any missing or damaged pieces leave gaps and make the picture incomplete. Some pieces have more weight and importance than others but each part, no matter where it sits within the total scheme, is relevant and locks into the other. Locked knees, for example, prevent the voice from breaking free. A slumped spine or a ramrod one means the breath cannot pass easily up the body and work sufficiently to give the voice the ballast it so desperately needs for extended speaking.

The problems or weaknesses inherent in one part of the body are the source of what I call the 'physical domino effect'. It works like this: a physical barrier to the breath means that the voice cannot be supported, which means it cannot be freed or placed, which means its range is cut down, the resonances halved, the jaw tightens, the speech slurs . . . and so on down the line of falling dominoes. There are many other examples of this same toppling physical pattern.

Part of the troubleshooting we do in voice work is to trace back along this line of falling pieces to isolate the habits that caused the fall initially. You cannot release the natural voice until you've singled out that one flaw, the personal physical trap that triggered the chain reaction. And we all have them to one degree or another. Each time we speak that trap may be preventing us from doing it with ease.

There are many misconceptions about what constitutes the 'natural' when it comes to those habits which afflict the voice. Students stand slumped in front of me and say, 'Look, this is my natural way of standing.' It is not natural to slump. It is habitual. Or people might say, 'My natural speaking voice hurts' or 'I naturally clench my jaw.' Both these are acquired physical habits. The body does not naturally hurt or clench itself. Other common complaints I hear from professional voice users are: 'It's natural for me to lose my voice after I sing'; 'I never breathe naturally when I go on-stage'; 'I am never heard at board meetings.' Again, all of these are habits we impose on ourselves. It is natural to make sound, to breathe and be clear in speech when we need to communicate. Only habits prevent us from taking any of these rights freely.

Most habits are not mortally wrong. I am not saying that slumping is wrong. It is only unwholesome when there is no other choice. So slump, through choice; mutter, through choice; be inaudible, through choice. By understanding and sensing the natural – being able to distinguish the way it feels from the habitual – all physical choices should be available to us. And choice includes habits of all sorts. But take care when a habit leaves you with no choice whatsoever. Beware if it has started to control the way you speak.

Restrictive Habits

Our habits, when done without choice, cut us off from our potential voice and immediately restrict all other areas of our communication.

When someone starts voice lessons with me one of their first and most telling comments usually includes: 'My voice doesn't reflect me, my thinking, feeling or imagination.' The speaker's creativity is restricted most often, it turns out, by a nagging habit. Their voice has inevitably become less flexible. Natural personality has been masked by one or a series of alien habits. Gradually these habits, which we take to be natural, enslave us. We become restricted in what we can say and how we say it.

Have you ever noticed how people who speak inaudibly or with unusually low voices seem blankly inexpressive all over? Their eyes and faces are lacking in expression in direct proportion to their voices. Just a habit like the lack of vocal power and resonance, just not being heard, can make us seem practically invisible.

At their worst, habits can seriously damage a voice. Some habits like pushing the voice, for instance, put enormous pressure on the vocal cords. For some reason speakers will happily risk serious vocal damage long before they would hurt themselves in other ways physically. It happens time and again, especially to young and untrained singers. Surely no actor, if asked, would dive from a ladder head first onto a concrete floor! However they would freely push and strain their voices, risking permanent damage. To take another example, many a school teacher takes it for granted that their voice will hurt over the weekend after five solid days of teaching. There is no reason why it should. A habit is compounding the hurt day by day.

If your voice hurts your body is simply saying 'stop'. Pain is a warning. Observe the warning always. Stop and troubleshoot the problem. It is important to point out here that the full range of vocal qualities and tasks that a voice needs to do – like acting every night or teaching five days a week – can be performed safely with technique and training. In Part Two of this book I will go into all that in greater detail. Short cuts, however, can be dangerous and damaging.

The Birth of Habits

Just as we need reminding about how easy it is to damage the voice through thoughtless habits, we must also remind ourselves of the voice's natural resilience. Imagine a baby playfully cooing, laughing, crying and eventually screaming; tiny vocal cords producing an enormous sound and never seeming to tire until they are out of breath from body fatigue. Babies also display an extraordinary variety in vocal range, pitch and rhythm. Their breath is free and their body unheld. No useless tensions are evident. The natural voice of birth is still theirs.

As life and its pressures infiltrate the infant and then the child, habits grow and take control. The natural voice begins to slip away and is only sometimes rediscovered and remembered in heightened moments – often either perilous or hilarious ones – when we really need emotional release or when our need to speak overrides our restrictions or self-consciousness. I believe that everybody retains some memory of a free, natural voice. It usually releases when the defence system of our habits is momentarily dropped. Many people I work with bear witness to hearing a sound escaping from them, not feeling it contained or held within them: a cry for help, a really loud belly laugh or suddenly being powerfully articulate in a critical argument. The sound we make in these instances is so clear and loud that only after a few seconds do we realise it is our very own voice!

Sudden Freedom of Heightened Moments

A common experience underscoring the free, clear voice in action is a heightened moment when clarity of communication is so vital that we actually reach out with our voices and words and bypass all restrictive habits. As a child starts to run out in front of a truck after a ball we don't mumble 'Be careful', we yell 'Stop!' The vocal release is free and clear. The words have to save a loved one or stop an object. We don't find ourselves in this kind of heightened situation often, but when we do the voice really does come into its own as an instrument of power and the body springs to its aid, helping it to manufacture the appropriate sound.

I will frequently refer to these heightened moments. I simply mean those times when we have a sudden need to communicate and find the best way to say it. We usually break all restrictive habits in order to arrive at this release. Most of our daily speech transactions are either unnecessary or, more precisely, are only uttered to pass the time of day, done to accomplish some prosaic business or discuss trivia. We usually speak in diminished moments not heightened ones.

Often our words do not confront a situation directly. They either deflect it or circle around it. This evasion of the straight and narrow can often be vigorous, especially as our voice and speech habitually manufacture devious, entwining twists of phrase. Many of us take pride in our ability to be subtle and speak as if we are in a play by Harold Pinter. But more often this habit engenders a flabbiness in communication that comes from neither the desire, need, care nor passion to touch someone with words. Why bother to speak clearly if it does not really matter? But then try listening to a speaker who suddenly makes it matter; a great orator like the late Martin Luther

King, for instance. They are clear, defined and infused with energy. They hit points squarely on the head. They are also wholesomely direct. Their communication only deals with the essential. All the tangled bits have been straightened out. Well, I claim we can all capture this same heightened, declarative, verbal energy for ourselves.

I have worked with completely disconnected, incoherent speakers who suddenly come alive as they speak about a passionate hobby. Suddenly a heightened subject enthrals them. I recently had a meal in a London restaurant on a slow evening. The waiter was bored and uninterested, barely communicative. For some reason I commented on a nearby tank filled with tropical fish. The waiter came to life. He loved those fish and was responsible for them. He knew each of them and spoke with such precision and care about them. I found myself in the midst of an exciting and vigorous discussion – about fish. The man's voice became clear, focused and vital. A good note to any public speaker is always 'if it matters to you it will matter to us'. We all have the capacity to speak on the crest of heightened moments that rise above diminished ones.

The incident with the waiter and his fish might seem like a prosaic example. However when pain, loss, betrayal, love, joy or delight becomes so great to the point of bursting, we always break through to a heightened plateau of communication. Suddenly we need a voice, we need a word and we find both. We make contact. We can even surprise ourselves by our eloquence. Often, too, we find ourselves speaking a language we never usually experience. We leave the prosaic behind and will often become poetic. Speakers at weddings and funerals always captivate us in this way. None are usually professional speakers. The moment, however, imbues their voice with a compelling motive to be heard.

In these heightened moments, I will argue, people are at their most vocally clear and released. They are also at their most natural because they are most themselves. The moment might not even be linked to a word or sentences but purely to a sound: a scream, a laugh, a wail, a groan, a whoop of delight. Those expressive sounds that signal an instant reaction to life and often result from pure heightened spontaneity.

I would also suggest that the great classical plays of all cultures that confront the universal issues of humankind are all exploring heightened moments. We have only to look at the plays of the Greeks to find example after example. Shakespeare's writing could be described as life with all the boring bits cut out of it but all the thrilling bits left in. He might give us thirty seconds of normality in a character's life before plunging them and us into the terrible tests he imposes on them. Think of *Hamlet*, *King Lear*, *Macbeth* or *Othello*: all heightened plays full of heightened moments. Bearing this in mind it does seem stupid when actors try to impose their disconnected everyday reality and unfocused speech habits onto these heightened texts and then claim it is 'real' to mumble their way through *King Lear*. The heightened need to speak gives us the heightened right to speak. One without the other leaves the whole enterprise sorely out of joint.

Natural Release

We have to learn to release sound naturally in order to release ourselves. Then all that energy will flow into a word, a sentence and a need to reach out to the world, purely through a combination of sound and language.

I often speak about drunkenness when I do voice work. Many people experience a free vocal position when their social and behavioural barriers have been dulled by drink. They are also most physically relaxed. Suddenly someone who wouldn't dare sing sober, releases their voice completely as they become intoxicated. I am not advocating drink or alcoholism as an aid in vocal performance but the 'memory' of intoxication will often help liberate a voice from sobering habits.

In the West we live in such vocally and orally suppressed societies that the sudden experience of vocal freedom can severely shock anyone trying it out for the first time. By touching off our vocal power we begin to sense all sorts of other powers. Our society simply does not encourage us to be vocally free or expressive. You have to go to other areas of the world like the Mediterranean, Africa, the Orient or the Caribbean to experience genuine vocal freedom in action. Such a riot of sounds will often jostle most Westeners.

Many of us have been taught *not* to feel easy about expressing words and sounds openly. Our society likes to control the volume and keep us vocal hostages; it doesn't want to hear the thoughts and opinions of certain groups like children, women and minorities. Too often we only like to hear the voices of so-called 'first class citizens', well-bred and well-toned. Ironically, it is usually the 'other' classes of citizens whose voices still retain the habits of natural release.

The natural voice is lost to too many of us as different factors, oppressions and influences – often of the most mundane sorts, like conformity – erode our self-confidence. We first learn to shut down and then begin to shut up. Some of these factors are profound, others are banal. From class to fashion, environment, family, religion, peer pressure, sexual dilemmas, our work places, the state of our bodies, geography, dentistry, physical injury . . . well, you see how the list could go on and on. I will explore the purely physical factors later on. Suffice it to say that all of these pernicious influences, plus the ones I have yet to name, chip away at our natural voice and obstruct it with habits.

It is very useful to understand some of the ultimate causes of any debilitating or even mildly irritating habit, but often just releasing the physical tension that has found its way into the voice by whatever means will be sufficient. Perhaps we should not always have to talk about the source, but just work the tension out! Just relaxing and taking your time, for instance, or just saying one word at a time are wonderful ways to start experiencing the right to speak.

Many voice teachers agree that our habits, the ones that directly affect the voice, take hold of us between the age of eight and our early teens. I don't have a hard and fast opinion about this because I have seen habits begin to influence the adult voice where there were none before or completely new habits appear. Divorce or the loss of a job, for instance, or the set-back in one's career that ignites a mid-life crisis can all lead to habits that suddenly smother the voice or compress speech. A blow to our self-esteem or just an embarrassing moment can equally do the trick.

Or it can happen at an age far earlier than eight. Some years ago I was working with a group of doctors. We were discussing the natural cry of a baby. After the session one doctor showed me some of the infants in his care. Following him I found myself entering a ward full of battered children. Already their cries were erratic and strained; strangulated, actually. Their experience of violence had already pierced their voices and created habits. Would they, I wondered, ever have the right to speak again?

Holding On to Habits

The one thing you can say about habits is that they are comforting. You grow to like them and they grow to like you.

People generally hold on to habits for their familiarity and security. Human beings are creatures of habit; we all know that cliché and retain habits that become part of ourselves to prove it. Sometimes we hold on to habits for good reasons, other times because of fears, misconceptions or simply because a habit has become so habit-forming that we no longer notice it.

Naturally we all have a right to our habits, our personal

quirks and ticks. But if we have cultivated one, I only hope it is out of choice and not for a more negative reason. Habits, after all, can be addictive and even unhealthy.

Breaking habits can sometimes be alarming because you can suddenly feel empty or naked without them. A habit might seem so important to us, so much a personal trait, so very interesting and expressive, that we have invested a great chunk of our personality in it. Vocal habits are of this sort. A particular delivery, tone, speech impediment or affected accent draws attention to us, gets us noticed. Sometimes we exaggerate habits like these in times of stress. Without them we think we would be dreadfully dull and, at worst, very middle class. So we might, for instance, speak with weak 'r's as in '*w*abbit', or babble in a pseudo-excited delivery as in disc jockey speak, or settle into the quiet confidential tones of 'the comforting voice'. Each is a habit.

We are so often under the misapprehension that vocal habits add colour to our speech and zest to our personalities. Generally the opposite is truer: a habit drains our speech of colour and usually sets us further adrift from our real selves and voices.

Many popular performers and public figures have made both a living and a legend from their vocal peculiarities. Here I think of British comedians like Tommy Cooper or Ken Dodd who used speech habits to superb advantage or the late American President John F Kennedy whose pronounced 'Boston' accent was widely mimicked. On the screen, television or radio this kind of put-on vocal habit works incredibly well. But it will neither carry nor be clear from the Olivier stage of Britain's National Theatre. Voice and speech habits work best in close-up. They are used to supreme advantage when they create a very tight circle of sound around the speaker, particularly when used in conjunction with a repetitive physical action or in combination with other habits. This is why they serve comedians so well. Habits used with choice can make some performers seem like weird and wonderful mechanical dolls.

Those kinds of habits are priceless ones that are consciously cultivated.

I have had actors and people with thick regional accents pace around me as though they were in a gladiatorial arena and I was a lion ready to pounce on a lucrative habit. Among students and younger actors a favourite habit nowadays is the voice that affects 'street credibility', a kind of 'hey man, you know what I mean' honesty. If you take that kind of habit away from them or they are suddenly left without it they feel vocally naked. They are back to themselves. But what I am usually offering in its place is an altogether better choice, I think. The right to speak in your own personal voice, uncoloured and unflavoured by anything artificial.

Both kinds of speakers, those with either good or restrictive habits, labour under the same fear – that they might lose something special that is very much a part of them. No habit will disappear for good unless you actively will its disappearance. Really *will* it out of yourself. Voice teachers, whatever any of us may claim or proclaim, are not wizards. If you like a habit, feel that it gives you aura and power, by all means keep it. But recognise it for what it is. Keep it with the knowledge that under certain circumstances it will be wholly inappropriate for clear and telling communication.

Affectations always get in the way of honesty and clarity. It is what makes 'beautiful voices' sound to me like ineffectual or so-called 'bad voices'. You can't be clear in the large padded auditoriums (any modern theatre or lecture hall designed with soft materials and wall coverings) if you do not use your voice openly and fully. A borrowed voice won't help here, a voice that trails off at the end of words or sentences will only lead to a dead end. A forceful vocal push will shatter an audience's ears if used over a microphone or transmitted by radio. A clamped voice will surely suffer damage if forced to speak in large spaces night after night. A heavily glottal or 'attacking' sound tires very easily from this affliction. Habits have a way of destroying voices – and sometimes professional careers. If you are suffering vocal abuse of this kind it might be time to look into it. Is this a risky habit you like well enough to keep?

Habits Linked to Fear and Sexuality

Some habits that make us hold back on our voices are connected to human fear and sexuality.

These habits are more complex and harder for a voice teacher to pinpoint and eradicate easily. Often they can never be eliminated completely. So many of us hunch in telling ways (shoulders up, breasts and genitals protected) to insulate ourselves physically from others. If it is too frightening to let go physically then don't. You will do so when you are ready. Generally when you are feeling quite pleased and open you do it without noticing.

The so-called sexual revolution of the 1960s and 1970s followed by the sexual confusion and suppression of the 1980s and 1990s have brought with them their habitual hang-ups that have left telling effects on the voice. Students – both male and female – are ashamed or uncertain of clinging to their virginity and are expected to have lost it by a certain point. I have actually heard some voice teachers in Britain and America exhort their students to 'go and lose their virginity'. 'You cannot breathe,' they will say, 'because you are holding back your sexuality.'

Now there is little doubt that an awareness of sexual energy is useful in the process of placing the lower breath (the breath that reaches down to and releases into the pelvis and groin). But this is where voice work naturally leads into delicate personal areas where it is subject to abuse. One ought not to venture in the direction of deep breathing and the deep feelings it taps until fully committed and prepared. I know of many people who, once they have released the sheer power of their full breath and voice, frighten themselves by their new found strength. A full voice can do that to you only because you never knew you had it in you or have blocked it for years on end. But finding it too soon can confuse and shock you.

I raise these issues here (and will raise them again later on) for the sole reason that finding your voice is sometimes a frightening process. We all have the right to find it, I believe, but have to do so at our own pace and in our own good time. This is not work you can force. Our genuine voice, the one that is habit-free and guilt-free, may have been locked away and hidden for years, deeply tangled and enmeshed in a web of habits. Drawing it out has to be a gradual, deliberate and delicate process that we take one step at a time. The fear of butting up against forces that block it will diminish over time as you play and experiment with your voice during the discovery process. The caution you should carry through this process is that up to the moment when you fully experience and then accept your voice, you should hold on to certain habits as a kind of tightly woven safety net. Sometimes you have taken habits on for protection, so do recognise that fact and use them to catch you should you fall. But habits, like crutches, can be cast aside once the body is fit to stand again on its own without any artificial supports. The same is true for the voice.

Habits that Manipulate and Control

A whole host of the vocal habits we acquire are not just used to defend us but to manipulate and control others. Sometimes our reluctance to address them has to do with an unwillingness to surrender power. I am not just speaking here about the overbearing, aggressive speaker. To be brutally honest for a moment, a heavy stammerer might have learned to enjoy making people pay attention, making us listen and wait for the word to burst forth. This is neither true of stammerers in general nor do I say this to slight those with this speech affliction. But I use this as an example of manipulation because so many stammerers have admitted to me that this is part of the habit. The listener is left dangling, hanging on to the expectation of a completed word or phrase, and in the process the stammerer can gain time to fill out a thought. This only works, though, with sensitive listeners.

A more frequent habit in this category is that of the 'devoicer' or whisperer; someone who speaks so low and confidentially that we must literally lean in to hear what they have to say. This kind of manipulation is used by 'guru'-like figures or anyone who has created an aura of power and control by simply speaking softly. This may sound contradictory, manipulating and controlling by speaking softly, but it is true. We have to go to the devoicer to decipher what is said. By speaking softly the speaker has figuratively made us bow at his or her feet in order to receive the word. A precious attitude perhaps, but an awfully effective one.

Quiet people use this habit to wonderful advantage. And I have encountered this habit interestingly enough in people whose job it is to exert control: theatre directors, upper echelon business executives and leading politicians. I suppose it can be called 'the speak softly and carry a big stick' syndrome. Quiet, steady, hypnotic speech can often signal either confidence or deep sincerity. It rarely signals danger or competitiveness. Lots of very powerful women, I have noticed, use this technique to entrance their listeners and not to frighten men. We all become devoicers when stopped by a traffic policeman or when caught in the act. I usually think that devoicing as a manipulation starts in childhood and never outgrows some of us.

The 'waffler' is another in this category of vocal manipulators. He or she is the kind of speaker who abandons clear speech and succinct, definite language in favour of an incoherent delivery and wandering thoughts that ramble through our minds. This is the sort of speaker who habitually delights in obfuscation and obscurity. If the language sounds learned, profound and embellished and the points being made appear to have growth potential, the listener is then left with the uncomfortable feeling that he or she is at fault for not being able to crack and decipher the waffler's coded message.

Often, however, we are simply being vocally and verbally duped. The waffler takes us on a verbal wild goose chase in search of sense and meaning. This is a very useful habit that we all adopt, especially when we try to waffle and avoid answering direct questions, avoid unpleasantnesses or just refuse to speak the truth. We all waffle, don't we? But the next time you do, try and notice the speech and voice habits you adopt in order to do it. We put up a whole blind of sound, posturing and rambling ideas and phrases. In my experience this is the kind of habit cultivated by public officials, so-called experts on various issues, theatre directors unsure of an answer and doctors trying to avoid telling patients the whole truth. Wafflers are often delightfully gnomic and envelop us in linguistic bear hugs which we are then left to straighten up from on our own.

At first glance the 'hesitator' seems more a victim than a manipulator. He or she leaves us waiting for a reply. In fact, the reaction from a hesitator is often a delayed one, like the reaction we sometimes get over intercontinental telephone lines! The rhythm and pace of normal conversations are not part of the hesitator's brief. He or she doesn't lead the listener like a well-rehearsed speech partner should, but holds us back or steps on our toes in a hesitant, stabbing search for the right word, phrase or answer. The organic stream of natural discourse seems continually dammed up into little stagnant pools where we wait for the conversational flow to be released again. This habit works as a form of manipulation if the listener is kind or gullible or even subservient. The speaker may be a powerful one, practised in the use of hesitation as a means of keeping a roomful of listeners in thrall. A hesitator can often steer a conversation in a manner that a clear, fluent speaker never could. A whole room can wait for a reply from a hesitator. There are lots of speech teachers who advise speakers – businessmen particularly – to rely on hesitation techniques as a sure means to gaining a captive audience. What we are made to feel is the notion that thoughts and words are being formed before our very eyes and ears. But when hesitation becomes such an afflicting habit that we cannot even give an answer to whether we would like tea or coffee, then I think the hesitator has ventured into a habitual danger zone from which he or she ought to retreat. We usually excuse the hesitator or other types of non-communicators as being shy or reserved. Many, in fact, are severely blocked and inhibited speakers or need to face the fact that help is required.

I know a couple, both flamboyant conversationalists and wonderful hosts, who continually entertained a female guest for whole evenings and days at a time. She would sit in the midst of our group and contribute nothing or very little to our involved conversations. She just sat, watched and listened. Discussions, debates and verbal passions whizzed around her head and we all thought this must have made her too dizzy to talk. I began to resent the fact that this woman was taking in so much experience and not giving back one word in return. Here we were revealing ourselves, speaking freely on all sorts of levels, and there she sat behind a wall of silence. So shy, so *hesitant*, we thought. We were all silenced some years later when we appeared – our dialogue quoted and our stories revealed – in her stage plays. We had accepted her hesitation to join in our discussions but were duped in the end.

All of these common habits adopted by some speakers – the reluctant speaker who stammers, the devoicer who whispers, the waffler who overelaborates, the hesitator who dams and clams up – are both weaknesses and sources of power. A speaker will never give up one of these habits either willingly or easily if it is serving him or her favourably. But here is the problem: there will certainly come a time when each of us needs to reach out vocally and verbally, when we will need to take the right to speak but suddenly find ourselves helpless to do so. The sore point about these kinds of habits is that they atrophy our vocal range and equipment. A voice that has settled into devoicing all the time cannot be extended on command. The waffler cannot be simple and direct. The hesitator only taps a fragment of the full capacity to speak. The devoicer can be deadened into silence. When we surrender to habits we surrender many of our vocal rights too.

4   The Growth of Habits

I often wonder if our society actually likes to hear children? 'Children should be seen and not heard' is an all too popular and widely accepted axiom.

A child should always say what's true
And speak when he's spoken to,
And behave mannerly at table:
At least as far as he is able.

Robert Louis Stevenson

We see parents in supermarkets constantly shaking and 'shushing' their children in the most threatening manner. When we do allow children to speak we discipline them to say only what is polite and unthreatening. 'I was brought up with one saying ringing in my head: "If you can't say something nice, don't say anything at all!"' That's how one of my students in Texas summed up her early verbal training. Yes, I do think we are told too often to be quiet on the one hand and only say what is nice on the other. Think of the habits those two directives engender!

It seems to me that as a society we violate the child's right to speak and enjoy sounds . . . the 'bum notes' and the 'grace notes'. Obviously there are many families who engender a right to speak from the very start. They encourage an imaginative exploration of verbal dexterity, a feel for words, debate and discussion at the dinner table and a choice to speak one's own mind. Even if you are just five. Yet the experiences I have collected from both students and adults I have worked with and from other teachers are dismal. People have been disciplined from the earliest age not to speak and certainly not to make noise. To be 'mannerly', yes, but in the process to become too mannered.

A well cared for baby, nurtured and encouraged, makes the most extraordinary range of 'mewling and puking' sounds. Babies have a free, tireless stream of vocal energy always at their command. The hard part is keeping them quiet. New mothers and fathers can certainly tell you that. They are in fact eager to speak and become suppressed only through conditioning. To our adult ears the sounds a baby makes may not always sound attractive but they certainly are natural and open ones. Just listen, for instance, to the variety of notes a baby can intone. The sheer experimentation in harmonising or distorting sounds in the resonating organs – head, mouth, nose, throat, chest – and in the articulating organs of the mouth, tongue and throat muscles that will prepare them for later speech, all this and the sheer *volume* they can achieve in cries and shrieks leaves a voice teacher like me astonished. And to think that all this is done with only 3mm length of vocal cords makes you stop and ponder: a) how it is possible and b) why do we surrender that capacity as we 'mature'? Do we not, in fact, seem to 'immature' vocally as we grow away from infancy? What goes wrong?

As a child develops, first vocal and later speech restrictions are levied on them by parents and teachers. We are first told to hush and then told what not to say. I can remember at a very early stage sitting in the back seat of a car with my friend's father driving, making those childish nonsense sounds that invariably led to words: 'auck, buck, cuck, duck, euck, f——' Suddenly, almost as if from out of nowhere, the back of a hand struck my mouth and I heard an enraged 'Don't you ever speak or make that sound again!' I never stopped experimenting with words, but I probably hesitated for a while and kept it limited to *nice* words.

The point is that all sorts of pressures, well intentioned discipline and even a benign finger up to the lips limit a child's access to his or her own voice and the capacity and right to speak.

Obviously as the baby tunes up, babbles and toys with first one sound and then another – almost duplicating a series of vocal exercises like the kind I'll be offering in Part Two – certain expressions are encouraged or discouraged depending on the parents' language and culture. Try, for instance, getting a group of younger or older adults to: blow a raspberry; move their facial muscles in ways that resemble funny faces; or play with non-intellectual sounds like 'la la la' or any number of tongue twisters. They all collapse in laughter or embarrassment at any of these commands. Probably in course of experimentation the baby stumbles on the sounds 'da da' or 'ma ma' and the baby is encouraged to cease experimenting but focus energy instead on 'daddy' and 'mummy'. We learn rather swiftly to stop pleasing ourselves and please others with the sounds we make.

I am certainly not trying to make any deep and original discoveries here on the level of child psychologists like a Piaget or Bernstein. But I do want to make you aware of how our own voice and speech begin to get manipulated from a very early age.

For the sake of education, a necessary step, a large bit of our vocal potential also becomes sorely limited. We remember the slap across the face, the mouth washed out with soap, the repetitive focus on 'daddy' and 'mummy' to the exclusion of other sounds. Our sounds are focused to gratify and impress others rather than ourselves. A powerful instrument full of sound and capacity is suddenly curtailed by limits of one kind or another; fertile ground for habits to develop.

A baby on waking will gently warm up and play with its voice before getting down to the real business of the day and calling out to the world. How many of us, as adults still do that? How many of us would rather go through the early part of the day in total silence, not uttering a word to anyone?

At night many babies and young children will wind down the day's activities by chatting through the day's events. Every day to a child is another vocal excursion into novel and exciting terrain. They speak in order to know the world, to identify it, to give it names. The exploration is unabashed and honest in its directness. I'm not suggesting that we should maintain our childlike wonder into adulthood, but even simple childlike activity like warming up the voice is essential to any professional voice user as is the adventure with words. All of us, especially those of us who use our voices professionally, simply cannot afford to abandon the right to explore the vocal potential of linking words to the experience or object they express.

We need to speak, and come by our birthright to speaking, by sounding words aloud, breathing them into the air, so that we understand their significance and the very actions and emotions the words describe. A child seizes ownership of a word by sounding it infinitely until its tones and proportions, the thing itself, is clear. Spoken language – sometimes I think more than written or read language – makes experience, ideas and emotions concrete and tangible. When Hamlet speaks his great soliloquy that starts 'To be or not to be', he gives voice to his dilemma just like a child in a series of sounds that first coordinate and then negate each other. Look at any other great Shakespearean speech or scene and you find characters using language literally to voice out loud experiences escaping and taking shapes in sounds.

Those of us who don't talk about experience often find ourselves cut off from it. It seems to me ironic that so many people go into various forms of psychotherapy just to learn how to speak again, to find an arrested or repressed voice and make sense of themselves once more through language.

Suffer the Little Children to Sound Like Me

What I have discussed so far may seem patently obvious but there are more subtle influences working on a child that inhibit future choices in voice and speaking.

I have never yet taught a group of students when one or more of the following causes for blocks do not surface. Usually the force has been a casual comment or series of comments from the family, a teacher or just a friend. A child being told they are too loud, for instance, or their voices cruelly mimicked or their stumbling over the pronunciation of various words. The cynic might say, 'Well, life is cruel, children cannot always be protected, they have to fall off the swing some of the time.' Fair enough. But it's helpful to begin exploring how restrictive habits evolve and why we seem stuck with them.

One restriction we all encounter very early is over the right to sing. I believe anyone can sing. When I say that to a roomful of students at least thirty per cent will disagree.

'I can't sing. I'm tone deaf.'

'Who told you that?'

'A teacher at school. I had to mime in the school choir.'

Tone deafness is, in fact, very rare. It is one of those myths that needs exploding like the myth of a bad voice. In talking to ear, nose and throat specialists and physicians in general none has ever come across a clear condition that one could radically term 'tone deafness'. I have never worked with anyone who could be clinically labelled in this way. A powerful delusion perpetuated by an unthinking teacher can effectively cut any of us off from a singing voice for the rest of our lives: 'You're tone deaf. Sit down and be silent.' Most of us stop trying to sing in childhood though we hum to the radio or even sing out loud when we are on our own. I think we become terrified easily early on but probably innately retain the belief that 'God doesn't mind a bum note.'

What about something simple, like posture? How has that

affected our voice? Young people are normally taught that good posture means pulling back their shoulders to avoid becoming round-shouldered. But that rigid pulling back is one of the best means of cutting off the breath and tightening the throat muscles, thereby impairing our vocal variety and delivery. The trouble with discipline is how much vocal restriction it dictates.

If a child appears to have round shoulders, the centre of the spine is usually collapsed. If you can lift through the spine, keeping the shoulders relaxed, the shoulders will adjust to their normal position.

By and large children have naturally aligned postures even though to adult eyes they might look awkward enough for us to bark commands like 'Stand up straight!' Look at four-year-olds watching television. Frequently they will loll about, but often they will sit up quite straight and are beautifully aligned. It is only when their self-esteem is attacked that they begin to cave in. Criticism, more than anything, bends them out of shape.

Once while offering a poetry workshop for teachers I was, as usual, suggesting ways they could encourage children to speak and revel in the rhythm and muscularity of spoken verse. I was shocked when one teacher said, 'Oh no, I love poetry too much to allow the children to speak it. They would spoil it. I read to them.' I instantly had this appalling vision of thousands of children she had taught never being allowed to speak or quote from the great poetic texts; now all habitually frightened of poetry. They were allowed to experience poetic literature through her voice alone.

Yet is this attitude rare? Too many students and adults, including experienced and terrific stage actors, openly admit to being frightened away from speaking great texts by a similarly restrictive or proprietary attitude. They quake and sweat at the thought of tackling Shakespeare. It usually emerges that they were made to feel vocally and verbally inadequate, not up to speaking it, by a teacher or overbearing adult. Each will report they were told they couldn't read out loud expertly enough or their regional accent was jarring on the teacher's ear or that one specially gifted child, whose voice the teacher praised consistently, was given all the honours. This is how resentment to spoken verse starts.

Many eighteen-year-old students start vocal training with a very soft, almost whispered quality, completely lacking in confidence or vocal focus. This vocal position, which I have already mentioned earlier, is called 'devoicing'. Only a small portion of the voice's power is being utilised. Apart from vocal potential being halved, this position is tiring for the voice. The remark used to explain many of these voices is, 'I was told I was too loud and noisy, so I cut my voice down.'

Other students go to the opposite extreme in order to sound more vocally overconfident. They use an overly mature vocabulary that doesn't sit happily with them and actually seem to be speaking like their parents or in a manner that will win adult approval. As children many of us suffered to sound like them.

Stuttering

Girls are consistently told to speak quietly and nicely, boys to be assertive and fluent. Every child, at some stage, stutters. We all do as we search for words, become fatigued, frightened or thrown off verbal balance. At the stuttering stage, children are exploring language and how it is physically made. Stuttering, or stammering, only becomes problematic when it is continuously commented on. There are so many schools of thought on this topic. Like tone deafness it is hard to clinically isolate stuttering or stammering as a physical affliction. Most experts do agree, however, that somewhere along the line a stutterer has been bullied to be vocally clear. Outside forces usually account for this entrenched habit.

Statistically more men stutter than women (four out of every five stutterers are males). Perhaps they are expected by the world to be in control of their words and are consequently picked up more than women. Women, on the other hand, find it much more difficult to speak about important issues. Most intelligent women will claim that bright boys were listened to before them as children. Sitting in a classroom with your hand eagerly held aloft waiting to answer a question – at what point do you cease to bother? Women are allowed to gossip but not to have strong opinions. Perhaps adults listen more attentively to boys' rather than to girls' opinions. That certainly would have been true in past decades and probably still persists. Habits, you see, begin very early.

Mumblers have been bullied to speak clearly with remarks like: 'If you want me to listen to you then make me understand.' Children generally speak very clearly if they have an attentive audience. As adults we have to ask ourselves whether we actually want children to sound themselves or only the way we want to hear them. Do we really give them the right to speak or do we want them to express only what we rightfully find acceptable? How many adults really listen to children and engage them on their own level? How many times do we interrupt them? Only use my words, only speak my thoughts, only express my opinions. Is it any surprise that young people are frightened of speaking? That they stutter? Should they not have the right to say what they wish? We usually blame them for being inarticulate, but I think the fault lies just as much (if not more) with us.

People enjoy speaking and playing with sound, it is not a joy we abandon easily. Whenever anyone discovers a delight in words and verbal images you simply cannot stop them. Within days, weeks or months anyone who has been taught to shy away from language can become immeasurably articulate once given the right incentive to speak.

When I express views like these, as I often do, there will always be one person who will assure me that he or she was brought up 'to be seen and not heard' and it never did him or her any harm. I can never help but notice that this assertion is often pronounced in too loud and too pushed a voice. I am usually being spoken 'at' not 'to'. That vocal push in itself is a kind of reply.

I'll end these thoughts by simply pointing out that in my experience the most vocally and verbally repressed among us usually overcompensate. Their voice has become insensitive to the natural world. So they push, are loud and grating, force their sound upon us. The victim has become the victimiser; the unheeded is now in no position to listen to anyone. Voice work usually uncovers these kinds of vicious circles that produce habits.

Adolescence

The rush of physiological and emotional changes that course through the physical system as children move into adolescence creates a whole set of noticeable vocal adjustments. This is another point at which lifelong habits, some of the most radical we are likely to experience, are incurred. For boys, the 'breaking' of the voice can be traumatic and difficult. Girls' voices may not change quite so dramatically (they don't experience the breaking as fully as boys, for instance) but adolescence can be the time when once open, chattering girls withdraw into shells never to re-emerge. It is a difficult stage for most of us to get through; a time when either being giggly or compliant, shy or tetchy shapes the whole way we speak. It is certainly not a period when intelligent forthright communication rules our vocal lives.

Boys' voices break anywhere between the ages of eleven to fifteen. 'Breaking' is a loose term that attempts to approximate the process of the changing adjustments the vocal cords are undergoing during these years. It can be an unsettling process as the cords stretch into new shape, grow and thicken. This growth can happen in as short a space as a couple of days (quite rare and dramatic) or, more normally, over several months to years.

To illustrate the changes we undergo during adolescence here is the pattern. The vocal cords, or folds, of a six-year-old are approximately 8mm long. By the age of fifteen the average length has stretched to anywhere from around 9.5mm to 23mm in young men and from 12.5mm to 17mm in young women. You see how for females it is so much less dramatic. After the surge of this growth process, the muscles surrounding the throat and aiding the vocal process have to settle and adapt to the change. Physically, a boy has to learn to reuse a natural function in a new way. Not only is the voice physiologically transformed but new muscles have to learn to re-orchestrate the vocal tune. It is a bit like moving from the reed instruments to the brass section of an orchestra, from say piccolo to trombone in some cases.

As I've said, the settling down process may take some years (as many as eight to ten) before the full vocal mechanism is coordinated. I never like 'stretching' or extending the range of a male voice until about twenty-five years of age. Some voices are ready for this at twenty while others have had to wait until twenty-eight. At about twenty-five, though, all the muscles and ligaments surrounding the vocal cords in the neck have settled and the voice is ready to develop its full potential. But during the early stages of this breaking-in process exquisitely voiced boy sopranos, for instance, will find they can no longer sing and may have to wait out the years to discover if they will settle into the tenor, baritone or bass range. This is a critical stage in the life of a male voice for which there are no hard and fast limits. There is also no way to predict how the sound will turn out.

A female voice also breaks but at a much earlier age, between eight and ten. The physical growth and change to sound made by the cords are less noticeable. The changes usually occur when the sexual stakes in the adolescent world are not as critical, so few girls notice the breaking as much and it draws fewer comments from peers. In training a female voice, the breaking-in process begins to settle around eighteen years of age. So young women have a slight advantage here in terms of beginning to stretch their voices. However as girls mature physically into women their posture and breath can suffer a decline, perhaps in an attempt to hide their changing bodies. They get tighter and more withdrawn, more round-shouldered and protective of their sexuality. In effect, they close down.

Physical aspects of breaking put aside, the period of this process exerts pressures that put restrictions and develop habits on the ways both genders speak. Adolescence is the time when we consciously begin to map out our sexual roles and take our sexual space in society. The way a boy's voice breaks is usually the source of comments and snickerings, either vague or open reflections on sexual prowess. The breaking voice is fair game for mocks and teases, especially as the voice uncontrollably but naturally swoops through notes as it breaks. So in order to avoid jibes most young men 'sit' on their voices by artificially lowering them to suppress the register and manufacture a 'male sound'. This can result in a lifelong habit of being stuck in the pushed-down position. Some voices stay there the rest of their lives devoid of colour or higher registers. This is most prevalent in the West and not such an issue in the East. Male Oriental speakers tend to be much freer than Occidental ones.

It is at this time too that boys will learn to be male by showing more vocal authority as a means of masking other changes. This comes across as vocal 'bluff': too much volume, too much laughter, too many grating sounds, too much vocal competitiveness. Girls, on the other hand, are encouraged to sound feminine: less loud, less challenging, more demure, more reticent in speaking. During this time girls usually learn to devoice, or tone down, and not to inter-rupt men. Giggling and shrieking are acceptable (mainly in female company) in a way that articulate vocal assertiveness is not. I still find in the young women I teach a tendency to heighten the pitch of their voices to accent feminine sound. This is still very common in the East and also throughout the United States (particularly in the South, Midwest and West Coast).

The pressure exerted on both genders to assume sex roles and prove acceptable to their various peer groups – the pressure to avoid ostracism – is at its most intense. This is understandable. Who among us has not been through some phase of this adjustment or breaking-in to society? Every cell of our body and all our attitudes seem to be under a constant shift and swell. In an attempt to find some concrete foundations many adolescents choose to reduce or deny themselves in order to fit the mould of a role. It is a dangerous time to be different, a prime time to conform. Mostly adolescence is a period when vocal playtime is over for the individual and group vocal traits appear in its place: the singing style of a favourite pop vocalist, the latest sayings and jargon, the braying and chanting at sports events. The childhood affair with sound for its own sake and the unabashed relishing of individual words ends for the time being. Exploring the realms of the voice and speech becomes horribly straitened and even predictable as one teenage speaker begins to sound like another. Here again habits put clamps on individual vocal prowess.

Parents hardly know how to deal with or speak to adolescents during these trying times just as young people have trouble responding or instigating communication that seems adult. Personal confidence as we break into the world at large, going out on our own, can fall to a low ebb as confusion rises with the tide. It is at this point in our lives that many of us are attacked as being 'mumblers', 'inarticulate', 'naive', 'selfish' and 'arrogant'. This is the period of grunts and groans and linguistic shrugs. At least our voices seem to signal this. It will often seem to adolescents that in conversations with adults they can never win; that they are always under interrogation and attack. I have often wondered if the celebrated communication breakdown that solidifies between adults and their adolescent offspring about this time isn't sometimes just a result of the vocal breaking down going on inside adolescents' throats! Certainly neither adults nor their children will allow each other the vocal freedom to sound and speak as they should.

Different Voices

During adolescence, as a means of hiding our perceived inadequacies when we are at our most vulnerable, we can adopt one or several voices to express different facets of our lives: a family voice, a school voice, a voice for friends, a voice for the opposite sex, silly voices or serious voices. We become expert mimics and imitate incessantly the way other people speak. All forms of this vocal defence system, as overcompensations for a lack of confidence and maturity, can remain with us throughout our lives and become serious habits. A silly voice is an excellent means of avoiding serious subjects or the truth. We all consciously use this kind of voice in jest and should do so, providing we don't fool ourselves into adopting habit-forming modes that undermine our authority as speakers. Who wants to listen to someone who is silly all the time like a character out of Monty Python! The struggle we face as we move towards adulthood is whether to accept a vocal role or just be ourselves.

Middle Years into Later Years

As I've said above, most voice experts believe that the optimum time to train a voice is in the mid- to late-twenties. The body and mind are still flexible enough, the vocal system has settled into its own and is ready to be extended, and most of the student's emotional and sexual problems have been addressed or are on their way to being resolved. The voice now has its own persona. At this age, too, we are eager to improve and motivated enough to make the improvements. Even during the late teens, as much as students desire it, the heart and mind are never fully focused on the work. But remember, too, that the voice isn't completely ready to benefit from the full effort. As the body ages and we become more rigidly set in our habits it becomes harder to change our attitudes to sound and the use of language.

Admittedly these are gross generalisations. I realise that as someone ages certain vocal functions, like breath and posture alignment, can get rusty and harder to shift without willed effort. Yet I can point to many examples of people desirous of vocal change who have transformed themselves despite being in their seventies. So age should not be considered a barrier in voice work but just a stumbling block along the way. There are lots of exceptions to general wisdom in this type of work. A respected seventy-five-year-old poet, who wanted to keep giving public readings of his verse despite his age, thought he was too old to improve his voice. After we had been working together for three lessons, he actually strengthened and enriched his voice dramatically.

However let's examine the practical problems of ageing. I believe it is true to say that the voice needn't age dramatically if the body stays healthy and exercised, showing no serious sign of fatigue or debilitating illness, and if the voice in particular shows no sign of abuse or injury. To train and release a free voice does get harder as the muscles and joints lock or soften, or if the mind sets or the imagination deadens. In fact the longer you live with a dulled vocal imagination the more distant the whole natural potential of enlivening it becomes. Unless they are addressed, habits deeply embed themselves and penetrate to the core of our being over the years. The seemingly shapeless habits of youth, like slumping or pushed shouting, can begin to deform the body and vocal apparatus, seriously undermining the voice's potential.

As we age, simple release and freeing exercises get harder to perform. The shoulders and spine can become so rigid that many basic breath and voice exercises become increasingly difficult to achieve. The hearing diminishes and becomes less acute, especially if we have spent a lifetime of not listening carefully enough. The voice, like the body, can suffer from a sedentary lifestyle. Older persons can resist lying on the floor even though floorwork is probably the best and most relaxing way to begin work. As muscles age and weaken the vigorous use of support and vocal extension in the abdomen and upper chest will be curtailed. A life-threatening illness, a heart attack or stroke can all make us feel that any subsequent vocal exertion is beyond our means. We can easily fall into a syndrome of overprotecting our voices and through our voices appear weaker than in fact we are. Look at older people in nursing care, for instance, and you will hear how feebly they use their voices. It matches the frailty of their bodies and the general climate of frailty that engulfs them. But then compare this to the plucky resilience and command in the voice of the late Dame Peggy Ashcroft who, up to her death, had the kind of commanding vocal presence any younger actress could only envy.

The voice teacher might have to rethink exercises for elderly people and apply them with tremendous care and consideration. But vocal release, if gently done, can affect and change all age groups. The younger student might be open to more physical bravery which for an older person would be inadvisable. Yet less exhausting means can be found to achieve the same results. Later, in Part Two, I'll refer to some of these exercises.

As we age vocal abuse is more dangerous. The youthful heavy drinker and smoker will not notice the effects on the voice apart, perhaps, from the morning after a fitful bout with either. Healthy, young muscles can withstand the abuse along with more vocal attack and push. The price to be paid comes later when they will certainly notice the voice becoming incessantly rasping, hoarse, showing inflexible range and phlegm accumulation along with chronic coughs and wheezing. This is not a polemic supporting temperance but just an observation of two very destructive habits. The choice and right to pursue these habits, as ever, are yours entirely.

5   Settling into Habits

Habitual Roles

Physical problems aside, there are many insidious habits that can dull our vocal capacities as the years go by.

As adults we adopt roles that lock our voices into place. This is especially true of professional types like bankers, teachers, and salespeople. Real vocal release, joy and play become more infrequent as a professional role weighs down on us and becomes a leaden habit. Many older people locked into a role will feel embarrassed or vulnerable if they are asked to do even the simplest and most neutral vocal exercise like humming. A role has hardened into a habit. They have not allowed such sounds to reverberate through their voice for years. The sound does not fit their ideal sound of themselves.

But many voice training exercises in the early stages are like child's play. If we believe and have invested in our role in life then we quite often cultivate a voice that matches it. This is even true of some very grand voice teachers! The 'professional' voice, the 'parental' voice, the 'couple' voice; any sort of special use voice is really a habitual one if we cling to it too tenaciously and it becomes our everyday voice. To experiment vocally is hard because it does initially feel like we are stepping off the path too much and venturing into new, unknown areas. Not only does it shock us but also those around us who have grown used to the way we speak. So a word of caution: if you engage in any serious vocal work expect it to change the way you sound to others.

Most professions have a voice that is deemed 'suitable': doctors, lawyers, teachers, bank managers, vicars; even manual labourers, housewives, nurses, or any life role you can name. Roles require and have a way of reinforcing tones and rhythms that infect daily speech. The difficulty sometimes comes when we have to cross boundaries or cross-pollinate with a different vocal role. Can a bank manager, for instance, easily step outside his or her vocal persona to converse with a child or ticket collector? Can the housewife easily tackle or challenge the doctor? Can the parent express grief in front of the child? Can the teacher be vocally vulnerable in front of students? If we have invested much of ourselves in our vocal roles how do we break the habits?

I constantly deal with the physical manifestations of this kind of vocal entrenchment. Physical release and alignment are necessary to break barriers, but so are experimentation and the vocal ability to throw off roles and accepted personae. Too many people feel that they will lose a piece of themselves if they shift a vocal pattern. None of this, of course, is true.

There is, as in all things, another side to the debate. Age can enhance us, liberating us from the fears and uncertainties of youth. Any liberated person will sound free. The right is there for us to accept. Any person who sounds organically interesting should be naturally curious enough to explore what they say, how they say it and if they can say it better. Age can give us renewed confidence in a new voice. Suddenly older speakers, once attempting to break vocal habits, become enthusiastically childlike in their interest and not the least bit ashamed to let youthful feelings echo in their voices. Questions of vocal roles are moot ones once we accept ourselves for what we are and stop fighting or bluffing the world.

The voice is as it is, reflecting the impulses that move through the head and the heart and there is never a need to cheat or artificially produce a sound. It comes of its own accord. The securer we feel as whole persons the more likely we will be able to listen to others and respond without effort.

We have more time to give them. Perhaps that is why younger people find older grandparents or family friends easier to talk to. Their voices have lost the habit of judgement. They have learned to accept and enjoy their voices. That may also be why they are such good and free storytellers. By that point we have stopped fighting our voices and have again found our natural ones at last.

In some ways we might hold all ages within us at any one moment. The child can sound mature, the aged can sound like a baby. If we allow the full range of age to fill and mellow us like wine in wooden casks and add colour to our voices by letting all sorts of experience shade it, then mere physical deterioration will be outweighed by the richness of experience found in the voice.

The Glass of Fashion and the Mould of Form

When I taught in India it soon became apparent that many of the basic exercises I used in the the West to release and align the body and breath were completely redundant, particularly for women. You can't do a head roll in a sari! The traditional draped cotton and silk clothes that women wore made it difficult for them to be physically free. I had to adapt all my exercises to suit the fashions of the country. Now I am not suggesting that a Westerner should be smug and judgemental about a sari. I only use the example to show how clothing and modes of dress become habits that impede us.

Some fashions make it extremely difficult for the wearers to be fully free and support their voices. Lots of us who are vocal victims are also fashion victims. We learn slowly. Not too many years ago it was 'correct' for voice and speech teachers to wear very conservative clothes. One famous American speech teacher in particular would lecture her students on make-up, hair and their general appearance. Many drama and speech schools were also a form of finishing school.

This approach was radically rethought as the advantages

of floorwork became apparent during the late 1960s. Lying on the floor in twin set and pearls was both ridiculous and counter-productive. A few years back another American voice teacher came to London to study with me. She tottered into the studio on the highest high heels I have ever seen. She said she was having trouble getting her breath low and was amazed when I told her just to remove her shoes. As she felt the floor through the soles of her feet, she was able to centre her voice and her breath lowered instantly. Nobody can get in contact with their lower breath standing in heels. I constantly find this same problem in Texas where my male students wear cowboy boots. And although trainers or track shoes are great for running and physical workouts, you cannot really feel the floor through air-cushioned Nikes.

Do bear in mind that any article of clothing that restricts the body in any way whatsoever will block breath and ultimately the voice. Any shoes that defy full, natural contact with the earth will throw the wearer off centre. Any impediments around the facial muscles, neck or jaw will make speech harder. I have had many students suffer deep frustrations because they cannot achieve the speech dexterity they desire even though they have done all the prescribed exercises. They could have been wearing heavy framed spectacles which once removed suddenly allow their facial muscles to work. Half-glasses cause the chin to tuck in with a resulting speech habit. Neck tension results from the wearer having to peer over the spectacles. Beards and moustaches can tighten the jaw and lips. Hair that shrouds the eyes creates neck tension and untold distractions. Heavy cosmetics will make you feel that you cannot move your face without disturbing the image.

Some of us have been encouraged to wear more restrictive clothes than others. Obviously women fall into this category. Their clothes are often designed to close down certain physical features and accent others. Corsets and bras, if too tight, naturally impede the breath. No wonder upper class Victorian women fainted at the slightest shock. Their ribs couldn't swing, allowing them to breathe. In a desperate pursuit of fashion and a slim waistline women still have ribs removed, destroying their breath potential forever and cutting away with those ribs hundreds of vocal choices.

When actors play in period costumes they have to first find ways of adapting the clothes to suit their voices. For instance, never allow a corset to impede the full rib-swing or a tight high collar to squash the larynx. We can become so self-conscious about our clothes and how we move in them that we suddenly speak differently and accommodate our voices to what we wear rather than the other way around. Tight belts, collars, shirts, skirts, jeans and jackets – the Levi look – can all impede the voice.

When I have taught in places like France or Italy, for instance, students will come to a voice class laden with heavy jewellery: earrings, necklaces and bracelets. They cannot begin to work properly until it all comes off and with it the distracting noise! Even finger rings can distract and hinder the voice process. Once you have unburdened yourself and experienced the right to total physical freedom, then you can easily work around a fashion habit and adapt to it. Unless, that is, it takes control of you.

A famous singer who works with me regularly came for a class after appearing in a film in America. She was having trouble reaching her higher notes. Her face appeared to have changed and she couldn't fully open her jaw.

'What have you been up to?' I asked.

She did not answer but just squirmed.

'It was the film company's idea,' she finally replied.

'What was?'

'It looks better on close-ups,' she confided.

She then revealed that she had had the extra fat from her non-existent 'double chin' *vacuumed out*. I think they call this process liposuction.

In order to resume her singing career and regain the proper function of her voice she had to have extra surgery performed to counterbalance the first session. All at vast monetary and emotional expense. So you can see how cosmetic surgery, implants, orthodontic bridgework all can affect the voice and speech process. Vanity is one of the chief reasons some speakers will not release their lower breath – 'In case my stomach sticks out.'

Many politicians and businessmen I have taught have been amazed to realise how restrictive their ties and buttoned-up collars can be. When I work with speakers who will be giving an important after-dinner address I always ask them, 'What will you be wearing?' The reason for the question becomes obvious later once they realise the restriction of full evening dress regalia: white tie, tails, cummerbund, braces and perhaps even a chain of office around the neck. All of this formal wear is designed to impede the vocal process unless worked around and adjusted to suit the right voice.

It has been speculated that the high military collars worn by British regimental officers during the late eighteenth and nineteenth centuries helped create the so-called 'stiff upper lip' sound we now know so well. The chin, almost as if set in armour, was so held by the uniform that the jaw and lips could not move properly. Rigid and heavy hairstyles, wigs, necklaces, ruffs or head pieces can seriously restrict the neck. If you feel you can't move your head freely because your hair will be ruined or your hat fly off or your appearance otherwise marred, the neck muscles go into hold and freeze the capacity to speak properly.

Television broadcasters, especially news readers, find themselves strait-jacketed to chairs at the correct camera angle, their jackets, shirts or blouses pulled tightly across their chests so that no wrinkles appear on camera. The head and neck barely moving so as not to draw attention away from the delivered message. Listen to any of them speak and you can hear the rigidity in the voice.

I have also noticed that people who need to wear heavy clothing and footwear because of climate have much more constrained and muffled voices than those who habitually wear lighter, freer clothing. The sheer weight of material around the neck, shoulders, ears and head all affect the way we sound. To always be in a warm climate without the need to wear restrictive clothing must be enormously freeing for the body and the making of sound.

All the fashion situations I mention above can be managed and need not become restrictive habits if we are aware of their potential to strain our right to speak. Even unbuttoning a tight collar or loosening a necktie can provide miraculous relief. The adjustments can be that simple.

Fashion has also done much to dictate how we want our physical body to appear. We will actually spend hours remoulding our natural shapes into unnatural ones. Many physical workouts, particularly weight and Nautilus training, literally put clamps on our throats, shoulders and abdominal areas. Listen to the way muscle-bound athletes and performers sound. Their voices are tight, muffled and often disconcertingly high. You can actually notice the problem in the neck area where the head seems plugged into the shoulders like a cork. The press-ups they do have made their neck muscles so thick and inflexible that their voices literally have become as muscle-bound as their biceps!

By all means, exercise and work out your body, but you must also pay particular attention to releasing the neck, shoulders, chest and abdominal areas afterwards. Keep these areas especially flexible, otherwise the locked effort of a strenuous workout will produce that high-pitched voice you sometimes hear coming from footballers, wrestlers and boxers. I have worked with a lot of muscular actors, particularly in North America where the body beautiful has a greater commercial appeal than it does in Britain, and getting their voices lowered back into place is always an effort if they continue voice work in tandem with body-building.

The issue of weight, particularly for women (but equally for more men nowadays), is really more of an obsession and has critical bearing on the voice. Continual dieting, for instance, and attempts to control weight, leave some people so physically weak that they have little energy left to supply to vocal support. Lots of actors, for instance, who have to gain and lose weight for different roles will notice a range of vocal changes during this process. An anorexic voice cannot find power. It is common for large and overweight women to devoice and speak in either a 'little girl' voice or a whisper, actually using the voice to disguise size so as to sound 'small'.

Fashionable Sounds or Speech Impediments

> *And speaking thick, which nature made his blemish,*
> *Became the accents of the valiant:*
> *For those that could speak low and tardily*
> *Would turn their own perfection to abuse*
> *To seem like him.*

> *Henry IV, Part II* (Act II, Scene 3)

Shakespeare's Lady Percy uses the above lines to describe her dead warrior husband Henry Percy, appropriately nicknamed Hotspur. Hotspur's manner of speaking throughout the first part of *Henry IV* receives a great deal of attention from others in the play and he obviously became something of a speech model to his troops. His sound ('thick', 'low and tardily') became a fashionable sound that even voices of more 'perfection' aped.

Just as with fashionable clothes and fashionable physiques, there are fashionable voices and fashionable speech. This has included, for instance, the very odd practice among upper class males or public school types to stress a weak 'r' that approaches a 'w' so that 'rabbit' sounds like 'wabbit'. The fashion among lower class, comprehensive school types might be to overstress and rap out the 'r' sound to such a degree that 'rabbit' sounds like a rabbit punch. Both are fashionable habits anchored to the way we perceive ourselves.

Women have been known to affect a lisping sound for any 's' (the 's' sound transforming to a 'th' sound) in order to sound cute or '<u>th</u>weet'. Among actors there are habits that have been picked up from their acting or film heroes: John Gielgud, Laurence Olivier, Humphrey Bogart, Bette Davis, Al Pacino, Robert De Niro and an infinite number of others. In the 1970s there was a joke making the rounds that many Royal Shakespeare Company actors pronounced an 's' as a 'sh' (as in 'I <u>sh</u>ay'). Hundreds of young actors would come in for auditions with this affectation, turning 'their own perfection to abuse'. In the 1920s the rolled 'r' (as in '<u>rrr</u>round' or 've<u>rrr</u>y) was in vogue among both British and American actors. John Barrymore even used to pronounce his name in this way. Today we ridicule this kind of affected, actorish sound just as we are starting to do with much overplayed Olivier and Marlon Brando imitations.

Whereas speech and vocal affectations once mimicked the upper classes today these have gone decidedly down-market for models. The vogue nowadays is for inarticulateness and almost slouched speech filled with lots of meaningless sound fillers and phrases like 'you know'. Just like words and phrases, sounds and pronunciation can date us. It would be ridiculous to use 'pshaw' today although Restoration fops invested mightily in that sound which once carried the weight we give to certain spoken expletives. Equally no modern feminist would dare affect a lisp to sound 'thweet'!

Class Attitudes

I opened this part of the book with some offhanded and harsh remarks about the upper class always feeling the right to speak was theirs alone. I do believe that class sound is being rightly attacked more and more today and its importance as an indicator of 'proper' sound is under reconsideration by the vast majority of us who do not speak this way. (I have actually had requests from British MPs to help them iron out – or maybe crinkle – their 'public school' voices!) Yet we still remain enslaved to this class sound.

Those who come from less privileged strata of society with their own accents have been victims of this elitism as well as the vast middle class. Regional accents are only now being accepted by broadcasting companies. The BBC actively searches for presenters with rich regional accents. In America you can drive between the states and hear a rainbow of accents like an arc over your journey. Regional speakers are beginning to be thought of as 'intelligent' and with something to say.

I realise that the re-education of prevailing attitudes plays an important role in this debate about class sounds. I am not shirking the issue but I think there is sufficient evidence to prove that even very well-educated and brilliant speakers, with evident regional accents, have reported fewer initially positive reactions to what they say than their more 'proper' colleagues. I have sat in drama auditions where regional speakers have suffered from the panel's indifference or where doubts were raised about intelligence levels even though these candidates had qualifications galore from top schools and universities. Until quite recently, in fact, the Standard English or Received Pronunciation (RP) taught in drama and speech schools was not the natural, neutral, well-placed and effortless accent now being taught but a distorted, upper class public school sound. Actors in their thirties and forties, for instance, will swing wildly in private conversations between the way they actually and naturally speak and the affected way of speaking they were taught in training schools.

My British students are always shocked when I say that British royalty does not speak Standard or RP. They speak an upper class accent that is often incoherent, quite exaggerated and never neutral or clear. George Bernard Shaw was so convinced by the power of accents that he passionately campaigned for a standard form of English that would eradicate the class system of Britain.

Physical Injuries and Illnesses

The body adapts very quickly and efficiently around pain. In order to stop feeling pain or its memory we can numb all sorts of areas around an injury. Long after the injury has healed, we can be left with muscle tension and physical blocks that are restraining unrelated areas of our bodies. Lower back pains will tense the neck. A twisted ankle will tighten the pelvis.

Identifying and coming to terms with old physical injuries can sometimes be very important in order to release some breath and vocal problems. Let me mention a few of the problems I frequently encounter in this area. Spinal injuries or aggravations, from either a serious accident or just by having to work as an actor on a steeply raked stage, can trouble the whole breathing and vocal process. Knee and foot problems will affect our ability to centre and feel grounded. Any jaw or facial injuries, even slight ones like a slap to the face, a toothache, a cut lip or facial and skin blemishes, can result in speech difficulties and a self-conscious, tightened voice. Injuries to the ribcage and shoulders are also evidenced in the breath. Surgery, particularly in the areas of the stomach, spine, breast or groin can prevent the releasing of deep breath.

I never pry too deeply into my students' present or past lives but it is very important that a voice teacher knows about any major injury or illness someone may have suffered, in order to provide the best kind of work. One also needs to know where the delicacy of the work resides. Certain exercises, for instance, would be dangerous and aggravating to do if the spine is frail. I will always ask for another opinion, a medical one, if I feel that a physical habit is the result of something beyond my scope. Good osteopaths, orthodontists and Alexander technique* teachers are valuable allies for a good voice teacher. Voice work includes working with the whole physical apparatus.

* The Alexander technique was developed by the Australian physiotherapist and performer F M Alexander (1869–1955) as an aid to realigning different parts of the body and posture to overcome habitual voice problems.

I would also say that the distant and small injuries are more intriguing to me – the needles in the haystack – though often less obvious and harder to root out. These kinds of afflictions affect the voice in subliminal ways. Here the domino effect of habits is probably most apparent.

If as a ten-year-old you were hit across the face with a lacrosse stick, you wouldn't really expect that injury to be affecting your speech eleven years later. However, this actually happened to me. To accommodate that intense pain, I very deliberately froze all my facial muscles and never let them thaw again until a voice teacher at London's Central School of Speech and Drama encouraged me to release them. And as I released those muscles, I had an immediate and painful memory of the lacrosse stick hitting me again. More recently I noticed that an injury to the fingers of my left hand made me so protective of the hand that within days my shoulder had tightened, followed soon afterwards by my breath. The physical pain we suffer is kept locked in the memory of the breath and then transfers to the voice.

These sorts of stories about injury or childhood illness unfold too often in the voice class to be dismissed easily as fictions unrelated to the problem with speaking. Harsh experiences in the dentist's chair or a violent childhood toothache have spewed out of students in the process of releasing their jaws. Memories of ancient operations have been experienced during low breath work. Falls, accidents, fights and major to minor blows are regularly rediscovered in the process of serious work on the voice. But once these memories are gradually revealed in the open, held muscles can be released around old wounds and encase them healthily, the body can slowly realign itself, the breath can drop into place and the voice and speech be freed.

This freeing process, if gently done, is rarely traumatic and mostly a huge relief to anyone. We simply never know what or how much we are holding back until we get into a safe climate for release. I would never claim that voice work is psychologically therapeutic (that's one of the dangers to be avoided), but as a kind of physiotherapy it does release hidden memories encased in the body. To that extent it is exceedingly therapeutic.

Students who have or have recently had a debilitating illness, like a persistent cold, flu or viral infection, will need to postpone voice work until fully recuperated. The body just cannot be asked to do too many things at once like heal completely *and* set off in a new direction. When a student at the Guildhall School has been ill for a term, we always make him or her repeat the work after health has been fully restored. It is a necessary measure and the voice (if not the student) is always grateful for it.

As a teacher of twenty-six I was amazed to experience that, after a severe bout of chicken pox, my breath, voice and placing abilities were set back four or five months following the recovery from this fairly common illness. It made me realise why so many performers lose their voices a month or so *after* suffering flu. During the bout with the illness the body's marshalling of resources pulls them through, but once performances are over and body defences relax, that is when the illness seeks its revenge. Any illness suffered during a long theatrical or speaking tour usually compounds, through exhaustion, and surfaces once the job is over. There were incidents a while back when Britain's Prime Minister John Major and US President George Bush both suffered bouts of illness and then exhaustion. The effects of these became habitually manifested in their voices. The strain you could hear in the voices of men and women reporting day and night on the 1991 Gulf War showed what a different kind of tensity exhaustion could produce. Actors, politicians and other heavy voice users working under considerable strain are often not aware of danger signals developing in the voice (weakness of breath, the voice quickly tiring or early morning hoarseness). But once we are off guard our voices will be vulnerable and real damage can happen. Laryngologists say that many actors don't lose their voices on-stage, where they take natural precautions, but at the parties afterwards where they throw caution to the wind!

I recently worked with the star of a big West End musical. Her voice was tiring and she was losing her top notes. It turned out she was in the position, enviable for most actors, of having been in constant work for four straight years; one musical after another with only a few days off during that whole period. She had caught a cold and her whole vocal system had naturally surrendered. Her breath had shortened and become fragmented. Only rest and relaxation during off-stage moments would allow her to win back full breath and her whole voice. She did but it took time.

So do remember that some of our most insidious habits are unlinked to deep neuroses or pubescent abuse but come from injuries and illnesses: perhaps a cricket ball or baseball smashing into our cheek at the age of nine, a flu virus at fourteen, a painful menstrual cycle at seventeen, a fall from a roof at nineteen, a chronic backache at twenty-five and so on. If you scratch a tough little habit that refuses to go away, like a tightening in the back of the throat (even if it is scarred over, like a small one on your chin) it could be that you have pinpointed something about your voice and the way it sounds. You may have begun to explore the means of finding a solution to a previously undisclosed ill. The lesson to leave you with here is that you should never underestimate the long-term weakening effect of any physical malady. Life and its physical ghosts could be haunting you still.

Environment and Geography

I have met some speech experts who swear that the geographical terrain in which we live determines our speech intonation, stress and variety. The flatness of the American Mid-West, for instance, has resulted in an equally flat and inflexible accent. The craggy coastline of Maine is reflected in that version of the New England accent. Likewise the lilting qualities of the Welsh accent match the hills and valleys surrounding Welsh speakers. Landscape shapes speech, or so the theory goes. The theory intrigues me but I'm not sure how reliable it is. I do know that with so many voices on television and radio becoming more and more predictable, despite attempts to stress regional variety, a blander sound is surfacing all around us, devoid of any accentual roots. The rural character of speech is fast disappearing and nostalgia for it makes the idea of landscape informing the sound we make seem very appealing. But nostalgia instantly evaporates when you recognise both that the landscape is disappearing and that rural areas have been undergoing colonisation for decades by urban folk. What it suggests to me is that we are becoming more and more cut off from native sound.

Regional accents are in a state of crisis. They are continually being broken down and neutralised by schools and the media. Older people who still retain a rich regional accent are becoming increasingly rare national treasures, prized when discovered by folklorists, ethnologists and linguists. It is as if they are a lost tribe of some sort. Sad days lie ahead for the survival of the richness of language.

It still amazes me, however, to be able to travel an hour north from London on the M1 motorway, stop for petrol and be greeted by a completely different set of sounds. I suppose the same could be said about travelling from Washington, DC into more rural parts of West Virginia and Tennessee. The language and sound map does change when you shift only slightly. It can happen in London and New York within the space of an underground ride. Britain is still comparatively rich in accents and dialects, and people are battling for the right to preserve their own particular mother sound. A North Londoner still sounds quite distinct from one on the south side of the Thames, an East Ender from someone living in the west. So perhaps there is some truth in the belief that the natural boundaries of rivers, valleys, plains and mountains have separated people enough for them to develop happily their own version of a vernacular language.

In my experience there seems to be a great deal to suggest that certain features of geography and place infiltrate our voice- and speech-creating habits. Urban speakers are generally much louder and more insistent than rural speakers. Combating the noise and high volume stress of city life raises the speaker's volume, creating a harsh, grating city sound. Moving from a city shop to a country shop, you quickly notice the difference. Rural conversation, and transactions of all sorts, take more time to complete. The leisurely pace of the countryside is in the speaker's delivery. It is calmer and slower. It is also true that speakers in modern cities produce a more nasal sound as the result of a vain attempt to keep filth and pollution from entering through the nose. The habit is to block it and produce a blocked sound.

Urban speakers do appear to be more aggressive, more impatient, less inclined to finish sentences. The fullness of language is more random and fragmented. A farmer friend of mine always complains about the city people who walk through his woods. 'They talk so loudly. No wonder they never see any wildlife.' My Guildhall students, coming to London for the first time from rural backgrounds, will always comment on the loudness and brassiness of Londoners coupled with the fact that so many seem to be speaking in isolation rather than in conversation. Urban speech can be alienating. Surely the loudness is just a bluff so as to sound important in a mass of competing voices.

Urban life has given the voice a brashness, a quality of irony and mistrust with no room for answering. The glottal attack, push and vocal strain so very perilous to the good health of the voice are found mainly in urban speakers and in their accents. London cockney, Glaswegian, the New York accents of the Bronx, Queens and Brooklyn or any sort of 'ghettoised' speech is riddled with all these habits. They are so prevalent in these circumstances that they seem almost genetic rather than environmental. The urban breath is shorter and more shallow, the speaking more rushed, clipped and careless, the jargon and slang richer and the overall vocal quality more domineering and aggressive. Images, too, are more sharp, rapping and pungent.

The slowness and seeming dull-wittedness of rural speech have been endlessly mocked, especially in literature where town and country are pitted against each other as in eighteenth-century texts. We arrive at the mistaken impression that all slow speakers are dull or thick. In the so-called 'New Towns' of Britain, hybrids of city and village, you find the phenomena of urban and rural mixing together, with sharp vowels being delivered at a slower pace.

Those of us from urban backgrounds listen romantically to the sounds and singing made by 'the workers': the legendary ploughmen, boatmen and field workers whose work is performed in rhythm with their breathing and singing. There is, in fact, a substantial body of folklore surrounding the type of individual who works in the open air or on the vast seas (i.e. the plaintive and deep-throated blues rhythms that evolved among Black plantation workers in America). We ask ourselves: 'How do they make those free and wonderful sounds?'

Country speakers call and shout more effortlessly. Their breath is longer and they never 'wind' as easily. Everything in their process and metabolism is more naturally paced. Perhaps it is as simple as having and taking more time to breathe, the space to feel important and the physical freedom and right to call, chant or sing across a field or the sea. A Nigerian voice teacher recently demonstrated to me how forest farmers in his country communicate by means of a lilting open 'OU' sound that can travel for up to ten miles. Apart from sounding lovely, it is one of the clearest, simplest and most effortless sounds to make and sustain. Just by whistling commands to their dogs rural sheep farmers can control and direct whole herds into new grazing grounds or homeward bound.

Space plays a key role in developing vocal habits, especially when it comes to the freedom of release. It is very hard to be physically and vocally free in a small bed-sit flat overheard by neighbours. It is much easier to breathe in open unpolluted spaces. Our breath and our confidence in breathing change immediately when we look out across the sea or up into the sky or over a hill or mountainscape. None of this is just recreational, it is absorbing the right to a healthy natural breath that is just like a refreshing drink from a pure stream. Living for a while on a Norwegian fjord, staring up daily at a sheer wall of rock, I noticed myself cutting down on my breath. Suddenly I understood the essence of claustrophobia and why the characters in the plays of Henrik Ibsen seethe with repression. They cannot breathe. Hedda Gabler is suffocating. When she speaks she is breathless. Enclosure has compromised her right to speak.

You cannot work day in and day out in either restrictive clothing or restrictive workplaces the size of most modern office cubicles without your voice being affected in some dramatic way. I think the air filtration and conditioning systems in most modern buildings, which dehumidify and dry the atmosphere we have to breathe, are probably more damaging to the voice than most of us realise, even though all of us sense their effect.

I once worked in an inner London school set in the midst of massive tower blocks not unlike the sheer rock walls in Norway. These tower blocks were where the seven-year-olds I was teaching lived. The classrooms were open-planned, so the children had space at school. They were generally very good and well-behaved, but every Monday morning for the first two or three hours there was chaos. The children would rush wildly about and make an uncontrollable racket. It took me some time to equate this unfocused pent-up energy with the fact that on weekends they were penned up in those tower blocks. Monday morning was release time; back to the relatively open space of school. Back to freedom.

Family

Probably a good number of our most persistent and individual habits are family based. Our physical make-up, and therefore our voices, mirror our parents' and we probably pick up our parents' physical, breath, voice and speech habits just by ingesting them from an early age. Accent and dialect are the most obvious examples but there are many subtle versions of these habits passed on by osmosis, like breath, stress, inflection and vocal placement. There is a vocal umbilical cord which sometimes needs cutting as a step towards liberating our own voices.

Many students who leave their home environment to train elsewhere talk about returning there after the sudden revelations of the first twelve weeks of voice training. Here are a few of the more common reactions: 'My father pushes his voice just like I do'; 'My mother snatches her breath'; 'My older sister inflects in exactly the same way as me'; 'No one in my family ever talks.' Other students realise their parents' habits embarrass them so much that they have adopted ways of speaking at complete odds with the parental sound: 'I now realise I mumble because my father is so loud and clear'; 'My mother's shrillness annoys me so much that I have deliberately chosen to devoice'; 'Both my parents are so jolly that I've chosen to whine.' At home we seem to take our voices to opposite extremes. I really only heard my father's Dutch accent after returning home from my first term at the Central School of Speech and Drama. As a vocal trap and breeder of habits, the home is sometimes the first place we ought to look in order to get a clearer picture of ourselves and the way we speak.

Returning home after starting voice work and with a changing voice can also be traumatic. A family or a boyfriend or girlfriend may not like the sound of a different you. A changed person has entered their midst. 'You're sounding too posh, too assertive, too clear, too strong . . . You don't sound like yourself any more.' This last comment can be the most upsetting. In order to survive this sudden identity crisis we cover it over with a kind of vocal schizophrenia: speaking colloquially and speaking 'properly'. We instantly transform voices according to our audience, becoming masters of vocal disguises.

Students with newly attuned hearing capacities are always amazed by what they discover at home: they can now detect noise or silence in their home environments, whether the background is oral or not, whether speech itself matters or not, whether seriously engaging topics are raised around the dinner table or just trivial conversation. A friend in his forties recently realised after returning home that only his father was allowed to hold a strong opinion. The rest of the family was expected to sit in unchallenged silence as he held forth. Bearing family habits like this goes against our rights. They will ultimately prove unbearable unless we recognise and then confront them.

Friends and Peer Groups

The pressures exerted on us by close friends, colleagues and peers can lead to different kinds of habits from those that develop within the family. I am continually amazed at how we cleverly adapt our voices and speech to meet the expectations of any group. Parents have all had the experience of their nicely spoken children returning from school or from being with friends suddenly transformed by vulgar and raucous sounds. They begin to mumble, grunt and slur words, becoming generally incoherent. Again a sort of speech schizophrenia is in evidence. Children can develop several ways or more of talking, all aimed to please different groups.

Rarer, but also possible, is the child who gains a precocious mastery of language that intimidates a parent by its clarity, imagination and forcefulness. We don't like our children to go beyond their right too soon. So children are often punished for being too 'lippy' or 'cheeky', sometimes just for being too clever by half and outclassing the parent with oral feats.

In any of these instances the parent has to remind himself or herself that the child has been learning a new way of speaking, a new vernacular and slang to fit into a peer group. To avoid speaking in this way could mean ostracism. It is the unusual and solitary child who does not have this vital need to conform so as to fit in. That fitting in is what leads to habits.

Fitting In

My father, a native Dutchman, always says one of the things that enabled him to get on in England was his heavy Dutch accent. In a perverse way he stood out so much that no one expected him to conform. He became special. No one could place him within a rigid class system so he stayed outside it. Saying the wrong thing, using the wrong word, was forgiven because English was not his native language in the first place. Perhaps, too, the charm of some foreign accents can beguile us. The foreigner, we think, is at a disadvantage and should be tolerated. We still find French accents romantic and the Italian accent tempestuous. But we probably harbour less attractive views of Asian, Middle Eastern or Caribbean sounds.

My father experienced a rude awakening, however, in an Amsterdam bar when he returned some forty years later. He was chattering away happily to the barman in Dutch when suddenly the barman said, 'You speak Dutch in the most dated way. Where have you been all these years?' My father's rather wistful comment to me at the end of the story was: 'I don't speak any language properly. My speech is not accepted as normal anywhere.' What he was saying was that he did not fit in with any class of speakers. He had invested heavily in the oddity of his voice and speech for all sorts of situations in England but his rights to his own mother tongue had lapsed.

Male and Female Differences

You can tell the sex of a voice.

The voices of males and females are naturally different. Nowadays we hate to believe that there are these crucial distinctions between genders. But in matters of the voice this happens to be true. The differences are largely physical ones. For a start men have larger and thicker vocal cords. Their larynx is bigger and can visibly protrude in the neck (significantly called the Adam's Apple and more noticeable in males). The male physique is generally more developed and roomier so that the actual sound produced by the vocal cord is reinforced in greater resonating cavities like the chest, neck and face. Female breasts, on the contrary, can muffle chest resonance.

Greater lung capacity and rib power do not necessarily produce greater volume. No one would accuse top flight female opera singers of singing any less powerfully than their male counterparts. A man usually senses this capacity and authority and his right to it more readily than a woman. Any woman, after sessions of training, can begin to feel these powers for herself.

As their voices break, young men undergo the embarrassing sensation of hearing high-pitched 'female' tones in their voice. Despite the name calling they suffer, this is a natural transformation for the voice. Many transsexuals try, mostly in vain, to alter the pitch of their voices to sound 'female' but usually have to resort to habits as a means of so doing. Our belief in a drag act, for instance, is as much reinforced by the high-pitched qualities in the female impersonator's voice as by the wigs and clothing. It is so easy for groups who do not fit clear gender definitions and who have been mocked and repressed, to then hide behind a vocal caricature of themselves.

There have been numerous studies comparing the conditioned responses in the modes of conversation of males and females. Women will question more, listen more attentively, make supportive caring noises and use a greater variety of inflection. Men tend not to listen so obviously, interrupt more frequently, dispute and interject, make dismissive noises or silently pretend not to hear what is being said. They can also have more colourless inflection yet offset this by having stronger opinions and exploring a greater range of topics in conversation.

In other words, women tend to be supportive with their voices and men tend to dominate. One hopes these sorts of gender stereotypes are beginning to disappear. I do begin to notice that a change of habits is under way. But we cannot instantly escape from the history of woman's inferior role to man in areas of communication, especially when this superiority has left such deeply conditioned habits in the voices of both sexes. No wonder that a famous British female politician who became our Prime Minister actually began to soften her voice when she was criticised for being too verbally aggressive in the early stages of office. She toned down her voice and made it sound more caring, not only to charm her colleagues and the media in public but ostensibly to woo the electorate! The man who then succeeded her in the same office spent his early term trying to overcome vocal and verbal shyness, that even had touches of natural caring, by eventually choosing to adopt a more aggressive vocal push that seemed to go against the grain but made him sound like a world statesman. Our own innate vocal personalities and habits of articulation may resist our projecting the very stereotypes that life in the public eye dictates.

I have found that training male and female voices is quite different. The conditioned responses in each, from both the encumbrances of gender and innate personality, make each harder to shift. Let's look at women and men in turn.

Women

Throughout recent history (the past 4000 years!) women have been conditioned to seek and play a lower status role. We all know the popular myths that have resulted even if some of this has been shifting a bit. Women gossip and perform domestic tasks. They are not expected to speak about important issues, to have opinions or to rule; at least not to do any of these in public. Some cultures still drill women to be deferential where male conversation is concerned. When some women speak in mixed company they can entertain men but not challenge them. I seriously doubt whether most women, outside peer associations, are listened to by men in quite the same way as men listen to each other. The listening factor, as we all know, is what compromises and breaks down so many relationships.

Until quite recently well-reared girls were not encouraged to sound 'coarse' or to 'shriek'. They might be allowed to titter, perhaps behind the barrier of hands against their mouths, but never to emit a full belly-laugh. That was unfeminine. Nor were they allowed to express themselves openly through shouting, rage or even passion. All that was left to the operatic Carmens of the world but not to proper girls. Young women were taught to sound 'nice' and not to interrupt. Boys were too but they were almost expected to rebel. Because these well-bred girls were to be models of femininity, any girl from any class (or even from any country who wanted to learn English) aimed at acquiring the 'nice' sound. I always hoped that poor Eliza Doolittle didn't lose her ability to squawk once she became clipped and posh!

In Japan, for instance, women have traditionally been taught a particular set of feminine sounds and inflections to keep them separate and apart from men. A very strict set of vocal rules was enforced almost to the point of there being stock reactions and formal replies for any circumstance. Throughout Asia many women still are not allowed to speak in public and those who do attract considerable wariness.

There are some benefits to be derived from this history. Women do speak more frankly to each other about their feelings and fears. When they do so their voices are more open and natural. In that way they help to educate themselves and are more in touch with themselves. They are also better at keeping oral traditions and histories alive as a favourite family aunt might be.

Women are more physically closed than men. They also slump more than men. This is a fundamental difference that immediately reveals itself in any voice work. One major thing women have trouble accomplishing is standing with their feet apart and squarely under their hips. It is not part of their habit to do so. Somewhere along the line females learn to clamp their thighs together and only separate their legs at the knees. They also learn to protect their breasts and become round-shouldered. As a result their spines collapse in the centre, they stoop slightly and appear to be backing away even as they move forwards. Women will tuck in their heads, look down at the floor, devise hair and clothing fashions to hide behind. As their shoulders hoist and arch their breath tends to become higher rather than deeper, the intake more rushed or snatched, resulting in a breathy breathlessness. Physically they are taught and exhorted to reduce, not to spread or to take up too much space. To stride as a girl is unfeminine. All the natural expressive aspects, in fact, of one's physical life (except, perhaps, for dance) are censored and reduced. Each of these limitations infiltrates the workings of the voice.

Clamped thighs and tightened stomachs mean that the breath we need to fully vocalise is severely held in check and will neither flow nor issue in the right manner. It is quite apparent that females are not encouraged to be loud or to show rage. They are, however, allowed to weep and in some societies to wail openly. It is almost impossible, naturally and physically, to produce a fully connected sound if the lower abdominal area is seriously held. Yet this is the part of the body that most women constrict.

So what has to change first: physical or social conditioning? The two are mutually supportive when it comes to restricting our right to speak. They come in such varied combinations of habits that I think each individual has to address the task of separating them out on their own. It is very common that as we release tightened, twisted physical tensions, waves of emotion and social resentment are suddenly released as well. Often the reverse of what you might expect happens: suddenly women show rage and strength, men show grief and vulnerability.

Let me return for a moment to the idea of natural breath and what that means. The natural respiratory rhythm of 'breathe in, breathe out' is translated into speech by the formula 'breathe in, speak out'. That simple equation is what produces sound. But a perverse habit, common to women, complicates this simple task. They will 'breathe in' – then either hold or top up the breath – only to finally release and 'speak out'. This hesitation and suspension of breath is perfectly normal if we encounter a change of thought in mid-sentence. But when it becomes a repeated norm, as it is for many women, that signals hesitancy or loss of direction, it can reach the stage of becoming a settled habit. Speaking in this way can only come in short bursts and fragments. While I think that what I am about to say may sound far-fetched, I do believe that this habit of holding breath comes from years of thinking in this sequence: 'I want to speak / I breathe in / they are not listening or interested / I stop / I top up my breath / I'll try again / then again / to break into this conversation.' It sounds extreme and slightly comical but you can also detect in that fragmented scenario lots of frustration and struggle. It might account for the breathiness and huffiness of so many female speakers. Casual surveys amongst my female friends tell me that on nights out together they return to a more natural and relaxed breath pattern. Only in the company of less attentive male audiences does the snatched, held breath occur.

Until recently many women adopted an unnaturally high vocal pitch. There is a rather cruel joke amongst teachers in many British drama schools that you still hear those high-pitched voices from female candidates who have come from far flung parts of the country. Presumably they are cut off from feminism and themselves. The same seems to apply in the American South and Midwest where some young women seem equally disassociated from a raised consciousness. To squeak is still to delight! In order to appear feminine the voice actually takes on relevant disguises: 'niceness', 'vulnerability', the 'look after me I can't cope' voice. Please don't interpret my comments as being those of a radical feminist. Do realise, though, that the Women's Movement has given back to many females the rights to their own voices by getting them to drop artificial vocal guises and actually drop their voices back to the natural middle range. Too many women had it stuck in a 'shrill' top range, up in the head where it had no access to the chest. What a relief you feel once it is dropped! In the realm of voice work that has been a real bonus because the voice can suddenly explore all the lower resonances and shades. In the work I do the best and most well-rounded female actors are the ones who have developed the full range of their voices. Those still working in the upper range through habit are destined to play more limited roles no matter how great their potential talent.

Among all the female vocal habits, devoicing is the most common problem. It seems to indicate to the world at large a greater level of sensitivity and caring. We do not make an intrusive sound when we speak low yet we can also signal effects like 'I am really listening to you and being attentive.' The sound has a softness and lack of focus to it and can be immensely irritating for the listener. The devoicing speaker is frequently underutilising their potential and is not in serious competition with anyone else, especially more dominant speakers. Sometimes those other speakers relish it as Lear finally does that of his 'sweet' daughter Cordelia:

> Her voice was ever soft
> Gentle and low, an excellent thing in woman.

King Lear (Act V, Scene 3)

In speech, some women start and finish a thought with less than wholehearted conviction. Their sentences frequently fade, trail off or are left incomplete. The words they choose are less definite; strong words, if chosen, are more muted and held. Some men still hate to hear women swear, nor will they swear in front of them, as some sort of cultural taboo. Women carry that taboo within them and will normally drop to a whisper and secrete swear-words under their breath when they speak them. Profane expletives are normally a male preserve and women are denied the glorious physical nature of all swear-words. Habits in excessive swearing, however, can be both distressing and alarming when every other word is accompanied by one. There are plenty of women you meet nowadays who have this in common with men. Swearing does, however, allow the voice to tap its potential. Too bad about the words and what they signify!

In our age women together with men are in a state of transition. Fifteen years ago, to judge from my teaching then, the habits and distinctions between genders that I point to above were far more distinct and common problems. Women have adopted more of their vocal rights since then and are less prone to vocal habits. I still notice, however, when I teach in mixed groups, that the women are more likely to stay in the background with only a few joining the men in the foreground, both in work and general discussions. They will frequently blurt out replies to my questions, then show surprise and a little embarrassment that they have done so. So more aggressive tendencies are still in the process of being formed. A curious irony, however, is that those who have broken the barrier are taking on more of the male habits which I shall identify next. Almost as if to compensate for centuries of not being heard, some women go too far by either exaggerating or imitating the worst male habits of 'pushing' too hard, using excessive volume where unnecessary and, maybe worst of all, not listening and bluffing. 'Liberated' women, to stress their freedom and assert their rights, will be vocally insistent. It seems that to fight our way out of enclosed silence we are in danger of desensitising the voice and disconnecting ourselves from our bodies and breath. We have to learn instead not male attributes but something about human harmony: vocal balance and the smoothness of just 'being there' when we speak. The very best speakers in the world are not the overstated ones or the underpowered ones but those who have won the right to be balanced.

Men

The male habits I am about to describe are usually thrust upon men by prevailing views that a man must be strong, clear, assertive, individual, unemotional and wholly beholden to no one. It is also true that the shifting balance between the sexes through which we are working today means that some men are adopting the sensitive traits and habits typically associated with women.

Men, I think, have more pressure exerted on them as speakers. A statistic that I mentioned earlier shows that four out of five stutterers are male. Girls are allowed to make mistakes with words, be more extravagant with them; boys are not allowed either luxury. They are drilled to be clear and to speak without hesitation. Due to pressures like this many lapse into long silences at an early age. Challenge a child on a mispronunciation, a pause, a repetition or a hesitating tick once too often and you could be on the way to creating a stutterer. The first step to a cure is to relieve the pressure on the child. A more advanced step might mean resorting to speech therapy.

Because they are more verbally challenged than females, males have an assortment of weapons in their vocal arsenal. Let me start with the most typical male vocal habit of all, something that I call 'bluff'. Physically, men are expected to appear more powerful, more macho, more cocksure. They feel they have to be centred, balanced and 'there' without any emotional build-up. Sport requires them to have instant reflexes to both danger and competition, although they can also get locked into habits like being extremely physically rigid and lacking in all flexibility. You see both in developing boys. I think all this carries over into the voice and gives it the same characteristics.

Many male speakers brace and hold themselves across the shoulders, pulling them back, lifting their upper chests the way a pigeon does in the puffed-up power of a mating dance. Locking their spines in place men push their heads forward to confront the world. All this physical rigidity signals 'bluff' – the terrible fear of being perceived as either weak or unprepared. Oddly enough all this physical posturing can weaken the body and, in quite a different way to female habits, disconnect the voice.

Although men can freely open their thighs and spread their legs when they sit or slouch, taking up space in a way that many women would find difficult, all of this can be taken too far. Striding too much, creating heavy footfalls, thrusting the pelvis forward – none of this is conducive to a balanced, centred body but just a bluff.

Men, I've noticed, allow themselves much more time to breathe than do women. They are more connected to the right to breathe, especially if they have played lots of sports. They acquire natural habits in breathing but often take the right to extremes. Males will often cut off from their breath, however, if forced to show weakness or emotion. Security in full breath can produce some of the most droning and boring speakers; a speaker so certain and assured of his ability to hold forth and awe an audience of listeners that no real effort, excitement or need is put into the voice. All of us have heard this kind of speaker go on ad nauseam. The bluff here is couched in ponderousness. Male 'buffs', too, those hobby enthusiasts who wring your ear with arcane bits and pieces about their work or recreation, like railways or computers, hardly ever seem to have to catch their breath but can go on and on. I've rarely met women with that same capacity to bluff their way through hours of talk. Despite the enthusiasm, despite the interesting details, the bluffer can be an enormous bore. And just you try and interrupt that kind of speaker or change the topic of conversation – you'll either be bulldozed by an aggressive avalanche of new facts and figures or be seen as a threat.

In a desperate attempt to appear powerful many men speak more loudly than necessary and literally drive too intently through words and sentences. Listening spaces are shorter for them, the conversation more single-minded and one-sided. The 'drive though' habit leads to inflexibility in both range and intonation. This is quite understandable since listening and responding openly and emotionally to a dialogue between speakers is not something men give themselves over to easily. The male speakers who do are actually quite wonderful to listen to. Most of all they are attractively engaging because they take in what has been said and don't just limit themselves to a rhetoric of their own.

I speak so much about the emotional quality in speaking because I feel this is where verbal variety and colour are derived. Yet does it all have to be linked with grief, loss, pain and despair? It does not, in fact, need to have a thing in common with weakness or vulnerability. Men who talk with affection about a favourite sports personality, team victory or piece of crafted woodwork endow their speech with all the range and tonalities we usually associate with emotion. When we prevent any of this from entering our daily speech, however, or only show the emotional tones in displays of rage, assertiveness or even violence, we bar ourselves from one of the great treats of verbal discourse. Even when speaking about a balance sheet of figures, for example, an accountant can convey a world of excitement when it is released through the voice.

Rigid, unemotional speaking leads many men to suppress their voices down to a pitch that is lower than natural. The sound that emerges is anywhere between sonorous and gravelly. As a result many male voices are stuck and confined to the lowest bass ranges. This then leads inevitably to the voice dulling and rumbling around or being confined only to the chest and throat resonances. The result is that plummy sound which some men exhibit and take great care to cultivate. But it makes the placing of words forward in the mouth very hard to achieve. Lots of words get muffled by this habit and articulation is difficult to achieve. So although the voice is still capable of volume the words are harder to convey in space from too much bass feedback. Sometimes, too, speech trapped in the throat and chest, where the speaker swills and swishes it around like fine old brandy, can be mistaken for the clearing of the throat. That unattractive habit often punctuates this kind of speaking because accumulated phlegm is usually a hazard for 'throaty' and 'chesty' speakers.

Effective communication, as I have suggested above, requires the skill to listen. You develop your voice as much through hearing as through speaking. Many business executives in the highest echelons are good at their jobs and making their points because they concentrate on what their employees are telling them and they synthesise others' ideas into their own words. Yet one study has concluded that women hear and retain more information than men which is why, so the theory goes, girls achieve more earlier in schooling. Many males I have taught have the self-conscious habit of listening to themselves when they speak in a state of continual wonder about their voice. I have only come across a handful of women trapped in this same habit.

Men are much more confident in starting and finishing not only thoughts but whole conversations. They structure language and ideas more definitely, speaking confidently in entire paragraphs. They start and finish a word with more confidence too. The important topics are more their preserve, the frivolous ones not. Whenever I do playful voice improvisations, I always find that the women rise to the occasion and respond more quickly than the men. Males frequently lack the licence to engage in the more irrational side of verbal sport.

A startling change, however, is under way. So-called 'liberated' males are beginning to counter centuries of insensitivity to women with sensitivity, even adopting some female vocal habits. I and other voice and speech teachers have noticed that devoicing is on the rise amongst men, presumably as a counteraction to bluff assertiveness. There are more cases of men who exhibit the female habits of physical denial: slumping, round shoulders, hesitation in breath and speech. Men are beginning to feel the right to cry and speak more openly about their feelings. They are beginning to listen and not interrupt so frequently, allowing their voices to give and show sensibility as well as sense. All of this is enormously positive for fuller and richer voices. Nowadays, of all things, I have female friends who complain that their men are crying too much and being overly attentive and caring vocally. How we have changed!

6   Deep Habits and Release

The Terrors of Deep Habits

The range of habits I am about to discuss is common enough in everyday voice work to be mentioned openly and candidly here. These habits include those forced on some of us through serious abuse and physical or mental violations. This applies equally to women and men.

Psychic trauma of any sort – like the death of a parent in early life or of an adult mate – can easily shut down the voice which takes a while to recover. If damage has been done to us physically that too will echo in the voice just as it sometime echoes during a nightmare when we whimper or call out. Time and again in voice workshops I have experienced traumas of all sorts that are suddenly released along with the voice. The tightness held inside us seems to be interlocking. I think it is necessary to raise this aspect of work because it is a necessary part of rooting out habits and also expiating demons of affliction.

If the breath is affected and altered by even a quiver of emotion (the remembrance of a sad or funny event, a slight shock like a near miss, a gasp of recognition when we suddenly meet an old friend) as it always is, then it must follow that more powerful violations or grievings which are not immediately purged will penetrate deep into the breathing mechanism and lodge there like parasites feeding off the breath until eradicated.

Open discussions of some emotions in our society are still

considered either taboo or just in bad taste: death, incest, domestic violence, battering, sexual deviance, crime and guilt of every brand. By keeping silent at key moments of our life we lay the sort of unexploded mines that will tick away just waiting to be triggered. That trigger can easily be squeezed if we are encouraged to breathe deeply or voice fully at an advanced stage of voice work.

The voice teacher is in the front line of action in these instances and can receive both the impact and implosion of this sudden release. I never encourage a teacher to trespass into the lives of students but I would be naive and less than truthful if I said I have not been hit by various bits of emotional shrapnel during these episodes. As a teacher I often have no idea what has just happened to someone outside the classroom. Have they just witnessed a road accident? Has their flat been burgled? Has there been a death in the family? Have they just been mugged, had a row with a lover, a friend, another teacher or a parent? All and any of that happens quite regularly, but breathe deeply after any one of these kinds of traumatic events and the result is something I liken to a sort of delayed 'vocal shock'.

I never force any student to perform an exercise that will make them panic or surrender emotional control. It has to be someone's choice to go in that direction when they feel ready. There are breath and voice exercises that I can guarantee will have eighteen out of twenty-five students in tears within five minutes. Voice work can be that powerful. Getting down to the deepest breath is sometimes a bit like a diver going beneath the ocean in one of those old fashioned deep-sea diving bells where you are suddenly sensitive to the enormous sea pressure pressing against the walls. I never use these exercises unless I am sure of their purpose and when there is a high level of safety and familiarity in the group or trust within an individual; usually this kind of work is done for professional voice students in advanced stages of training. A professional speaker who simply must develop deep relaxing breath capacity in order to meet rigorous vocal demands must head eventually in this direction, taking the voyage down past the ribcage and into the abdominal area; the one place that normally remains sealed off.

But let me explain what happens during these experiences so that you will understand why it relates to habits and our rights as speakers. Habits in the breath and voice, many of which I have already described above, can be either superficial or chronic. They can also create themselves as a means of blocking the memory of a painful and intimate horror. When that block is gradually eroded through proper relaxation, breath and voice work then memories long encased will inevitably spring forth. Suddenly a crucial event is relived, at other times rage and pain replayed or even felt for the very first time. This kind of emotional outpouring happens too often and too regularly to be ignored.

Each time encounters of the sort I will mention were disclosed, I was working solely on breath. In each case the person was someone holding back the breath in the lower abdominal area and we were in the process of releasing it. On at least seventy-five of these teaching occasions over the years people have spoken about various kinds of sexual abuse as youths and adults or instances of childhood rape. On most of these occasions I was the first person to hear about the abuse and 'witness' it through a vivid reconstruction by the victim. All seventy-five of these voice cases were evenly divided between females and males, younger and older persons of different classes. The vast majority were successful in their careers already or aspiring to be the best in their profession. So none had any reason to show inhibition or restraint or to be secretive in any previous phase of work. In other words there was no 'crying wolf' involved.

As the breath goes lower and lower past its superficial and then its normal capacity in the throat and upper chest, then down through the chest and diaphragm where a more intense capacity lies, and then deeper, yet deeper into the abdomen and pelvis, it settles down into and disturbs a habitation untouched by the intellect and rationality. When it does hit bottom it sometimes dislodges a vital clue to our being – the secret life held down under the deepest of breaths: 'I was six, I was walking across the heath from school, a man was following me . . .'; 'My uncle used to take me sailing, when I was seven he made me . . .'; 'When my mother was ill my father would come to my room . . .'

All the tellers of these stories said they had been frozen into silence by the outrage and all felt the deepest of guilt because of it. Some had never been able to find the right way to give the experience words or the horror a name. But the details were vivid and freshly felt. All then went on to examine and expiate the experience with specialists who could give them proper counselling and help. All said that as they found themselves breathing without barriers to contain them deep pain, deep experiences were suddenly released and, like a diver with bends, bobbed to the surface. All of them said that the guilt they felt had made it impossible for them to make any sound either during or after the violation. The victim was not even given the right to whimper, not even the right to release the feeling of injustice into a scream.

My conclusion about this is that we can block and seal the memory of a vile sexual penetration under the breath. We can hold and freeze it in the muscles of our groin and contain it there for a very long time. The breath can also thaw it. Air and oxygen can bring it to the surface. It has the right to spill over into a recognised experience. It has the right to be discovered and uncovered so we can finally be released from its grip.

Our habitual impulse is first consciously and then unconsciously to tell ourselves, 'If I don't breathe down there, if I hold it tight and wrap myself around the wound, I won't be reminded of the horror, the suffering, the guilt.' But experiences like this are an inevitable aspect of deep voice work. At some point in the life of a professional voice user deep breathing has to be on the agenda. After this kind of release some people reckon that they 'had always been looking for a reason to breathe down there.' The terrors of the deep had been broached and exorcised.

I have found this same holding pattern in women who have been raped. They were obviously more conscious of the violation than those who suffered childhood abuse, but not as conscious of the ensuing pattern of restrictive breathing. As we progressed further with work, each felt the hold and then the experience billowing up from within them and then uncontrollably releasing wave upon wave of rage.

Grief and rage are also released through the breath and related exercises. It is as if from adolescence onwards we are not encouraged to breathe, not allowed the right to wail or howl when we are abandoned as we did in infancy and early childhood. There are therapies based on the primal scream. Deep breathing is not one of these but it does tap a sound we have been forced to deny and forget.

It is a cliché (and a much too embracing one) that Anglo-Saxons pride themselves on their control and propriety. The display of grief is neither proper nor adult. As we colonised the world that control gave us a sense of superiority and maturity over races more emotionally open than our own. A demonstration of grief, however, is cathartic and not in the least disgraceful. I remember some years ago seeing a Portuguese farmer wail and wail at the loss of his child. He was beating himself and releasing strains of the freest sounds possible. Every cell of his body seemed committed to the sound. I felt a mixture of embarrassment and envy, envy that he was allowed to mourn, embarrassment that I had not been conditioned to accept or experience this depth of public emotion myself. Three days later I met him working in an orchard; he was obviously still in pain but seemed lighter and not so burdened by the grief. There he was at work again, not denying the pain but working and living alongside it. He had taken his human right to feel and express the deepest mortal sorrow.

If we deny grief as it is happening we open ourselves to a habit that can fester for years to come. By not releasing it when we should we endow it with a power that can deaden and overwhelm us. While doing some deep breathing exercises just last year I found myself purging the death of Nanna, my dearly loved grandmother, nineteen years after her death. I hadn't mourned her at the time of her passing and it took the loss of another friend to jolt my whole breath system into the right to grieve.

Loss becomes more insidious and infiltrates on a deeper level when society decides that grief is only appropriate for some and not others. We all recognise national days of mourning but what about lesser examples: the legal spouse, but not the lover, gets the right to grieve when a husband or wife dies; the death of a favourite pet is often mocked and not taken seriously; the embarrassment that gays are greeted with when a partner leaves, becomes debilitated or dies from AIDS. Some forms of grief fall outside the parameters of what is socially acceptable and make it harder to vocalise the deepest feelings. Families have a priority on grief above friends. Sometimes grief has to remain secret and go underground. At some stage, though, it is sure to haunt us.

Linked with the denial of grief – the 'lump in the throat' – is the habit of pushing down on the voice. In order to block pain and contain it the voice feels literally clumped in the throat like a mass which we neither swallow nor expel. Expression is obstructed. We want to cry out but stop the sound in the process and deny ourselves the right. Most of us have felt this clamp at funerals and even at sentimental movies. The jaw tightens and the throat constricts, the breath shortens, the lips quiver, the shoulders brace.

I once taught a student who had incredible tension in the jaw, throat and high breath. No exercise could shift the physical habits, everything failed even though he seemed so willing to try. Then one day in a text class concentrating on classical Greek drama came a breakthrough. Something in the

text touched him and as he went with the emotional discovery
his voice suddenly released with sounds I had never heard
him make. Suddenly he howled and howled and howled. He
could not stop and needed to be given time and space alone.
I and the rest of the class discreetly left him and some hours
later he came to find me to apologise (not that he needed to).
He had lost both his parents within six months when he was
sixteen. Being the eldest child he had to remain firm and cope
with the grief of his brothers and sisters. He had never been
given the right to mourn but had settled into a steely state
of restraint. Still he felt an apology was in order. From that
moment of unexpected release his voice never looked back.
It got stronger and stronger, never again exhibiting any vocal
tension. All of it was released in that one session. This is a
good instance where work on a text can be keenly related to
releasing a long held habit. For this particular young man the
Greeks' notion of 'catharsis' or purgation became a key factor
in his voice process.

Surely one of the uses of ritual is to provide an outlet for
overwrought feelings. All surviving forms of rituals that one
can still study involve some form of breath work and physical
vocal release. Chanting, humming, singing, dancing, keening,
kneeling and moving in processions are all expressions of the
breath pattern that the ritual imparts. Sometimes it is slow
at the start, then it becomes agitated with the advancing
crescendo. The mood of a ritual strikes the vocal tone. The
group aspect of ritual, the mutual support of many voices
and many breaths, gives safety and support to the expression.
You can still experience this at football matches if you are all
part of the same group of supporters. Many societies, in my
view, have sensibly and vigorously held on to many forms of
ritual and encourage active participation. The Irish wake is
a simple example. Theatre is obviously a remnant of rituals
that once purged audiences and now it just entertains them.
But when it does occasionally touch its ritual roots actors will
speak of the audience as 'being at one' with them, sharing the

same breath. However, most White, Anglo-Saxon rituals have become clinical, dead and boring. Perhaps when the modern age began to question whether God was dead a spark of breath was extinguished from our lives. Rituals are about the right to fiery beliefs, whether they are pagan or deeply religious ones, and they open the vocal instrument in ways most of us would deny is possible.

The severe forms of denial I have been speaking about, the ones that set as habits and are a result of physical abuse and violation and unexpurgated grief, can be so potent and dramatic that it is sometimes hard to give credence to lesser examples of the same habit-forming experiences. Children and young adults who are relentlessly mocked, teased, mimicked and ridiculed by parents, teachers, friends or partners may not have been beaten with 'sticks and stones' but 'words' do hurt them. The process of closing off is slower but often it becomes more insidious. No one root to the vocal problem can be traced. But the gradual erosion of self-worth – sometimes amounting to little more than legalised abuse or to a greater degree verbal rape – has a way of settling into the voice. Any criticism that threatens and attacks our essential being or upsets our balance is potentially lethal. Sometimes the result is as dramatic as leading to full silence. More generally it results in hesitancy, a distrust of ever being open and fully declarative, a resorting to sarcasm and snideness as a defence, a general sealing off from the openness of language and voice. If the comments are skilled and torturous enough the victim begins to believe them and adopt such a low self-esteem that being, breathing or speaking is a right easily abdicated. The next time you are fairly or unfairly questioned, either subtly or angrily, notice what happens to your breathing. That is the best test of what I mean.

Many faltering, frightened speakers, stutterers, devoicers or shallow breathers have described some past scenario that is crucially linked to their voice pattern. The child who is continually mocked or teased by an overbearing parent; the partner whose sentences are always completed by the other; the daughter not actually being touched by the father but subjected to physical comments; the wife or husband put down or belittled by the spouse; the teacher who victimises a particular pupil; the academic or executive who lords it over the less well-educated or less skilled underling. All of these examples, daily examples we all experience, are a kind of verbal terrorism someone, somewhere in the world is experiencing each second of every day; not just in jails but in domestic situations. The effects on the voice are simply staggering.

Many years ago I found myself defending a student who had physically attacked a teacher. I was surprised by my adamant justification for the boy's action. I didn't know why I was doing it except that I was aware of, and had myself experienced, the teacher's wounding superiority and excessive put-downs. The boy was a terrifically instinctive actor without any real formal academic training. He had too few linguistic skills to be any sort of match for someone so academically superior as this teacher. I knew he had been under continual assault and might break as a result. The boy was found at fault and made to leave the school. That teacher still teaches. I moved on from that school, no doubt thought of as someone who condones student violence and so-called student rights. So make no mistake: words can break bones and hearts and minds! The voice, especially a quiet, reasonable voice, has the capacity to infiltrate and shatter us. The memory of an insidious comment, as vivid as any physical act of violation, can lodge somewhere within us and become entrenched in our bodies, our breath and our own voices. It becomes an echo in our communication, reverberating in the way we speak . . . possibly forever.

Not surprisingly, many voice teachers have reported a sharp increase in clients who have been made redundant from powerful jobs or are failing interview after interview in a quest for a new position. They are not showing their best, they say, 'because their voice fails them'. A long, uncertain period of unemployment leaves them cut off from using their voice in ways they know how; sometimes their fear makes them sound exhausted, lacklustre, defeated or simply listless. Their self-worth has been damaged so dramatically that their usual vocal confidence gradually ebbs away in direct proportion to the length of unemployment. Suddenly a once powerful and confident speaker now devoices or hesitates. We can all understand this process and may have experienced it ourselves. As a barometer of life's pressure, the voice is unfailingly accurate.

On the other hand many frightened or unsure speakers choose to compensate for perceived inadequacies or lack of qualities by speaking with a push to bluff their way through a situation. Unlike reticent and uncertain speakers they fail interviews for being too assertive, for coming on too strong, for being too loud and declamatory. A different kind of vocal pattern betrays an essential flaw in ability.

Many actors describe this kind of desperation when they attend auditions after periods of lengthy unemployment. They try 'too hard' to feign confidence and lose control vocally. Having sat on many audition panels and having interviewed many candidates for work I can say that a loud 'bluff' is as disconcerting to a listener as an ineffectual mumble. I will often just stop an audition to get an actor breathing and listening properly before restarting the piece. Both are manifestations of being walled up behind fear. Both can seal off a potentially talented person from what they have to offer in those brief moments of an audition or interview.

It would be a very rare, protected person who could live life and never experience some bruise or damage to their self-esteem. Understanding its effects and controlling the fear are possible if you can root out how it changes your breath, physical posture and voice. Whenever I can detect an accurate source for one of these losses of faith I immediately ask someone to check the following: 'Did you find that you stopped breathing deeply?' The answer is usually 'yes'. So a solid piece of simple advice to carry along with your résumé is 'Keep breathing'. It does improve a situation. With the appropriate breath as a regulator thinking, feeling and communicating become more possible. So:

- Breathe as you walk into an interview or audition.
- Breathe while either is in process.
- Breathe while the other person is talking.
- Breathe as you wait for the results.
- Breathe as you walk on stage for the press night.
- Breathe as you face your parent.
- Breathe as you confront your spectres.

But whatever the situation never follow that old adage and 'hold your breath'. That will only dissipate what is an essential right.

Laughter

I have been discussing grief and the habitual traces it leaves on the voice to such a degree that I fear I am leaving you with a maudlin impression. So let's look in the opposite direction to joy and laughter. What happens when we deny ourselves these kinds of rightful liberties?

Some people simply cannot laugh. It's true and it's regrettable. Laughter is one of society's most acceptable forms of emotional release, yet not all forms of laughter we hear are expressions of delight and triumph over mordancy. Analyse a day's collection of laughs and you'll probably notice the grimace behind the grin. Laughter often hides more bitter feelings. For instance we mock through laughter, hide shame and embarrassment beneath self-mocking laughter, we develop the nervous laugh, the sarcastic laugh, the secret laugh, the laugh that conveys a sneer or leer. Sometimes, instead of being openly aggressive, a laugh can either disarm or be a more deadly put-down of an opponent. A distressing laugh is the one that is circumspect or hollow: 'The watch-dog's voice that bayed the whispering wind, / And the loud laugh that spoke the vacant mind' is how Oliver Goldsmith put it. Laughter accompanies barbs, called wit or irony, and is very hard to defend ourselves against. If we do try we are parried with 'Where's your sense of humour? It's all in fun. Don't let it bother you.' But it is usually too much in fun and it does bother us. Laughter can be superior. It bothers our voice.

Laughter can bond groups and exclude others. The 'in' joke or expression can be a very exclusive verbal domain. Giggling and tittering can be an initiation into an exclusive group with its own likes and dislikes and forms of exclusion. Those of us on the outside are typically bemused and uncertain about what to say when confronted with this sort of laughter. What is it saying, what is it disguising? How do we counter it in our own words?

One of the happiest things we can do in life is to laugh along with others without having any hidden agendas; laughing for the sake of pure joy without any intention to mock or sting. When we find people with whom we can laugh in this way we cherish them and are reluctant to let them go. What we usually notice is what liberal rights they take with the voice. The happiest voices I know are also the freest. They reach that same level of openness and release expressed through deep grieving.

Laughter can border on grief. It can serve as a welcome safety valve that releases pent-up emotions. We typically laugh after we cry, the cleansing tears of one emotion watering the other. A dear friend of mine who passed away arranged his own funeral. He prepared it with wit and flamboyance to capture more joy than grief. What people said about him led the whole congregation to double over in uncontrollable laughter until they were howling wildly in the church. He instinctively knew that if he gave us the right to laugh it would naturally hasten the right to cry. Without giving ourselves that licence we lapse sometimes into the smug humourlessness that tightens the jaw and restricts all but the passage of clipped reproaches.

I have American friends who refer to such people as being 'humour-impaired'. Lacking in humour is indeed a sort of handicap. Without doubt you can hear and distinguish one of these voices: a snort or dry chuckle under the breath rather than a rich resounding chortle. A laughter as thin as creased lips. This sort of humourlessness exhibits all the vocal denial that we find above in the grief impaired voice: tight lower support in the abdomen, restricted range, pinched reserve, a clenched jaw.

Just as it is natural for a baby to cry it is natural for it to laugh. Without holding the two in balance we arrive at a stunted emotional growth. If we keep grief and joy out of our life and out of our voice, only choosing to be deadly earnest, we miss the essential colours of the vocal palette. To play, to be silly, to laugh without disregarding others requires, I think, a sense of self-worth, balance and appreciation for life's abrupt absurdities. If we continually feel that the worst is likely to happen or that life and other people are set against us or threaten us, then spirited, unconfined laughter is denied us. You cannot, I think, be vocally whole but always vocally tenuous. The voice, once any of its rights are restricted, has a way of ducking for cover and avoiding expression. Disturb its balance and it most surely will cover itself and head downwards.

I remember leaving an underground car park and stupidly walking under one of those striped automatic barrier arms on its way down. It flattened me like a starfish in the sand, just like the coyote in the Roadrunner cartoons. At the time I was wearing a smart outfit and carrying an 'executive' briefcase. I must have looked completely ridiculous. What a blow to the self-esteem. I refused all offers of help with a vacant protesting voice, scuttled to my feet and set off for my office red-faced, humiliated and bruised. Only days later, after holding the humiliation inside me, did I release through laughter. How silly I must have looked! My self-image of being a smart executive had been knocked down and flattened on the oil-soaked floor of the garage. Isn't it true that we protect ourselves with these sorts of images all the time, refusing to look at the funny side even when absurd factors conspire against us?

Some of the funniest performers and comedians are totally devoid of a personal sense of humour. When you meet them off- or backstage you expect to meet hilarity personified. What you usually encounter is someone morose. All the humour, like all their breath, has been expended for the benefit of the audience. They have nothing left inside. Silliness to them is serious business.

So many people feel that they might lose control should they laugh too much. The look of laughter is slightly odd and even grotesque: again, that grimace reflected in the grin. Laughter is sometimes seen as a weakness, as a professional liability. When everything is turned into a joke it certainly is. A teacher, in the opening of term, will usually restrict laughter in order to maintain discipline and feel under threat when it gets out of control: 'a time to work and a time to play.'

Many gay men have asked me to recommend ways of helping them stop sounding 'camp' in public. We all respond with snickering humour to a camp voice. But until the speaker comes to terms with the humorous and parodistic side of that speaking style their voice and delivery will always carry that label. Hostility to homosexuals usually starts with hostility to their voices. The same is true with hostility to any social group that speaks up and speaks freely. Usually gay people have to survive a brutal onslaught of comments and repel them in a voice trebly affected. As a means of saving face and self-esteem some let an attacking humour enter their voices as a countervoice and as a way of distinguishing themselves as being part of a group. But Blacks do this too, along with any group under threat because of the way they sound.

All these vocal attitudes towards humour intrigue me personally because I think I was twenty-seven before I suddenly realised that I too had a capacity for humour but had been denying it, and suppressing it in my voice. I was repeatedly told by family and school friends that I lacked a sense of humour. I believed them. I was serious. I fell into the rut of a habit. My voice became controlled, terribly self-important and sounded arrogant. People relied on me for help, personally and professionally, so I became adept at a good discussion but wasn't what you would call a barrel of laughs to be around. With this kind of voice, I felt, my opinions were worthy and carried weight. I acted in a tolerant manner but sounded like an intellectual snob. My voice said it all. I was the perfect specimen of someone 'humour-impaired'.

Several events happened that shifted these habits. I found I could make my students laugh – not at me but with me. I began to lose some of that superior control over my life and actually shrug off responsibilities in ways that are necessary for the sake of release. I began to see my silly side. In other words I began to laugh the kind of laugh that is a great restorative. Just as there might be a howl waiting to be released, a resentment waiting to explode, there is a laugh waiting to jostle and settle our whole body and being back into proper working order.

Once I experienced that realisation for myself and began to see how hooked I was on the habit of being too serious, I noticed my voice changing dramatically. It still gets trapped in the serious middle range, but I find that taking the right to express humour will spring it to a higher, more expressive range. When I speak now I experience a new vocal flexibility and tremendous ease that I don't think was there before.

Deep support and breath work will often get non-laughers laughing uncontrollably. Laughing and crying involve the same physical activity. The techniques taught for natural crying are close to that of laughing. Each cry and laugh differ but both are activated by the same means: there can be no physical barriers in the jaw, throat, shoulders and upper chest; deep breathing is activated for an uninhibited flow of sound; there is no glottal attack or constriction in the throat, no devoicing or swallowing of sound. Significantly a good laugh or cry shakes us like an aerobic exercise, loosens us so that we get the full benefit of its effect. When a mime artist mimes he or she exaggerates this physical activity as a replacement for actual sound; an instance of the action speaking louder than the sound itself. We too are trying to achieve the effect of 'laughing until our sides ache'. That way we are physically experiencing a rich, loud laugh.

Received Attitudes

Often our voices become inhibited by received attitudes that society imposes on us. The attitudes are all around us, they are in the air, and we need to come to grips with them before proper voice work can begin. One of them is our demand for an instant cure for any problem which is, in fact, only counterproductive.

The natural voice works from a free, effortless position. Push, attack and overambition won't help. That kind of drive is usually the kiss of death where long-term benefits are required. It is like the energy that we put into faddish diets or exercise programmes. Many of us, particularly in North America it seems, live for quick results. You come across this most noticeably in students: 'If I read this booklist will I be educated?' A fine enough attitude if superficial facts and figures are all we want to learn. But knowing your body and learning to recognise what affects it and induces habits, is part of a self-knowledge process dependent on an astuteness and a sensitivity that is not part of some calorie count.

Physical and vocal changes happen in depth. You can achieve rapid results but don't cram too much into the work too soon just as you wouldn't read this book and expect your life to be changed forever. Many voice exercises fail if you do them too hard in the expectation of results. They work best when gently and gradually done and without too much mental analysis. Voice work is very much the opposite of weight work or aerobics. It is not rigorous cardiovascular exercise. In fact that kind of exertion works against you. Doing an exercise easily, just for the sake and fun of doing it, is probably the healthiest way of approaching the work. Once it becomes a rigour or an intellectual challenge, drop it. Many of my exercises are accompanied by the note: 'Do the exercise with the text and then speak the text before you give yourself time to think about it.' Too much thought at the wrong juncture will cut us off severely from our bodies, voices and emotions.

Many American students, in particular, love to write everything down. I have to ban note-taking from my practical classes. It is too easy to write down a physical exercise. By making a note we feel that we have dealt with an exercise and have learnt it. The intellectual basis of most education means we don't take the learning experience deeply into our bodies, feelings and souls which, of course, is what has to happen in voice work. To free the voice means we might have to alter some of these received notions about how we learn. Voice knowledge, I think, is felt in the breath rather than the brain. This is one of the reasons I object so adamantly to the sort of voice training that psychoanalyses or spiritualises the process rather than simply approaching it through the body. The body seems more adaptable and flexible than we give it credit for being. If we short-circuit some censoring thought processes to get inside so much the better.

Many zealous and over-ambitious people benefit most from simply relaxing and doing nothing more complicated than 'breathing in, breathing out'. If you are anxious about meditating on something during this simple exercise then meditate on the breath – its coming in and going out, its circulating and refreshing the entire system. I am always amazed how panicked people become when given the chance to take this simple right. There seems to be a lot of guilt associated with just 'being' and breathing.

With students I often have to strike a bargain. They feel fine about just being, breathing and presumably doing nothing as long as they have been ordered to do it, 'instructed' to do it. I have even received panicked telephone calls from performers and speakers backstage asking me to tell them how to relax. Often by short-circuiting the mind and just breathing, just doing nothing for a moment, the body and mind literally 'catch their breath' and catch up with one another. Over and over in voice work it is of key importance that you strike a balance between all areas of the physical and mental state.

The over-ambitious speaker, once he or she has entered voice training in earnest, will always exhibit any one of the following habits: tight shoulders, head jutting forwards, a higher breath that is more rapid and snatched, pushed delivery, overemphasis, speaking too fast, not listening, cutting into others' conversations, impatience, etc. In short, working too hard and too quickly to achieve a result. You cannot please a teacher in this sort of work ('Am I doing this exercise right; am I doing it well?'), you have to do it for yourself ('How does that make me feel now?'). By learning to monitor ourselves we take responsibility for our voices just as we should any life skill. Along with panic I sometimes see confusion in many students' eyes when I ask them to assess their own voices and progress. 'That's for you to tell me,' they seem to be saying. No. You have the right to judge yourself. You have the right to your own self-approval and to be fully satisfied.

The Right Sound Attitude

Early on I talked about the myth of the beautiful voice. Now I want to mention a slightly confusing and similar habit that is sometimes engendered by some voice and 'elocution' teachers – striving to achieve the 'right sound'.

This syndrome of believing that each of our voices can strike the 'right' uniform sound and that a teacher is there to tap it in us or fix what we naturally have already is one that many actors and professional speakers find a gravely disquieting notion. A fear develops that there is one right

way of sounding or speaking, especially in the delivery of
Shakespeare, for instance. There is a rampant belief (born of
the mistaken notion that somewhere locked away in a safe is
an 'official phonetics chart') that a voice or speech teacher is
out to get you to talk in a specific way. This habit is confining
because it restricts anyone's ability to work in the right way,
especially if we are under the impression that there is only
one right way to sound. Imagine the cold sweats this habit
produces. One wrong sound and you're out!

What results is an imagination and response to language
that are seriously blocked. Most of us, in fact, live under the
impression that words can only be pronounced in a certain way.
The habit of needing or relishing a word for its own sake has
been beaten out of us. Sometimes, too, the need to enunciate
overtakes the more critical need to experience a word's fulsome
texture no matter how it comes out of our mouths. Affectation
in speech then begins to suppress the organic. That hesitation
you always notice in someone trying to 'sound right' begins to
inhibit the sound that is right for us.

It is fair to say that some people, especially students in the
process of voice and speech training, always begin to 'put
on' a voice while on the way to finding their own voice.
Acting students, in particular, try to sound like their favourite
actor. Often this is just a temporary habit like the occasional
stammer. It is nothing to worry or feel self-conscious about
except when the 'put on' voice replaces the real one. Then
it can be worrying.

Every year at the Guildhall School auditions I hear damaged
voices. A person could, for instance, either have been screaming too hard at football matches or have been abominably
taught. The damage is tangible in the sound. More common is
the damage done to someone's vocal and linguistic imagination
by being taught the 'right sound'. They have usually been
drilled to speak in such and such a way and in a pattern
directly opposed to the centre of their being. Trying to unknit
that pattern from their vocal tapestry, trying to dismantle the

drilled-in habit is enormously difficult. The habit has hardened into a personal trait. Anyone can feel, quite naturally, that they are being assaulted and picked at unduly. A remote tendency has become habitual or they have been rewarded for making an acceptable sound alien from their own or for choosing to use words for some other reason than need. The student who has been strictly taught some form of 'elocution', for example, usually comes burdened with lots of disadvantages when entering an audition. Usually such a student is under verbal stress and has to be vocally detoxified and shown how to rediscover their natural vocal and language abilities all over again. They have to be given the right to be children all over again, allowed to discover natural language and vocal abilities all over again, allowed to have their rights once more. We all like to be shown how to do something and great teaching can usually change our lives. So can poor and misguided teaching. That can blight our lives irreparably.

Vocal Imperialism

Throughout these opening sections I have been aiming comments at a habit that I think might be the hardest of all to break and the highest hurdle to jump: the sound of one right voice.

If you are White, well-educated, middle to upper class, Christian, heterosexual, able-bodied and most likely male then the next series of habits might not apply to you at all. The people that fall into this wide category have had the right to speak confidently on their side for centuries. They wield it as a powerful weapon and speak to rule. I am not talking here about simple black and white issues, master and slave relationships, but just an obvious fact that all of us would probably agree is true. There are perceived and dominant forms of spoken English that are deemed right and acceptable. We do strive to match ourselves with this one right voice that keeps our language inviolate. One dominant group has coined and codified language, kept it pure and without corruption, separated and segregated language groups and voice cultures that fall outside their sphere of influence. They have used the English language as part of the process of colonisation.

Our innate prejudices, pro or con, White or Black, are registered in our voices, absolutely branded there. No one habit is harder to break. A clear indicator of this habit is the sound and influence of names and what they immediately say about us or where they place us within the culture. All of us, either openly or under our breaths, use epithets to stress the gulf: 'wogs', 'niggers', 'yids', 'queers', 'spastics', etc. Powerful words, just sounds really, that say it all and expose a tense inner life of feeling about other people. The very sounds of these words are meant to give us vocal distance from any group not part of our own. Our venom and spleen become incorporated with the sound we make just as it can be heard in the words of Edmund, the illegitimate son of the Duke of Gloucester in *King Lear*: 'Why brand they us / With base? With baseness? Bastardy? Base, base? / . . . As to th' legitimate. Fine word, "Legitimate!"' As opposed to 'base' and 'bastard' the word 'legitimate' is a fine word. And all of us, all day long, every day, make similar distinctions that set us on one side of right against another.

Must a woman be weak because she has been described as 'weak' throughout literature? Must we continually pray to a male God for justice? I can still remember feeling unsettled as a young child, singing hymns in a girls' school with female teachers: 'Dear Lord and Father of Mankind . . .' Language represses and stresses cultural division. And when we speak we are never very far from falling into the clutches of this habit.

No matter what side of any debate you happen to be on – socialist or democrat, liberal or tory – you imitate the language of your power group. It is most often that of a civilised group but it can be that of a wholly separatist one. The English language, some would say, has been contaminated by other cultures. It is probably truer and more accurate to say it has been enlivened and enriched by being spoken in different groups and ingested back into the mother tongue. As a voice teacher attempting to help anyone to find their natural sounds I have to plead ignorance on many issues like this. I freely accept, however, that dynamism of language through its exposure to multiple linguistic habits always adds challenge to my work. Once I myself stopped believing that there was only 'one right sound' and began agreeing that there were only 'sounds' my task suddenly took on a very wide shape.

A Black South African colleague tells the harrowing tale of being taught her own dialect in London by a White teacher who had learnt the Black South African speech from a White European living in South Africa who had in turn learnt the dialect from tape-recorded examples! The tape recordings were taken from televised interviews of torture victims recounting episodes of violence. Many Black actors talk about the trauma experienced at drama schools when they were either punished for not sounding 'White' or punished for not letting their Blackness colour their voices.

There has been debate in some quarters about whether or not Asian performers have the vocal energy to fill large auditoriums and can be trained for European-style theatre. I have sat on committees where voice teachers will make sweeping negative statements against them. Having taught in India I know this is false.

Whatever their cultural differences, the voice of every culture works in the same manner. The biology, mechanics and hydraulics of the human voice are the same everywhere. Only our prejudices lead us to find cultural habits where none exist: Italians, Germans and Americans are 'loud'; the British all have 'stiff upper lips'. The Irish are too 'garrulous' and not to be trusted because of it.

I once taught a flamboyant Greek. His peers and some of the teaching staff tried desperately to contain him. His 'Greekness' was thought a liability; he was too loud, too colourful, took up too much space. No one succeeded in controlling him, thank goodness. His first job was a West End singing lead and he is now on his way to being a leading opera singer. An authentic, open voice is irrepressible. It cannot be contained.

The English will often define vocal directness as rudeness, as a result of which whole nations are dismissed because of their clamorousness. There was always a confusing clash in my home whenever Dutch relations and English ones mixed together. The cacophony of Dutch did not pass muster with the English ears.

Other voices have 'quaint' or unusual sounds that are put on show, fossilised or imitated for commercial purposes. The Scottish lilt is not as powerful as English Received Pronunciation but it is beautiful to listen to. I have seen Inuit Indian throat singers of North America put on display at voice conferences as examples of a rare species of vocal freaks. The sacred songs, stories and chants of cultures are often taught as novelties. A vocal technique that takes years and even generations to perfect is learnt superficially by Western voice teachers and then taught over the course of a two-day workshop.

A native American medicine woman told me that she and others like her keep their breath and vocal secrets to themselves. They jealously protect them from contamination, and well they should. Indian cultures have learnt the hard way on that score. The West, which prides itself on understanding and reason, has no understanding at all sometimes when it comes to the right to speak.

A Final Word on Habits

So where does all this leave me?

What I have tried to lay out for you as a major step towards starting some work with your voice are just some of the patterns that need to change before that work can have beneficial effects. I have reiterated the view that the inner and outer judgements we place on ourselves and others, the lifetime of habits that settle into all parts of our bodies, hearts and minds, prevent the natural voice from finding its space and place.

We must open our voices without fear and repression, let them come through as far as possible without censoring judgements. Bearing some of the above in mind you will know when the right to speak has seeped through. You will know because your voice will tell you so. It will be clarion clear, unshackled, effortless and tinged with humour and will sound the healthiest notes you will have ever heard. It will sound eventually like you.

But do remember one piece of sound advice: the right to speak does not mean there is one *right way* to speak.

The gospel according to my singer friend expresses it best: 'God doesn't mind a bum note!'

Part Two
WORKING WITH THE VOICE

Everyone suddenly burst out singing;
And I was filled with such delight
As prisoned birds must find in freedom,
Winging wildly across the white
Orchards and dark-green fields; on – on – and
  out of sight.

Everyone's voice was suddenly lifted;
And beauty came like the setting sun:
My heart was shaken with tears; and horror
Drifted away . . . O, but Everyone
Was a bird; and the song was wordless; the singing
  will never be done.

Siegfried Sassoon
Everyone Sang

7   An Owner's Manual of the Voice

I have been discussing vocal habits and differences between various sorts of vocal personalities in the hopes of releasing you from the bonds that constrict the right to speak. I think of that as the 'troubleshooting' part of this book. So now let's see if we can actually break some of those habits, and change our vocal personalities in the process, through work. Let's see how we can take ownership of our voices.

In this section I will provide you with a compilation of exercises to use for working on your own voice and then take you through further areas of voice and speech work, ending with some crucial advice on voice care and health. So think of this whole part as representing an 'Owner's Manual of the Voice'; something you can resort to often for your own care and maintenance. From here on our path through the voice becomes quite technical and practical. I have tried, however, to keep everything as simple as possible so you can easily follow the process. My hope is that you can go off and work on your own.

The Necessity of Technique

I am going to advance the notion that voice work can often be most effective if we learn to work from the outside in. By that I mean working from the purely physical and systematic aspects of ourselves (the outside) towards the emotional and intellectual life (the inside). Over the past twenty-five years most vocal training (and most books on the subject) has stressed quite the opposite approach: working from the inside out. Technique, of the kind I now advocate, was thought old-fashioned; the world of inner feelings was new-fashioned. The word 'technique' became a dirty one and many useful approaches became suspect. The main fear in many minds was that technique would bind and inhibit the speaker's individual personality and muffle creativity through slavery to a robotic repetition of exercises. Technique, so the line went, disconnected us from ourselves. Ironically, technique now seems radical because so many people sense they must learn how to work with their voices.

Theatre directors, for instance, began to view voice coaches skilled in technique nervously. There was a belief (often well-founded) that voice teachers gave speakers 'line readings', that is, specific directions on how to speak, phrase or 'read' any line of spoken dialogue even if it compromised the sense or interpretation of the text. The voice teacher's prescription for everything was: 'Now say it like this.' Voice and speech work of the first half of this century had indeed been a steady repetition of phrases like: 'Repeat the line as I say it'; 'Inflect this word and stress that one'; 'Gesture on this phrase'; 'Breathe now on that word and continue with one breath until the end of the line.' So the pendulum during the late 1950s and throughout the 1960s and 1970s had to swing naturally away from outside technical training of the voice to intense inner work that stressed changing the self before we could change our voice and our speech. Rigid restrictions had made speaking a dull and deadly activity learned by rote.

Unfortunately, however, some of the finer aspects of technique were first purged and then lost and forgotten. What I would like to do is rethink some of these now forgotten techniques. But first let's take a look at the actual instrument we are dealing with before we begin to work with it.

A Quick Check-List of the Voice

I must admit that I hate looking at unsightly diagrams of the sort most books on the voice resort to using as illustrations. I hope, as best I can, to describe and illustrate the functioning of the voice through words alone. So this is how it works:

- The body houses the voice, providing it with shelter and protection. It breaks down into a series of convenient chambers each with its own separate and vital functions: the head, the mouth, the nose, the neck, the chest, the stomach, the pelvis and finally the legs and feet that earth us. In the best voices all of these parts work together in wonderful harmony.

- The breath, bellowed by the lungs and housed within the ribcage, gives the voice power and propulsion. The breath is that column of air that initiates, sustains and supports the voice. When you are 'winded' or 'out of breath' you naturally cannot speak. So breath is of crucial importance to any vocal action. We'll talk a great deal about breath later on.

- The larynx, that knotty chain of bone and cartilage situated midway down the neck, contains the vocal cords or vocal folds. As the breath passes over and between these folds they act in two ways: as a kind of valve that regulates air and as a vibrating mechanism that creates the actual sound we make. It is a bit like a set of wind chimes. If you stop now and put your hand against the front of your neck and quietly hum you will actually feel this process being activated as air strikes the cords. Concentrate on the action further and you will feel the sensation of the air passing up from the lungs as the ribcage, accordion-like, squeezes the held air and then opens wide once more for another try. Notice too that the stomach, which has not yet been mentioned, aids in the pumping like a helpful power substation. Continue humming and you will eventually need to stop and refresh yourself with another breath of air in order to begin again. That is the whole vocal process in one.

- The varying thicknesses of individual vocal folds produce different notes, like the varying strings of a harp when plucked. Hum higher treble notes or lower bass notes and you capture this effect.

- The notes of the voice are then reinforced and sustained further in various resonating cavities or chambers strategically situated throughout the rest of the main housing: mainly in the chest, throat, face, nose and head.
- In order for the sound you've just been making to leave the body, the voice most be 'placed' in the mouth. Just hum and then open and close your mouth in various ways, trying to feel the buzz on the lips when they are together. Now you are manipulating sound like a baby would and discovering the voice in action. Notice too that the jaw has to be worked at this point.
- Speech is the breaking up of these sounds into recognisable units called words. Any English-speaker, French-speaker, Russian-speaker or Japanese-speaker, for example, simply puts a different vocal spin on these units to produce their distinctive languages. Although any speaker produces the basic components of voice in exactly the same way (all of us around the world sing the same), our languages are shaped differently in the mouth.
- The speech sounds that produce this language are then interrupted further and 'chewed' by mouth organs: tongue, lips, teeth, soft and hard palates, the jaw again and facial muscles. These conspire to produce the huge variety of speech habits and distinctive articulations we hear. Try this sentence for size to experience some of this; it's Hamlet's well-known prose lines to the players:

  'Speak the speech I pray you, as I pronounced it to you, trippingly on the tongue.'

- Say it low, then say it in different volumes, trying to make different kinds of sense of the words. Notice all the action going on in the mouth as you do so. That is you trying to articulate and manipulate sound in all parts of your mouth, forcing or placing the sounds and words outside you into the world.

The Arc of Breath

Each point on the above check-list I shall be discussing in much greater detail below, but it is important, I think, to note also that the voice works like an arc from conception of breath to placing of sound. Women preparing for childbirth are taught ways of using their breath in exactly the same way as any speaker should. Breath for the very practised voice should come from its lowest and deepest source, the pelvis area, and then be propelled up through the abdomen, chest, throat and out of the mouth producing a rainbow of different sounds while keeping the motion of the arc constant and clear. As an example of the kind of release you are trying to achieve with the mechanism, think of calling across an open field to someone. You try and direct the voice, aim to hit someone with it. So like an object, an arrow for instance, the voice has to be sent in an arc. I say this here because most of us suffer the same basic problem when we work with our voices: we are cut off from the breath. We speak supported by short bursts or fragmented gasps of breath that overburden the whole vocal process and cut down its efficiency as a mechanism. The body and the voice are machines that you can learn to work extremely efficiently without hiccups occurring along the way. The greater resources of breath are both figuratively and literally in the bowels of the mechanism.

All of the above is by way of a brief summary of how the voice and its mechanism work and why the breath is so vital. Now let's examine all of that in detail and finally get down to the actual working on our own voices.

A Finely Woven Tapestry

When you do voice work it is crucial to remember that each step in the process comes out of and is connected to something else. The voice is like a tightly woven tapestry, all threads of the work are interconnected. Every idea I mention and every exercise we do is fused to something else within the scheme.

The voice is totally dependent on a speaker's moods, energy and intellect. The voice is actually a fine barometer of the atmospheric pressure within someone's body or life. Effective communication is not just about a well-produced sound. To teach you how to speak and articulate words is useless if done in isolation from the whole process which is the voice. In a way speech is like the final outer edge or fringe of the tapestry. So much of the colour and richness of the central panels lies in the deeper reserves and physiology of the voice. If we never allow our feelings, thoughts or imagination to enter our voices, the whole vocal production process will sound empty, unfulfilled and quite superficial. To get slightly mystical for the moment, the voice is an instrument that echoes the soul and it is the soul's energy that makes every sound unique. Matthew Arnold thought that 'genuine poetry is conceived and composed in the soul'. I think the same can be said for the sincerity of sound.

Daily I come across voices that are well-produced, clear and flexible but also dead-sounding, disconnected and boring. I always ask myself why this person sounds so dull and then I have to set about diagnosing the problem. Often the event they are speaking about has neither touched nor entered them to become part of the vocal tapestry; the voice has not been stirred and awakened enough to respond in all its full colour no matter how skilled they are at manipulating it. The soulfulness of the Black gospel singer I recalled above at the start of Part One is a good example of someone whose sound could be touched all the time. Love, grief, rage, joy, laughter, foolishness or just simple curiosity can stir this inner energy and stimulate the voice into action. Vocal imagination, I think, getting in touch with the soul of whatever you are trying to say, is the first place to start working with the voice.

Vocal Personality

Let the idea of the voice as a tapestry now just hang before you as an image and let's look at the voice in a different way.

All voices are unique. Each and every one has its own separate personality. When you link that vital personality to language you create an almost limitless instrument of communication. Various tones and moods are merged and manufactured in a limitless stream. When the voice is liberated from the pressure of habits and seizes its natural right to speak with unconstrained clarity, you become connected to what you are saying *in that very moment* and are never likely to say the identical word or line in quite the same way again. The moment and the sound produced will always be different. They become part of our evolving personality as we change from moment to moment, as we have new and different reactions to whatever ideas engage us. The duplication of sound and speech, the infernal 'sameness' and blandness, is what you want to begin avoiding when working with the voice. This is one of the reasons why great oral literature is always served anew and endlessly illuminated by coming into contact with different speaking voices. Imagine Shakespeare never being spoken twice in the same way! The combinations defy imagining. Yet individual personality and individual sound can manufacture endless combinations of meaning.

Working with the Body

In the quick check-list above I asked you to think of the body as a house. The body does house the voice and its state of repair in all aspects of its condition and functions is directly reflected in the breath and voice. If certain rooms of the body are tense or something is out of place or misaligned then voice work will be either a severe effort or impossible to do properly. So some renovation, or at least a little housework, might be necessary at the start: the roof may be leaking, the gutters trapped or the foundation sinking.

You cannot skip steps in the fundamental processes of voice work and so the body is the first place to direct attention. Any useless tension in the shoulders (a good place to pinpoint first), the upper part of the chest, the neck, the jaw, the spine, the lower back, the abdominal muscles, the feet and even the knees will lock the voice. These are those jammed doors of the house that usually need lubricating and planing for a smoother swing.

Let me first dispel a common misconception about tension. When I say 'useless' tension I mean just that. Not all tension is useless; some tension is very useful. Without tension as part of the framework, as in, say, a suspension bridge or a skyscraper, our bodies would collapse into a heap on the floor. And if you remove all defences to the body's natural tension, like when we black out, collapse is what we do. You can just look at animals and notice healthy tension in action: a cat setting itself to pounce, a dog alertly on guard. Part of the beauty of tension is that it signals expectation. Cats and dogs are continually alert and 'present' but do not carry or hold useless tension. They appear to be able to turn it on and off or have sensors that do the job for them.

So much of the tension that blocks our voice is used unnecessarily. It is beyond what is needed at that particular moment for that particular physical task. If you like, it is the too thick stitch in the tapestry that mars the overall design and is too noticeable. Healthy and appropriate tension, like the fight or flight tension required to survive an event like shock, is necessary to survival. So in a way the healthy tensions are those which come to the body's aid in times of stress and act almost as a counterweight. I recently had my hand trapped in the door of a lift. In order to save my fingers from being mangled I had to use extreme tension to pull the other way to get my hand out of the steel trap. Tension saved my hand from amputation.

When working with the body we have to address the useless tensions caused by fear, bluff and lack of ease, most of which are not necessary for survival but threaten us as habits. When we are relaxed and unthreatened, like a lounging cat or dog, we don't need to fidget, shift about, rock or shuffle. We feel at ease, we feel 'there'. When the great director and acting theorist Konstantin Stanislavski began to think seriously about the process of acting he reckoned that achieving a 'feeling of ease' was the most enduring task facing a performer. That is still true. Step one in working with the voice is finding for yourself that feeling of ease devoid of useless tension. Any unwanted, accumulated tension pushes our body in directions we call 'off centre', 'out of control' or 'out of body' like the sagging shift a house experiences during subsidence. Useless tensions are unsettling.

Body Language

To free and centre a body for working with the voice we usually have to rethink the vocabulary of our body language. There is a whole field of popular literature that seeks to educate us on how the state or placing of our bodies communicates power and self-esteem to the world at large. All under the heading of 'body language'. How we sit, stand and walk send out messages and cast us in an aura. Muggers, we are told, look for slumped, nervous walkers. Corporations train their executives to stride into a meeting and how to sit and shake hands. Physical skills are taught to maximise their effectiveness and to create 'a more powerful you'. Well, body language plays a large role in voice work, although the point of the work is more organic and lasting as a change and not just cosmetic.

Posture

Posture should be a key term in voice work. Unfortunately the term conjures up visions of school children walking around with books balanced on top of their heads or soldiers standing at rigid attention in a straight line. Posture to most people means the straight and upright, but for our purposes this sort of posture is the worst kind. Pulling the shoulders back and yanking the head up tightens the throat and stops the breath from sinking low into the lungs. This is the kind of posture that creates barriers for the voice. Upright students and soldiers at attention might serve society's notion of good posture but it doesn't help the voice do what it has to do. Besides, that kind of posture is meant to be accompanied by stern silence!

Perhaps our notion of what is beautiful and consequently 'artful' is to blame when it comes to rigid examples of posture. If you were to enter into a computer all the worst kinds of movement you can do to abuse the body and damage the voice, heading the list would be classical ballet. I have taught ballet dancers so I speak here from experience. Feet turned out, knees locked, chest lifted, spine arched back, jaw and head held tight. Beautiful to look at, lousy for the voice. Of course great dancers accommodate themselves to these learned habits and find ease within this strict form. But the terrible history of chronic dance injuries speaks for itself. It is an instance of art corrupting the natural with moulded tensions. Again, like the disciplined student and soldier, a ballet dancer works *en pointe* in silence. Add speaking to the action and it would be impossibly restricted.

The natural way of standing is based on achieving balance, ease and feeling centred. Leonardo da Vinci's famous sketch 'Man as the measure of all things' illustrates the ideal. So starting from the top and working down here is the natural stance for working with the voice.

A. Head

The head sits balanced on the top of the spine. Think of a ping pong ball balanced on a spout of water. It bobs and floats up and down, twists and turns sideways without the slightest effort. The spine threads up into the head like a continuous string holding up a puppet's head. Or think of one of those Greek statues harmoniously balanced on a pedestal. If you concentrate on any of these images and transfer that weightlessness to your own head you will immediately notice the useless tensions slipping away as the head becomes lighter and freer. It actually balances quite well without all that support from your neck and shoulders. It doesn't need to feel quite so 'attached' or 'riveted into place' does it? If the ball, puppet or statue were suddenly disturbed or abruptly pushed or its support removed each would topple over. Just the right amount of tension holds each perpetually in place. The head should avoid being jerked, pushed forward in a thrust, tucked back, its chin pulled in or the face arched to one side. Even excessive frowning disrupts the balance. Each and any of these motions or tensions disturbs the voice. Balanced and floating atop the spine, like a buoy supported by an ever-shifting sea, is something I'd like you to remember.

The jaw, a great zone of useless tension, should not be clenched, jutted forward or pinned back. It should feel loosely hinged and mobile. Tightness in the jaw is common. It holds the breath and disrupts articulation in self-conscious ways.

B. Throat and Shoulders

You can actually check to feel when the head has achieved a natural position: there is neither restriction in the throat to impede swallowing (try it), nor does the throat feel segmented but whole. You suddenly look out at the world to the point of the horizon, neither below nor above it. It should seem like a wonderful vantage point no matter what your height. The neck should actually feel slightly elongated and rather elegant. Again notice the absence of useless tension and a new lightness. That is balance taking over from imbalance.

The shoulders are neither braced up nor slumped down, neither increasing nor weighing down the head with useless tension. In fact the shoulders just hang naturally like any clothes hanger. They should be free and floating like the head. Shoulders are not constricting yokes holding oxen heads but the saucer that balances and steadies the cup for ease of movement and transfer. If you just stop now and hold your shoulders tensely and then constrict the muscles in your throat in a seizure you'll instantly feel how hard it is for the breath to pass and how much you hold your breath and block its passage. Now imagine doing that unconsciously all day long, 365 days of the year, year in and year out! That is precisely what the breath and voice can feel and it is not right that either should.

C. Upper Chest

The upper chest should be open and untensed so that breath circulates freely. Avoid pulling it up or caving it in. Place your finger between your breasts on the breast bone. Now lift the breast against the finger and then cave it in. In both cases notice the different difficulties in breathing. You might also notice how the position changes the way you feel or exerts tingles in other parts of your body like the ribs or lower back. Again, we do this daily more unconsciously than consciously. So think of what it does to the breathing.

D. Spine

The spine should be up and strong in the centre, neither snaked nor slumped like an attenuated 'S' nor rigid like an 'I'. Both positions cut off breath and vocal freedom. Both positions are self-imposed and learned habits that take more effort to attain and hold. The vertebrae of the spine need to evenly stack up one atop the other. It is not a position you are trying to get the configuration of here but simply something that feels balanced. Remember how much work the spine has to do: it holds the head and provides background support for the ribs, abdomen, pelvis and limbs plus all those organs, muscles and tissue. Getting the balance right here means helping to balance everything else, doesn't it? One way to experience the correct distribution of the spine's length is to lie on the floor. The spine instantly achieves its natural position and you can also sense just how much it is asked to support. You'll also notice instant relief to those parts of the body where a misaligned spine is exerting useless tension. One cannot say enough about the structural importance of the spine to the whole body.

E. Abdomen

The lower abdominal muscles are a sore point for all of us. Here is the place where a tremendous amount of useless tension is held in retention. The muscles should be unheld without being pulled in or pushed out in a bloated effect. In order for the breath to sink into the deepest regions of the lungs the stomach muscles cannot be taut or else they fight the process. The fear of appearing fat contributes to this hold. Heavy exercise to get thin and achieve a 'flat' stomach does something similar. In either case we add to the cut-off of the breath.

F. Knees

The knees must always be unlocked for voice work, the legs in a position almost ready to spring or sway in any direction. Too many of us use our knees rather than our feet to support the full weight of the body. The stress can be too great for these joints. Knee injuries (perhaps the most common sports injury), knee tension, 'trick knees' are each an inhibiting factor in working with the voice. Rarely do we think of the knees as affecting the voice but they do. It is part of the body's scheme of interconnections. Like the song says 'The knee bone is connected to the thigh bone . . .' But in fact locked knees do connect to restrictions in the throat and glottis, the pulled-back spinal column, the pulled-in stomach, and tensions to the calf muscles. Nothing in voice work can happen with locked knees.

G. Feet

The feet must take the full weight of the body evenly and not just on the heels, on one foot more than the other or the balls of each foot. Firmly planted feet is the ideal.

The Centred Position

Stand with feet directly underneath the hips taking the full weight of support, knees unlocked, spine up, back unbraced, shoulders unheld and head balanced on top of the spine. As you gently rock in this position you will feel the weight of the body find and return to its centre. If it is too far forwards or backwards something is out of natural alignment. Check again and make any adjustments. Now just stand that way for some time and experience what it is like being centred. It may feel like a new sensation.

> *He that has light within his own clear breast*
> *May sit in the centre and enjoy bright days,*
> *But he that hides a dark soul, and foul thoughts*
> *Benighted walks under the midday sun.*

John Milton

What you are actually experiencing is the physical fact that the 'centre' is distributed evenly throughout your whole body and not just confined to some mid-point in the stomach. This is a crucial fact to remember because any useless tension, even a useless thought on the brain, can throw you off balance. To test this assertion exert tension anywhere in the body: to an arm, leg, the back, shoulder, neck . . . anywhere. Slight jaw tension will pull the head forwards and the body with it. Even just let your mind wander adrift. The body will be unanchored and set adrift with it. The centre will not hold.

Recentring

Staying centred is a vigilant task. Obviously none of us can go through life with such concentration. We are, after all, only human. Resorting to tensions throughout the day to avoid dangers or confrontations (we slump to retreat or hide, for instance) is quite necessary for survival. They only become a burden and shift into habits when we cannot return to the natural, neutral, centred position but remain contorted like a petrified forest. Watch animals after they have had a confrontation. They don't stay bent out of shape with their back and fur up. They release and return to a relaxed centred position, sometimes after a scratch, a lick or a flop down. So do babies after a good screaming fit. Being centred (and what is more and more coming to be called 'in the zone') is fundamental to concentrated expertise in sports and martial arts. If you play any kind of sport or recreation regularly you will have noticed that your best winning shots are done with complete ease; all parts of the action work together. You are furiously active but centred. This crucial physical reference point is what we have to learn to return to again and again when we work with the voice.

Like a thoroughbred horse, if we are centred the world will view us as strong and in control. It is not just the horse who has to be trained to attain this but the rider as well. If we are not in the saddle firmly, riding centred, we are in danger of experiencing a nasty fall or a runaway steed. Imbalance, you see, can be a peril. Or compare the dog who is the leader of the pack with the one cowering at the tail end or off in the corner. Victims are always off-centre, always unawares, easy to push over. If we are honest with ourselves we know the people we can bully by the physical relationships we have with them. We also know who to talk down to and overrule with our voice. You can sense physical and vocal withdrawal. Technique or knowledge adds strength and suppresses weakness. It can even do it artificially like in those classes that offer 'assertiveness training' for women.

We could argue that our modern and often lazy, sedentary lifestyles have disconnected most of us from the easy, natural body position. Urban life, with its clinches and feints, clutches us and does not draw from us the same physical release that rural working life once did. I may sound like the bucolic romantic again but if you ever watch workers (or indeed try it yourself) labouring naturally on the land or at sea every action is centred, economic and paced with the breath. You yourself fall into a natural rhythm, like the swinging of a scythe, if you garden or just mow the lawn with a hand machine. You adjust and find a centre suited to the activity, even if it is just typing or knitting. Useless tension destroys the pattern, throws us off our rhythm, could damage and tire the body. Think of native people who have to survive in geographically extreme or inclement conditions. They learn to adapt and work with nature, not against it.

The centre alters to suit the task for optimum efficiency; body and breath patterns adjust in order to survive. This can be the case for anyone trapped and faced with sudden survival. I remember as a child nearly drowning at sea. The waves were overwhelming and furious, the undercurrent strong and pulling. I had to go with the conditions and not fight them, to get to the calmer centre of the turmoil. It is like sliding the car into the skid rather than away from it. The body and breath had to adjust instantly to the threat and oddly match its rhythm. Eventually the sea threw me up onto the beach. Survival meant the body and breath now had to adjust to a calmer, safer rhythm. So the centre of physical effort, you will appreciate, is constantly shifting and never the same. What is the same is the continual need for adjustment.

In certain situations we should not muck about with useless tensions or try to pry into their sources. Newspapers are continually full of stories of the woman lifting a heavy weight to free her trapped husband, or people trapped in mine shafts reserving breath in tiny air pockets for days, even weeks. Human beings have the endless capacity to touch off hidden reservoirs of breath and strength whenever they must. It is a deep power, hidden within us, that training and will can discover. But it will always be an undiscovered country if superficial tension and habits seal it off. In times of peril nature gratefully releases us to do the tasks that need accomplishing. Sometimes she takes us too far and we break down in hysteria or fitful states unable to breathe properly or think and act efficiently.

On a more daily level we have all experienced the urgent need to stand or speak up when passionately debating, arguing or noticing a wrong in progress. We have all had to 'rise to the occasion' at one time or another. They are usually emblematic vocal moments, for without even preparing or warming up the body and voice we automatically shift into gear and make true sounds. We seize the right to speak and be heard. The voice is confidently used to maximum potential. We are grounded and rooted. Each part of the body finds its place in the speaking act, becoming a perfect speaking machine. Can the whole system achieve this without suddenly rising to the occasion or being under threat in some way? Can we work with our voice like this all the time? Yes, I think so. At least we can try some techniques that will certainly help.

Being Rooted

When standing to do voice work we need to make contact with the earth – really feel rooted. We have to experience the contact through the soles of the feet.

Why? What is affected in the voice? The foundation of the voice is its contact with the earth. If you cannot feel the whole body through the feet as well as the earth balance is easily thrown off. Like a magnetic charge we have to be grounded. To feel fully centred and in touch with the breath, the lower part of the body has to be balanced as well as centred. Only proper even distribution of the weight over the feet gives this. A full voice works upwards from this support, it does not float. So the feet must take an even proportion of the weight and, to sense a state of readiness in full, you should be aware of the balls of the feet. You are standing alert and ready to begin.

The most common drawbacks here include too much weight on one foot or resting back on the heels so that the lower back is taking too much support. Misalignment can easily creep up through the legs, knees, pelvis, back, spine, shoulders and neck like a vine, sapping these parts of the body of breath. A loose foundation weakens the whole edifice.

In very tense people foot clenching or foot tapping robs the stance of centre and power. I'm sure you have probably noticed all the agitation and aggravation we put into our feet. Waiting impatiently for a friend or a late bus we pace and put our feet through all sorts of gymnastics. It is almost as though we were exercising the impatience through our feet. All of it stops as soon as the anxiety is relieved in some way. The joy of seeing that friend or bus suddenly appear brings the stance back to centre.

I have already mentioned how fashion is one of those habits that robs the voice and breath of power by our wearing of shoes that throw us off balance or cushion our contact with the earth: high heels, trainers, heavy boots, thick-soled shoes. Wear any shoes you like but never forget to give your feet and body the opportunity to realign properly. I know many singers who will not sing standing on a carpet because they cannot feel the floor through their feet. I remember at a North American voice conference the schedule was thrown into chaos when a Japanese Noh actor refused to demonstrate his technique on an expensively carpeted stage. He was accustomed to a hard wooden floor where his feet and body could feel solidly rooted for his exacting, calibrated movements.

The Knees

Many of us have the all-too-common habit of standing with our knees locked back. This is sometimes in tandem with the accompanying habit of pulling our back in, stiffening the whole lower half of our bodies. In this position the body is off-centre and unprepared to move quickly or with agility. It is also more leaden as though we have put braces around our legs. Knees have to be unlocked before an impulse or breath can move through the body and activate a movement or sound. If you stand, lock your knees and then produce a sound, notice the difference in quality when you unlock and try again. A certain pressure has been relieved in the second attempt, a strain felt the first time around. Officers and sergeant-majors on parade grounds usually emit strangulated commands from the locked position. The voice is not projecting up and out through the system. Imagine a tennis player or goalkeeper waiting with locked knees for play action to come their way. If you try picking up a heavy weight with locked knees (and many of us do) this is a sure way to suffer strain. The knees, like the suspension system of a car, bear and distribute weight.

I plague hundreds of students about unlocking their knees because I know it cuts off their breath and actually makes them self-conscious about breathing. Kabuki actors in Japan have adopted a technique of keeping their knees bent and their torsos lowered in order to tap a deep vocal sound. To some extent the bent knees help lift it through the body. There is enough medical evidence to suggest that a domino effect, starting from locked knees, creates a tightening in the throat. Again perform a test: stand locking and unlocking your knees. What you should feel is a ripple of pressure working itself through the system and then releasing. Now imagine that pressure as your breath. You cut it off when locked, release it when unlocked. Just like the locks of a canal.

As you stand your knees should feel loose and your back muscles untaut. You have to feel balanced without the imbalance that would topple you over in any direction. Stand waiting to receive the action.

The Spine

This is one of my main target areas as a voice teacher. When someone enters the room for an initial voice class with a collapsed, slumped or stiff spine I know that the whole vocal system has to be opened and realigned. Clearly half of the body, the crucial torso area, is under restriction along with the vocal instrument.

Many years ago a very famous and rather grand actress said to me: 'When the spine goes you age.' I understood some of the explicit relevance of that statement by taking one look at her body. This eighty-year-old with a supple spine could have been in her thirties. Her movements were that free and flexible because her spine was not rigid. It had not collapsed but was up. Her motto is one we can all share as a constant reminder.

When the spine collapses like a shrinking daffodil stem the whole body caves in. The lungs cannot properly fill with air so we operate at less than half-power and support. We also put pressure and constrictions on the neck and jaw area, the kind you feel if you nod off. In fact, let your head slowly drop a bit and you will feel that pressure first in your neck and eventually in the jaw. People with collapsed spines, sometimes suffered through injuries, have severe mumbles and difficulties being understood. Their vocal power is at a very low ebb like a long-playing record winding down. Also the emotional and intellectual energy in the whole body becomes numbed and depressed. Nothing can flow. The body sometimes feels like it has surrendered to a huge weight, and when not as the result of injury, the spine sometimes collapses through sheer laziness.

I once worked with a radio actor who was damaging his voice on the microphone. He did not require terrific amounts of breath or volume to be heard and yet his voice was tiring and showing the first signs of serious strain. I asked him to show me how he sat or stood in front of the mike. He showed me. He was completely collapsed down through his spine whether he stood or sat in front of it. Within a single session he was able to realign his body to a more correct and productive vocal position just by straightening up and adjusting his head. Any spinal weakening immediately throws the head off balance. The tension on the throat, where muscles are then asked to bear a tremendous weight, can be enormous and damaging. Many of us who work at computer screens which are too low are beginning to suffer from this tendency already. This tension on neck muscles can also lead to neck- and headaches. Once that radio actor released the tension on his neck and jaw and got the head upright, the voice instantly sounded and felt unforced. After this simple adjustment and physical centring, the voice strain was relieved. But it could have led to something more chronic and severe.

At the other extreme a too stiffly-placed or rigid spine will produce appalling shoulder and neck tension that can instantly freeze the entire vocal apparatus. I have taught sergeant-majors, town criers and masters of ceremonies on different occasions. All came to classes because they were losing their voices. No improvement was possible until the spine was relieved, breath allowed through the system, neck muscles relaxed and the vocal cavities opened. All these men had an initial horror of letting go of this spinal tension. They believed that their posture would suffer. The work that needed to be done was also frightening to them because all feared that shaking out their bodies and spines would interfere with their dignity and authority as speakers. But the ease they experienced as they let their spines relax was ample reward. The spine and its position and condition do seem to reflect the way we perceive ourselves in the world. The collapsed version smacks of low self-esteem. It will often subliminally communicate surrender, laziness and fear. The rigid, overly taut condition can be perceived as a bluff or self-righteousness. Watch a four-year-old sitting and you will notice how strong and easy his or her spine is. It settles into natural positions and the child is 'there' and not contorted. This natural position erodes as we age but it can be rediscovered by any adult. It profoundly affects all aspects of communication.

Shoulders and Upper Chest

Both these interconnecting areas are of crucial importance to any speaker. Habitual tension around these zones will block the voice and breath instantly. Here is where we immediately

feel the results of nerves, stress, fear and panic; that shaking
and trembling sensation that continues down through our
extremities. Watch any untrained, inexperienced performer
suffering from stage fright and you will see the shoulders
and chest begin to lift as the speaking event creeps nearer
and nearer. Without constant release in the shoulders and
upper chest the voice functions with limited results. The
shoulder-blades, in particular, lock and exert pressure on
the back of neck, closing the passage of air. It becomes
impossible to breathe adequately as tension begins to creep
into the throat and, mingling with tightness in the abdomen,
can produce a sensation of nausea. Most of us at this point of
feeling tension, as the grip on the throat tightens, complain
about being unable to swallow and unable to breathe. We
have all suffered this.

If the spine is in its correct position, up and flexible in its
support, then shoulders should hang down and slightly back
without tension. Habits that infiltrate the shoulders are a result
of holding, placing, bracing or lifting against a force trying
naturally to find its ease. In other words, we consistently go
against the shoulders' natural drift downwards by hunching
them in a different direction. Even as you sit there reading,
becoming more and more engrossed in the activity and engaged
with the words and thought, stop and notice how tension has
started to overtake your shoulders and upper chest. This is
the slow drifting tide of tension we have to fight against. In
order to keep this area free of contraction continual release
and monitoring are necessary. Even the slightest unease in
thought or gesture can make the tightness return so we must
put ourselves on constant reminder to release here throughout
the day.

Driving through heavy traffic, hunched with head in hand
over desk work, sightseeing, a spooky film, walking through
darkened streets at night, emotional frustration, even cold
weather will make this tension surface. The shoulders or the
upper chest will lift as a kind of barrier and take with them

the body's full weight. A vocal domino effect begins to take place throughout the body as tension is felt all over. As an instant remedy a small lift and drop of the shoulders back into their natural place can relieve the tension. But not a vigorous up and down action like you see most people do. That only displaces and induces more tension. You can also gently rotate the shoulders or swing the arms around. In other words 'let it go' easily.

As a voice teacher I have met so many people who have been deformed by this tension. Actors will particularly find this the root habit for much of their vocal loss. But I see this chronic tension in less regular professional speakers: stressed executives, doctors, solicitors and even actors who have been out of work for some time. Each tries too hard at pursuing their job, really pushing up through their chests and shoulders. Some of us are even unaware that our shoulders are practically up around our ears! We will complain of neck and shoulder pains, bad backs, fatigue or headaches but never make the simple association with holding our shoulders and upper chest. Once experienced, the relief of releasing tension here is immediate. Just stop and release your shoulders right now. I bet they have begun to creep up. Let them drop down and find their natural placement. You might even experience a sudden relief elsewhere in your body, like the lower back or abdomen or even in your thighs and calves. You will certainly notice your breathing becoming freer and perhaps more regular. You have just quickly understood a prevalent habit and have monitored it correctly. Now do it often and regularly. It does make a difference.

I have, however, met many people who love this tension. The effort of holding ourselves tightly here is associated with a sense of being active and hard-working. Release of this tension is too much like being at ease and off-duty. Generally during the start of a holiday, for instance, this is a part of the body where we allow tension to remain and one of the last to let go. Letting shoulders and upper chest drop surrenders to the notion that life is suddenly too easy. It can also signal that a burden has been lifted.

Other forms of tension in the shoulders and upper chest can be formed by misconceptions concerning 'good posture'. We have all been told at home and at school to 'sit up straight, shoulders back'. Wrong. We become round-shouldered from a weak spine and no amount of sitting up straight with shoulders back can cure that. So heap one complication on top of the other: the collapsed spine and the braced shoulders and chest. This can lead to the most contorted stance of all where vocal energy is now completely sacrificed. A common stance of this sort is one where the spine is slumped forwards along with the hips, the shoulders and chest forced backwards and then the head pushed forwards as a counterweight. Do try this yourself. It is a grotesque sort of posture more befitting to gargoyles but a way that lots of people stand.

The upper chest lift is also a misconceived habit we have, especially among men. It results in the large macho chest you see in advertisements for action movies. Pigeons and roosters exhibit this puffed-up strutting look as well. The sense it gives is that we are taking in vast quantities of air when in fact we are reducing our breath capacity by about fifty per cent. Many dancers lift and hold in this area in an attempt to shift their balance. But the upward lift here will only provide temporary strength and gradually weaken the body and reduce breath power. The speaking range then becomes sorely limited as well. You also cannot easily fight, throw a ball, lift or carry heavy objects freely or work manually with this tension robbing you of power. This is bluff power which has to be released before the voice can release along with it.

Head Position

The head should naturally balance on top of the spine, its weight economically distributed. If you balance or juggle a heavy object on top of a pole you will instantly see how even the smallest shift will topple the object. Our heads don't drop off but a series of muscles in the neck and shoulders have to work overtime to compensate for any misalignment we are suffering. The entire work we do here at righting our wrongs creates vocal tension.

The head can weigh up to twenty pounds so any imbalance creates a strain that becomes immediately evident, crippling the voice, clamping the larynx and tightening the jaw and back of the tongue. All of this is done by the off-balance of the head.

Common habits that pull the head away from its natural alignment include jutting the chin forwards or tucking it backwards. Each habit results in a vocal shift. If you test either of these extreme positions and speak you will see what I mean and experience your voice shifting quite remarkably. Don't do it too much or too hard or else you will feel some strain. But some of us do this all day long. Thrusting the chin forwards we seem to be saying, 'I am really trying to communicate.' The resulting vocal sound is pushed (because we have to use more air to push out the words) and tight (because every part of the neck is squeezed). The head pulled back squashes the neck and pulls back the sound into the throat resulting in a sound many of us find pompous. Sometimes this sort of locked-head position indicates withdrawal or even an unruffled or laid-back attitude. As listeners we pull back from a pushed speaker and lean towards a pulled-back speaker. Communication of this sort can be a veritable tug of war.

Many of us have the habit of looking down at the floor when we speak, not making eye contact with the listener and although the voice is in no danger of damage from this habit, it cannot easily move and gets set in an inaudible mode. It can easily sound flat and boring. It also exposes the fact that some of us find it hard to face the world and meet it eye to eye.

Other reasons for an unbalanced head position can be more simple: tight collars or tie knots, or spectacles (particularly half glasses which make the speaker tuck in the head in order to peer over them or frames that are so heavy that they pull the head down and sandwich the larynx). Short sightedness, too, can push the head forwards in compensation, as can an aggressive attitude towards the world. All of these everyday habits tighten the neck in some way and obstruct the ease of sound. None of them are wrong if we can remember that they destabilise the voice in some way and that we must seek relief from their strictures. Actors may sometimes have to adopt one of these habits as part of a role they are playing and have to modify the habit so it does not harm the voice and so a free position to speak can be effortlessly attained. A famous actor I was working with made a decision to play a Shakespearean lead with his head continually thrust forward. His voice was on the verge of going and beginning to hurt. Just by moving the head back a fraction of an inch the throat area was opened. The visual effect was the same but without the vocal abuse. Performers must bear in mind that these small adjustments are continually necessary for proper voice manipulation.

The Jaw

Many of the physical tensions we have already explored will eventually creep into and solidify in the jaw. Sometimes even after we have relieved the tension elsewhere, the 'memory' of it will remain locked in the jaw and become a permanent habit. In the falling chain of dominoes the jaw is usually the last piece either to fall or set back upright. Jaw tension is the final barrier we usually face in freeing the voice. It is the last of the unwanted tensions to disappear and the first to reappear. Jaw tension is necessary in certain situations as a means of 'holding back'. It is probably better to clench the jaw than to hit someone or say unspeakable things. Daily we are faced with straining situations where we have to 'hold our tongues' and that usually means clenching our jaws. But that residue of accumulated tension which you can actually notice in so many people's faces has to be released. If the jaw doesn't swing open easily or only becomes used to opening slightly, a sound or a word cannot escape fully and the whole vocal act itself becomes clenched. The jaw can actually trap a sound or word that is on its way to being fully released and muffle its delivery. The right to speak includes the ability to open the jaw and let a word out into space without obstruction.

As children reach adolescence they will always start mumbling; life is rapidly changing and the expressing and speaking of ideas (particularly to adults) becomes difficult and self-conscious. Inhibitions set in and the clenched jaw becomes for the voice what folded arms are for the body: a 'keep-out' barrier. Speaking takes place from behind closed jaws and an expressionless face. Even though we outgrow the set mind and attitudes which are the embryo for this habit, some of us never outgrow it. We also may be imitating the habit of someone in our family. Habits are not necessarily genetic but they can be accumulated by example.

A jaw at rest means that the teeth don't actually touch even though the lips are together. The lower half of the jaw should not be thrust forward (this impedes sound) or the lips tightened and pulling the jaw back (this muffles sound and makes it difficult to say certain words). As children we play with all these facial positions, scrunching our faces and mouths into elastic poses, but we usually release. Sometimes the tightened jaw is just a leftover from one of these habits or just our natural way of showing displeasure or even delight. It becomes a danger if it freezes in a habit.

Urban living in particular is fraught and threatening enough to make us often tighten our jaws (just as we raise our shoulders and upper chest) as a means of containing energy and preparing for the next blow. But I have also seen jaw tension develop as a result of dentistry, grinding teeth or the need to hide bad teeth. An old facial injury is another common possibility. The body encircles itself around the pain and needs the authority from us to open back up again. A blow to the face while playing too near a garden swing thirty years ago can still be remembered in the jaw.

Certain accents are connected with jaw tension. I suppose the most popular and probably apocryphal story is one that concerns the formation of the Australian accent. Many of the first convicts shipped to Australia were cockneys from the East End of London. To punish them they were confined to the most inhospitable, fly-infested areas of the country. The resulting accent is cockney with the jaw shut to prevent the flies from getting in! You could also argue that not opening the jaw and mumbling, as many powerful people do, is a way of showing your high status. Many members of royalty and upper class speakers speak through clenched jaws that barely move. Marlon Brando found a certain vocal quality when he acted in the film *The Godfather*. People have to stoop towards you in order to hear your commands. If you are powerful they will learn to make sense of your incoherence and hear you through your affectation. Sometimes, understandably, debilitating diseases or disfiguring accidents will bring this habit to life, yet the jaw habit, for most healthy speakers, is one we must try to break.

The Tongue

Most of us think of the tongue as consisting just of the front part that works in our mouth. The tongue actually extends right down the throat and is a large muscle that can fold back and choke us if we become unconscious or suffer a fit. We are so conscious of the sensitive tip and blade of the tongue that we forget it is like a tree with a network of roots. As a child I remember looking in butchers' shop windows at calves' tongues and thinking, 'Blimey, poor calf with that in its mouth.' Proportionately, a human tongue is as extensive. It is the back of the tongue, the part we don't see, which can block the freedom, placing and resonance of the voice.

Tension at the back of the tongue or an immoveable tongue

can muffle sound and make it sound undefined. Some accents naturally have this swallowed sound formed on the back of the tongue as in the way some Londoners pronounce words like 'ba*ll*' or 'kett*le*' or the way speakers in Birmingham pronounce their city's name. In the USA the so-called Bronx and Boston accents sometimes sound as though they are located here as well. In all these cases the sound is trapped at the back of the tongue and sounds as if it is being swallowed.

The gentle stretching of the tongue out and down across the chin will help release any block. Don't be hesitant about really stretching the tongue out like an animal and then releasing it to find its natural placement. Try not to control or force its placement. The jaw must always stay free when you do this, opening as widely as you can.

The Soft Palate

If you run your tongue upwards from behind the top front teeth you first feel a ridge (the 'alveolar ridge', crucial for the production of many consonant sounds), then you feel the hard palate at the roof of the mouth and finally higher back as your tongue curls a softer, fleshier flap that moves. This is the soft palate. Its function in voice and speech work is to separate the nasal cavity from the mouth. When it is down air can pass down the nose; when up, all the air has to stream out of the mouth. There are three nasal sounds in English Received Pronunciation (RP): 'm', 'n' and 'ng'. If you make these sounds you will feel air vibrating and releasing down the nose. If the adjustment to the soft palate is too sluggish then the voice will sound too nasal and words muddied.

When we have a cold or a throat infection, phlegm will sometimes stop the operation of the soft palate, creating the blocked, stuffed-up nasal sound.

To exercise the soft palate if it becomes lazy try bracing your tongue tip behind the bottom teeth, keeping the jaw open and free and make the sounds: 'k', 'g' and 'ng'. Say them quickly and repeatedly several times. They may sound more like gagged sounds. But they will shake up the soft palate.

Breath

In working on the breath we touch the true foundation stone of life and the powerhouse of the voice. William Wordsworth put it aptly in *She Was a Phantom of Delight*:

> *And now I see with eye serene*
> *The very pulse of the machine;*
> *A being breathing thoughtful breath,*
> *A traveller between life and death.*

Breathing is the first and last thing we do. We enter and depart the world gasping for air and life. Every feeling and thought, every mental and physical condition is first experienced and manifested in the breath. These are stored and remembered in the breath. To live we need to breathe and breath is our lifeline. Our most traumatic life experiences – grief, rage, joy and sexual contact – are held in breath patterns. Even the slightest event in life, like suddenly bumping into someone around a corner, registers a change of breath. As major international events unfold they are always accompanied by the headline: 'The World Holds Its Breath!'

Breath is so fundamental to us and yet so invisible an entity that any discussion or examination of it can send some people spinning into instant confusion and panic. Largely these are the results of total ignorance about the way the breath is manufactured and how it can be controlled. The breath is something we would rather not be too self-conscious about. Yet we cannot live a full life without breath. We also cannot fully vocalise without breath, although many people consistently try. Breath, when it comes right down to it, is the key to most vocal problems.

Each time we use our voice to communicate, some portion

of breath is used to propel and expel the sound. The calmer, deeper and more regular the breath, the more chance we have of staying centred and in contact with our feelings and thoughts. Under stress the breath lifts higher into the chest and shoulders where it shortens and becomes more erratic. This kind of breath is needed on certain occasions, i.e. for purposes of flight or for certain sporting activities like sprinting. Asthmatics or allergy sufferers will hold tension in this part of the body as they fight for breath. We need to return to calm, regular breath after any panic even though some of us in a constant state of anxiety never do. Often we stay trapped in one breathing pattern only.

Some people hardly dare to breathe, as if by doing so they would offend or seem intrusive. Breath barely enters the body to the lower cavities but stays trapped up around the chest, denied its full life. For others it remains a luxury to take the size and length of breath required to cope with specific experiences. Too often we do not allow the body time to rest and take the needed breath to get over one task before taking on another one. To breathe well is natural, but life experiences can defeat the natural breath and cause it to seize up in a different rhythm.

To breathe low and calmly into our whole body is to touch deep, deep feelings. Is it better not to feel? What might a deep breath reveal and release down inside us? A hidden rage, love, tenderness or fear? So, unlike a baby who operates totally from a natural capacity, we can actually make choices not to allow our bodies the full chance to breathe deeply. We can starve ourselves. This can be caused by something as banal as vanity: not allowing our stomachs full freedom of movement lest we appear fat. But can vanity also cut us off from our feelings and voice? It certainly can.

Most of us can recall moments in life when we stopped breathing. In such moments we held our breath in order to deny feelings, to bottle them up with a stopper. It is as though by holding the breath we suspend time, disappear for a moment in order to avoid dread. Every sensation is on hold and this can last for several seconds before the body begins to fight for oxygen. Children usually compete to see who can hold their breath longest but this action, if elongated, can be severely counter-productive. First we can die! But more realistically, the stopped breath moves steadily into a more regular denial of breath leading to the sort of avoidance that cuts down our whole ability to think, feel and react to experiences and situations that demand full alertness. We start to deprive ourselves of sufficient oxygen in all of life's critical and gradually uncritical moments. All parts of our life become studded with breathlessness and resulting tensions. Next time you are in a dentist's chair for just a check-up or a filling, for instance, give yourself the right to breathe. It is amazing how much less trepidation and pain you will feel as a result. The drill actually becomes less fearsome. Breathing allows us to cope. Too many people live their lives on half-held breaths which are synonymous with half-held feelings and thoughts. The whole of our potential as intellects and organisms is sorely reduced by any locked, insufficient breath. The important thing to bear in mind is the fact that the body was designed to breathe efficiently.

The Natural Breath

It's as easy as breathing, they say. This is a natural breath:

- You breathe in and then you breathe out. Inhale and exhale. Do it now, without thinking much, just so you remember the sensation.
- The quantity of the intake is what the body, emotion and thought capacity require in order to fulfil a given task at a given moment. Breath and action are equalised.
- The system accommodates itself automatically to the breath required: 'If I lift a huge weight I take in and hold a very deep breath; if I pick up a feather I scarcely notice taking in air.'

- When you inhale, a crucial series of actions happens simultaneously: the lungs fill and expand as the sides, back
and front of the ribcage open, the diaphragm moves down
and out and the lower abdominal muscles release. All this
in one superb motion. With large and deep breaths –
say after you've just run long and hard – you can feel
this movement right down into the groin area. After a
purging of heightened feelings many people experience
muscle aches here.
- When you exhale, all the body's muscles move in together,
converging simultaneously again, to support the exhalation
of breath. (Really exhale all the way now and you'll note
this extreme muscular sensation.) This exiting air creates
a current which contacts and powers the voice like heat
suddenly rising, hissing and rumbling though an air shaft.
This current or column of air fills and sustains the voice
as we make sounds or speak.
- No movement is needed in the shoulders or upper chest.
This area remains free and relaxed. Return to the image of
a baby. As it screams all the action of screaming is visible
around the centre of the body and not in the shoulders
or upper chest. What you see is really a pumping action
born in the abdomen. Any tension or movement in the
upper part of the torso blocks air from going down into
the lungs and conversely impedes the outward release of
breath.

The simplicity of the natural breath, becoming conscious of
how easy it ought to be, terrifies many people. It terrifies them
because the process can be subject to so many unnatural holds,
blocks, hesitations and panics that have been built in. Some
of us find, or are forced to find, every possible breath hold or
reason to stop living and being in the world. These barriers
are constant and come from the myriad of sources I explored in
Part One. Sometimes they are extremely difficult to pinpoint
and illuminate like the centre of a black hole. What always
distresses me is the fact that so many people deny themselves
the power of a full natural breath and so few live with the right
to breathe at all times. I rarely come across anyone constantly
in the process of breathing naturally. As an early step in the

process of working on the voice, one must never forget the sensation of an honest natural breath.

The naturalness of breathing is one of those healthy processes that become corrupted and perverted by life's pressures. If, after each of those darting experiences life hurls at us in constant repetition, we allowed our breath the luxury of returning to the neutral unheld position, then our breath would always stay natural. Instead we allow our breath to bear the full brunt of life's blows. As a result turmoils are imprinted onto each breath we take and retained there. They haunt every breath we take in branded breathing patterns.

A baby cries. It is nursed, comforted and then stops crying. But the nursing adult does not return the infant to its cot until its breath has returned to its natural in and out release. Usually a sigh informs us that this has happened. If only we would all treat ourselves to that most contented of luxuries.

Breathing Faults

Here is the litany again: You have the right to breath. You have the right to take the breath you need. You have the right to take the time you need to breathe. So what goes wrong? A series of 'holds'.

One of the most common faults in breathing is the following pattern: breathe in – hold – breathe out. Try it. That critical hold tampers with the natural breath pattern you tried above. The hold disconnects us from an organic and releasing breath position. At certain times we need to exert this hold naturally. For instance, you breathe in, change your idea of what to say and then have to hold before reassessing your thoughts. This hold can also stop us from communicating a vital emotion, like showing rage at an inappropriate moment or the way we fight to hold back tears. Many of us are so unsure of our own ideas and feelings that we are encased in the holding habit. It is a breathing habit very common to women who are neither listened to nor respected, one which they have to exercise out of existence. It is not there as a habit if you choose to have freedom of expression.

How Much Breath?

The breath taken should be enough to serve the speaker's needs. For this to happen the body must be free and relaxed enough to allow the breath to open all the breath areas: the ribcage, the entire area around the centre, sides and back of the torso and the muscles around the pelvis and groin. The bigger the emotion, the longer the thought, the greater the passion then the more breath we need. The bigger the space our voice has to fill or carry across then the larger the breath needed. Expression and space both require a strong breath-release capacity.

Any holds in the body will mean that certain areas of breath cannot be opened and this will result in the feeling and thought being disconnected. Holds are found in the shoulders, upper chest, back and lower abdomen. The reasons for any hold can be found in injuries, vanity, bad posture, held shoulders etc. Any tension stops the breath from flowing in, swelling the lungs and releasing muscles all through the torso.

Keep Breathing

When the body is free then the breath needed simply drops and falls into place. The process is quite organic and you will never need to think about it or force the process. We only begin to think about breath and have a growing awareness of it when it is either irregular or when useless tensions enter the body. Breathing becomes a problem when we dam up the breath and when the system is being controlled or manipulated. Animals never think about breath.

The free and lower breath gives us access to our feelings. Actors who don't breathe easily and low have to push for all their emotional responses and are quickly fatigued. They have to then stop and think about breathing. They cannot trust their feelings or even begin to take enough breath to match a felt moment. To compensate they can produce a pushed or ragged vocal quality to indicate: 'I am feeling.' Remember, too, that it is another form of denial to take too much breath. The amount of breath should precisely match the thought and feeling. I cannot stress this enough when you work with the voice. I have seen actors take an enormous amount of breath just to say the word 'No!' Yet they wonder why they don't sound real. The breath and action are out of kilter. If any speaker is in complete contact with whatever he or she is saying and why it is being said, and the body and breath are both free and relaxed, the speaker never has to mark or plan where he or she breathes. Breath will mark its own time. It will happen as it happens for a baby. Organically. To run out of breath in life is rare. Usually it comes as a result of something abnormal happening inside us or an exertion of some sort: perhaps a terrible shock to the system, a fearful panic or a blow to the stomach. Any event that winds us and throws off the breath's timing.

Breathing is the most dramatic part of voice work. The state of your breath reveals volumes to the world. Recently I was teaching a group of therapists who became excited by the notion that observing their patients' breath patterns could provide another key for understanding and unlocking their emotional state. Most of these therapists remembered noticing distinct changes in a patient's breath just before the moment of an important revelation.

We must never be frightened to show we are breathing. So many people don't seem to be breathing at all. Many actors and singers feel it is part of their job and a measure of their dignity *not* to show any audience that they are breathing. Nonsense. Their function as performers is to show us all of life and its complexities and details. Breathing is one of these. If we attempt to hide our breath we lock the breath higher into our chests and begin to travel along a path that leads to hysteria. The higher the breath, the more perilously close we are to panic and loss of control.

Breath Tension

As we become tense in any situation the breath rises up. The upper chest lift cuts down on our capacity to take a breath fully and deeply into the abdomen and lower. As this happens we cannot take the full breaths we need but only fractional ones. Ironically, these are the heightened moments when we most need a full breath, need oxygen, but deny it by fighting our natural breathing process. We may have added to constriction. Victorian ladies fainted at the slightest unsettling event not because they were weak or coy but most probably because their tightly-corseted torsos would not allow them to take a natural breath easily when it was most needed. One slight shock to the breath system and the ladies collapsed! Swooning must have been a daily event. The body takes over, keeping us alive even when we've plotted on our own all sorts of intriguing tortures to disable ourselves: cinching belts, corsets, waistcoats and braces. It is depressing to realise that we haven't travelled very far in our physical awareness from the point when women still had ribs removed in the name of fashion. In fact, there are cases where it still happens. But some of us today live in such a state of high tension that we manage to cut off our breaths even without the aid of corsets or operations.

Another habit that provokes the high, tense breath is one of not exhaling all the air we have taken into our lungs. We hold it back as a reserve. Releasing the whole breath can panic a speaker into thinking, 'I'll never get breath again!' Of course you will. Your body will see to that. Every opportunity is taken to breathe, even when the body doesn't need it. A speaker will frequently 'top up' with breath, even when the lungs are sufficiently filled, and it has to squeak out. This too can bring on a kind of panic. Breathe in without exhaling, then again, and again. You will notice your body responding to the confusion of too much breath with no place to put it. That is a tension we must avoid.

The Thinking Breath

It is very difficult to think clearly when any part of the breath is disturbed. Use the analogy of what any pain does to our thought process; a headache or a toothache. We simply cannot think clearly when under stress. It is equally hard to stay in touch with emotions and feelings unless the breath is low and free. Censoring the breath equals censoring our thoughts and a whole web of responses to life. The breath, in a manner of speaking, simply must be free to think for itself.

The Good News about Breath

Here is the good news to counteract the bad. After a few weeks of basic release and breathing exercises, the whole body and vocal potential can change. To breathe naturally changes our perspective so radically that our entire view of ourselves plus the way we are viewed by others can transform us. You tap a source of elemental power that is probably the most underused one in the physical network. If you consciously pursue natural breathing you can feel the difference in hours and change a lifelong habit within ten days. I have seen this happen again and again.

Obviously, speakers who require extended vocal skills must perform regular breathing exercises in the same way that musicians must perform scales. These daily chores are necessary to maintain the breath, once it has found its natural pocket, and to bolster the power and flexibility vital to sustain a voice in space or in the process of speaking heightened language or singing. Recognition of natural breath and taking the right to it can show immediately. I have seen actors and singers shift habits rapidly. Once you understand the need, or your profession and livelihood demand it, change can occur in a very brief interval.

Living with the pressure of breath tension is not only exhausting but uneconomic: some of us breathe more in order to live less. Think of unfortunate asthma victims who have to fight for breath just to stay alive. Then shift that analogy to your healthy self and how you may be breathing just as hard but not for the same life-saving reason. Yet when breathing problems arise for unaccountable reasons we turn ourselves into invalids.

Finding our natural breaths can be an emotional and frightening journey in some extreme instances. Changing our physical lives, however, undoubtedly causes us some discomfort, so as the next step in learning to work with the voice, we all have to learn something about the positions we take in order to extend the breath's capacity, control and power.

Breath Support

Now you have learned and experienced what a natural breath is and how it gets complicated and confused. So how does it become more regular? More importantly, how does the breath connect with the voice?

As you breathe in and the muscles around the centre of the body open, the ribs swing out and the diaphragm and abdominal muscles move down and out of the way to accommodate the expansion of the lungs. Hold your hands up against your ribs to feel some of this as you take in air.

When we breathe naturally, the ribcage swings up and out rather like the flexible handle of a bucket. The muscles of the diaphragm move down, an action you can feel if you press your hand between your ribcage and above your stomach. The lower abdominal muscles should move and release to create a bedrock of muscle support. They don't need to be pushed out but need to be free enough to release with a huge intake of breath. Swim underwater and as you come up for air you feel this opening action most dramatically as the breath whooshes in. You recover breath easily as you breathe out and the muscles move in to empty the lungs of air. This muscular action creates that column of air that we call 'support'. So support is not just the actual muscular action alone, or the ballast of the air itself, but both working in tandem.

This support of air should connect to and with the voice. Support starts and stops sound as we increase or cut off the air supply, just as you experience with an air hose used to inflate one of your car tyres. Think of the sound of the voice as starting with the support from the centre of the body and *not* from the throat. We need the full use of the body's pump to produce sound and not just the neck or head of the nozzle. Producing sound in ways opposed to this is where we encounter problems. The lower muscles of the body connect us behind or underneath the sound, giving it a healthy uplift. Obviously the louder and more sustained the sound, the more muscle power or support you will need. Small sounds are still supported but require fractionally less muscle power, yet all sound is created by breath which should be driven and propelled by these muscles. Without full support, the voice is powered by extra pushing in the throat. Consciously refrain your body from the neck down from offering any support and just try to speak aloud. Notice that the burden of all shifts to the throat and through the upper chest. There is no support here, just temporary shelving for the voice. Eventually, as you take in shorter and shorter bursts of air to help you, you will tire and cave in. That experience you just felt of producing unsupported sound through the throat alone is one of the most common forms of vocal abuse. You may have just solved a nagging problem! Now try producing the same sounds with the aid of support from lower down. You should feel the pressure in the throat and upper chest reduced. That is a supported voice.

Speaking without support creates an uninteresting voice and it can also damage the vocal cords. It is also possible to have an understanding of how support works but fail miserably at connecting thought to the actual physical process. I have met many actors, for instance, who have complete knowledge of the process after years of training, who have wonderful swinging ribcages like saloon doors, but who fail again and again at timing support with their voices. They get out of sync with support when they speak. It does happen, especially when you speak nervously or get ahead of or behind yourself. Support might be there only part of the time but not at the beginning or end of phrases. The support is irregular; another common problem. To feel in a constant state of support we must learn to trust and acknowledge the muscles that do the work, giving them the time needed to take and recover breath. Sometimes mind and body simply have to come to an understanding in order to get into sync. Timing is a critical factor in support work but natural timing is something all of us can achieve with a little thought: 'I breathe in, taking only the breath I need to say this, and simultaneously I sense the support getting behind and underneath the next sentence or phrase I say, and then I breathe/speak out as a twinned action, supporting and connected to the voice.' This sounds more complicated than it is. But it is the breath's natural thought process for each sound we make so you might as well eavesdrop. Wait and need to breathe, take the breath needed to act or vocalise. A lioness, roaring or pouncing, would never attempt either without the right preparation, without the right support. Support is balance and harmony in action, without which we are thrown off key.

Support skills are taught to students of the martial arts, particularly preparation and timing of actions. But the skills are crucially linked to breathing and in fact hang on the breath. I think that any dynamic speaker has to put himself or herself in this exact same frame of mind. We may speak without support (most of us do) and therefore without making contact, but we are then only communicating without muscle power or vigour – we are flaccid. On the other hand, with support we can aim to target and hit someone squarely with a sound.

Sounds made by humans – that shrieking child – before habits have invaded and taken over have sufficient breath and muscles supporting them. This is the bit that gets flabby or contained, so what we first do in working with the voice is shore up the foundation so the voice has a seat from which to function.

I meet hundreds of people every year who speak without support. These are people who come from every walk of life and are not just performers: teachers (their voices 'tiring and hurting by the end of the week'), executives (their voices 'not being dynamic enough in the boardroom'), politicians (finding themselves 'losing their breath speaking at a party conference') and others with similar problems. Some of these people know about breath, certainly they know how to breathe, but have forgotten to use the breath to support the voice. Their natural support becomes disconnected. Many actors and singers support when working but forget to support their voices when off-stage. They create compartments in their life rather than integrating the parts into one whole. There is much speculation among laryngologists and other physicians that this off-duty, off-support mode is precisely when many professional speakers hurt or tire their voices, especially at parties (where we try to speak over loud music, talking, smoking or drinking), football matches, talking in the dry, noisy confinement of an aeroplane, shouting at the children etc. In effect, some people respect their voice at work but show disrespect after. But 'after' is when most of us live our lives.

The Link between Support and Connection

Imagine breath support and connection as a unit; both work together fluidly and are completely interlinked. That fluidity is the factor which keeps the voice safe and powerful all the time. I must admit that it has taken years for this notion to settle into my own thinking. When I first started to teach I was too frightened to assert the old-fashioned, traditional view that support work was needed as a daily routine in the life of any professional speaker. Those of us teaching speech and voice were in flight from that theory, debunking it as a means to creating artificial voices. I knew that we needed support in professional situations but somehow felt it was much more the fashion to be less rigid and even to encourage unsupported sounds at other times. I believed that right up to the mid-1980s. I am now against that thinking. Unknowingly, I was encouraging disconnection, divorcing the speaker from feeling and experiencing the whole support process the whole time. No, all of this is something we want to avoid.

If an actor uses a vocal process only for performing and does not connect it to his or her life, he or she is usually left with the impression that the 'work voice' is put on. The natural voice feels unreal, the real unnatural. Many younger actors in the first stages of training and performing professionally think a supported voice is a booming one that intrudes at parties and announces: 'I am an actor.'

All qualities and shades of sound can be supported. The large, imposing voice is simply an oversupported and overproduced voice as lacking in the natural vitality of support as the undersupported and underproduced voice.

As I will say countless times, we are striving for a natural voice. Once we achieve a natural voice, which embraces a full breath with each sentence, the easier it is to support the voice all of the time. You will feel clearer and stronger each time you speak. Abuse of the voice will diminish substantially. The voice is almost always healthier if support and connection are present. So support is one of those crucial good habits we must begin to acquire.

Not only actors suffer from the 'fear of support at all times'. It is a strange and unreal sensation when a business person or conference speaker uses support on the podium and then retreats into inaudibility during the less formal question and answer sessions that follow a main address. Many speakers, in fact, suffer the inhibition that to speak with support in both informal and home situations will be greeted with teasing derision: 'Who does he – or she – think he's talking to?' Work on the voice becomes problematical for some who think it will change the pattern of their personality, never realising it will actually let the personality emerge. What I am suggesting is that we learn to use the technique of support effortlessly and without embarrassment so we can let the process filter into all aspects of our lives. Remember, we are what we speak, we are *how* we speak.

Once we feel supported and ready to speak we connect to real vocal power. Any previous temptation to push, bluff, embellish or even retreat from words is lessened. These are, after all, only manipulative habits we use to compensate for our fear of trusting our innate means of support. With support we begin to feel self-sufficient. The whole scope of the voice opens and widens. Any listener feels comfortable and secure in the speaker's control and power. A well-supported voice is infinite in its capabilities and possibilities. The unsupported voice frightens me. I find it teeters on the edge of possibility and power but has nowhere to go, sorely frustrating the speaker and forcing him or her to take dangerous risks. At such a stage you can almost taste the potential in your voice but have not yet developed the full appetite for the whole vocal feast. When someone reduces or minimises their support, vocal choices go down the same path. We get stuck in the narrowest of ranges.

Sometimes when we come face to face with a heightened choice – a moment of grief, pain or joy – we can experience support as never before. The habits of the body and voice are overridden and suddenly we go on automatic pilot, almost as if the moment can only be purged through sound. When we laugh until our sides ache, someone new to support work will feel their ribcage beginning to work. After bursts of crying, shouting, wailing or screaming many people, even ones with extensive voice training, will experience muscle aches in all those support areas that are not used to work. Often, when laughing or crying, we naturally hug ourselves to encourage and help the support. Some of us feel like 'bursting', so intense is the activity around the support areas. As the muscles around the sides and chest are stretched they do feel as if they will snap, split or crack. When we 'cry ourselves to sleep' we give in to the purging along with the exhaustion and fatigue suffered by these very same support muscles. Any actor playing a heightened tragic role, where support is being stretched fully, will experience the same physical exhaustion at the end of a performance.

On an everyday basis, support muscles can work without any noticeable strain. They are there to be tapped, exercised and controlled for the express purpose of helping us to produce sound. Actors and singers, who demand a heightened sound, must exercise these muscles regularly and intensively. Their craft is reliant on both support and contact. And the demand on both regularly increases, especially in long runs and lengthy performances. There are exercises that teach you how to extend this support availability (see p 203).

It seems that our lifestyle, in the decadent and often senti-mental West, has cut many of us off from physical processes, including support. If we were allowed to be more emotionally charged and powerful on a regular basis, if, each day, we had to work physically and be challenged to respond to our bodies, then I don't see how we could get confused over the use of this function. Urban life does cause us to live unnaturally sedentary lives all underpowered by the very muscles we permit to go flaccid. Our language is underpowered, too. We do not have to connect orally or physically with others but shy away. We can box ourselves away for days and weeks without the benefit of an absorbing or passionate conversation or let television and radio do the talking. False tensions and redundant, repetitive activities take the place of vital ones. Our true feelings are held in check. But try living in a rural setting for several months, fending for yourself. Suddenly, without benefit of gyms and health clubs, we become more a part of living routines. Our bodies and voices have to express and say more to help us survive. We are suddenly freer to use either.

I have taught in cultures that are far from being White and affluent. What always intrigues me is how close other cultures and races are to both their breath and natural support, which never need to be artificially summoned as they do in Anglo-Saxons. These people comes from all sorts of places – Southern Europe, Africa, Asia, parts of America – yet they all share one similarity. They are each more firmly rooted to the earth, each more in touch with the growth of a feeling. They all have a great and compelling need to speak, they take it regularly and efficiently without suffering guilt or remorse, and fit comfortably within a community of voices. Most of all these people speak with a passion that we in the West lack. We speak with tact, occasionally with compassion and understanding, but rarely use our voices to fully release and realise a thought. As soon as we stop denying ourselves and surrender to the passion in the spirit, then breath and support enter our voices fully. One hesitates to go overboard and liken the experience to speaking in tongues, but that is what it's like: speaking with unbounded passion about any topic we like. We have, indeed, cut ourselves off from an oral tradition that transmits knowledge and experience from breath to breath rather than just from mind to mind.

In starting voice classes with some twenty-five European or North American students, there will usually be two voices that are naturally supported; fewer than ten per cent. The two are usually upper- to middle-class males, privileged with the right to speak. The rest have an uneasy relationship with both their voices and language, particularly the women. In India, say, all twenty-five persons in a similar class would probably be supported already. Language and daily vocal chores are more a fact of everyday life. Yet in this sampling as well, the women are less prone to use that support in public though they may easily do it in private.

I have gone on at some length in praise of support because I think it one of those crucial techniques that we can begin to build into any vocal transaction. Support releases the natural on a more habit-forming basis. If you want to be heard, must be heard, *need* to be heard, or need to find a power spring that will trigger a thought fired by breath out into the air, then support is a crucial factor. If breath is the foundation-stone of the voice then support is the mortar that cements the breath to all other areas of our work. Few of the areas we will tackle in voice work can be done without either breath or its connecting support.

Freeing and Placing the Voice

Once we have gained control of breath and begin to understand the benefit of support for any vocal act, then freeing and placing the voice become tasks we can think about mastering.

A 'free voice' simply means a completely effortless and efficient one. The basic guideline here is that you should never feel pain or resistance in the throat. If any is there the voice is not free. Any catch in the throat, tickle, scratchiness, hoarseness, 'clamping' or 'pushing' is a sign that something is not right. If you feel all or just one of these obstacles then the voice is not free. A blockage is damming the sound. Some of these blocks are more dangerous than others but each will diminish vocal effectiveness and flexibility.

To 'place a voice' merely means allowing it to move up into your mouth, forwards into the face and then to leave your body. If you stop and hum and begin to feel a vibration on your lips getting stronger and stronger you are in the act of placing your voice. I best describe this phenomenon as a sound or word bobbing off into space and no longer ours. If the sound or word leaves us then we have committed ourselves to a feeling or an idea and both are now in the world as a kind of energy. We can neither recall nor reclaim them again, the words are no longer ours. It is much easier *not* to fully place sounds or words, to silently whimper or laugh under our breath, to mumble 'I love you', 'how dare you', 'no' or 'yes' rather than to declare these sounds and words with free undistorted energy, allowing them to travel forth without impediment. The ancient Greeks understood something about placing. They believed that if you spoke a word with the right intensity and energy the very thing itself then existed in the world. A voice that becomes well-placed speaks with authority and right.

Remember, though, our notion that each thing is connected to everything else. The voice cannot be free or placed if either the body or breath is not functioning and connected. The natural voice has to be able to pass freely up through the body, past the chest and throat and effortlessly into the mouth, to be sent equally effortlessly on its way into the world.

The Trapped Voice

Physical alignment and proper breath support are totally linked to the free and placed voice. The voice cannot be free if any neck, shoulder or breath tension is present. Vocal constrictions are a voice teacher's nightmare. It is in this habit that serious vocal damage or loss or tiring of the voice usually occur. A priority of any responsible voice teacher is to safeguard any student against vocal harm or damage. For this reason a teacher should never set exercises beyond an individual's or class's technical skills. This can be perilous. Much vocal damage is not immediately apparent to the speaker. An hour later, or even the next day, a voice can fail partially or completely. The excitement of speaking or shouting in a crowd can take away our physical awareness of going beyond our means vocally. Consequently the football fan, screaming with a packed crowd, feels the effects after the match. In time and with training a growing awareness of and sensitivity to voice will allow you to monitor its use. You need never feel hurt. Bear that in mind. A trained voice can sing all night and never experience loss or impairment. So what are these particular traps in the throat and how do they manifest themselves? Here is a list of the most obvious ones. Speakers can have anywhere between one and all of these holds.

A. The Push

Many voices are described as being 'pushed'. The listener feels spoken 'at' not 'to'. Actors, for instance, will often push their voices when they are bluffing a feeling or not trusting a text and its words. The pushed sound can be 'harsh' and 'ragged'. It can also sound 'inflexible', 'overly insistent' and 'distorted'. The instinct of most speakers placed in a position where they feel inadequate or out of control is to push. People who speak at meetings will often push themselves at the listeners in order to be heard. Notice speechmakers at weddings, the unaccustomed speaker in a church pulpit, the novice teacher with a difficult class – practically all will push and never dare to speak simply with support and ease. Usually we can hear the voice of a pusher but not any definition, the sound but no clarity. Remember the times you could hear an actor from the back of a theatre but you could not understand a thing he or she said. That was probably pushing. The sound is typically nervous and overstressed. The tension suffered in the throat makes it impossible for the voice to achieve any range. It will sound stuck and all on one energy plateau, generally aggressive. The push alienates the listener just as much as it disconnects the speaker from thoughts and feelings. We have all had the experience of being in conversation with someone who pushes: the heat of the discussion rises to a certain temperature and suddenly the speaker disconnects from the argument and seems vocally out of control and off the point. The push has taken over. We cease to listen and all discussion ceases as well. Pushers like one-way discussions.

A speaker's fear of a large space or theatre or even of a daunting, complex text or report will breed the pushed position. Language suddenly becomes confused and generalised. We easily wander from the main point. The push can also indicate a huge lack of self-confidence or just incomplete preparation. Speakers who try to improvise on the spot will often push. This is typical of stand-up comedians, for instance, and also of actors who come to rehearsals not knowing their parts. The push is a cover. In panic or when told to 'Speak up!' many speakers will push in order to be heard which is completely wrong. This only makes the push worse. I remember, as a child, speaking a role in a school play. The teacher had a novel idea that she would ring a handbell each time she could not hear any of us, even in front of an audience, creating a kind of 'Pavlov's Push' as a result! All of us heard this bell again and again and we lost our voices as we tried, in vain, to push our speaking across the space of the auditorium.

The push is experienced physically by a speaker as not having adequate breath or support to power the voice. Everything from the upper chest down is cut off. At the crucial moment of vocalisation the breath and its support cannot get under the sound because it will not come. The speaker is left stranded with no reserve of power to draw on comfortably or, more importantly, no trust in their vocal ability so he or she begins to push for power only from the throat and strains the vocal cords in the process. The energy needed to vocalise is 'head butted' or kicked from the throat. In the handbell incident I do remember feeling so under threat to produce a result that I could not take the time I needed to breathe and find the right power. I had no idea what I was saying (I had learnt the text by rote) but knew it required some emotion without having any specific idea in mind. I was totally disconnected from the whole act of speaking, my rights being directed by a bell. I was left with little option but to push. A sore throat was the result but it could have been worse.

Some actors *like* to push their voices. They feel that the

pain equals hard work and shows they are making an effort. Many believe that art is supposed to be painful. This only contributes to some romantic myth of self-flagellation that becomes manifested in the vocal push.

Habitual pushers will often go red in the face as they force sound out (particularly in heightened moments). The head could jut forwards, veins will appear along the side of the neck as pressure increases, the body will go off-centre and very little breath will be taken. These are the classic signs of the push. The pusher will often compensate for lack of variety by getting louder and louder, and indicate stress by wagging the extremities in a desperate attempt to physically push the sound out further. There is a general sense of vocal constipation. Nothing flows easily through the throat and vocal fatigue or voice loss is the main achievement. If you push too often and regularly, the range of the voice becomes locked and limited. For all the wrong reasons, the speaker becomes exhausted.

The push is frustrating not only to the speaker but to the listener. I liken it to someone running up a down escalator or pushing everyone aside to catch a departing train. Force is matched to force. Suddenly the unnatural takes over. If we express natural grief, on the other hand, we release laughter or wail with intermittent breath and sound gushes out without interference or force. It might not be a beautiful sound but it is certainly not pushed. When we trust a word and allow its power to exert itself naturally the push becomes redundant.

There are a series of simple checks and balances that help anyone avoid the push:

- First check and monitor the neck, shoulders and jaw for any useless tension. If these areas are held rigid then the voice will get bottled up and the speaker might sense that only a push will provide release.
- Next breathe. Take breath in and feel breath underneath the sound, making contact with it. Sense support as a replacement for the push.

- A yawn, or even just thinking of a yawn, will take pressure off the throat and save the voice. A very useful trick. Up to the turn of the century actors were taught to speak 'on the edge of a yawn'. The resulting plummy sound was not very real but it was still a good ploy, at least, to prevent pushing.
- Begin to vocalise with a silent 'h' at the start of any vocalisation and especially before any words that begin with vowels. This eases the transition into speech and smooths its passage.
- Stay in contact with the word, *need* the word, trust the word, breathe the word. Don't rush ahead and lose the effect of being 'in the moment' as you speak. This last bit of advice is really about taking your right to speak. Don't let yourself be bullied by events, a speaking challenge, yourself or others when you speak. Don't start until you are ready. Most of all, don't push!

B. The Clamp

The larynx, containing the vocal cords, should bob up and down freely. Imagine a buoy at sea and you capture the effect. The buoy moves with the sea, it does not resist it. If the buoy is too tightly chained and the waves thrash it about, it will snap from its moorings. The larynx suffers likewise if clamped and not allowed to drift within the sea of the throat. My other image of the clamp is of a speaker either sitting on their voice or pitching their voice higher than is advisable. Some oriental women, for example, practise this high-pitched clamp as do children searching for forgiveness in a 'mummy' voice. It is rarer today since our society equates a lower, huskier voice with being powerful, sexy and competent. Many speakers clamp down their voices to try and create this fashionable effect. Some ninety-five per cent of male students effect this clamp. When I first work with them on releasing it they think I am trying to get them to speak higher which is not necessarily so. What I want is to hear *their* voice and to get the voice to move to different places so that the speaker can begin to experience range.

The common complaints of the clamper are: 'My voice won't move'; 'It won't reflect the range I know I have'; 'I have two voices: the bottom one and then a jump to a higher one.' The head of the clamper is usually tucked in and back. They feel vocal vibrations trapped in their throat or chest. Some clampers like this sensation even though it is uncomfortable for listeners.

The voice is not easily damaged in the clamped position but it does tire quickly and sounds monotonous. A clamper can even have good breath support and physical freedom in other areas of the body but through sheer will-power have locked their voice either down in their chest or up in their head. The lower clamp sounds muffled or gravelly, the higher one squeaky and disembodied. In both instances it is difficult for the sound to get into the mouth. We might be able to hear either voice at the back of a theatre but we won't be able to distinguish words clearly. Clampers have trouble articulating.

The habit of clamping creates an unnatural vocal dam. A few sound waves pass through but most are contained. Pressure builds, and since the voice works best in an up-and-out arc, the clamp is one of the voice's own worst enemies.

The clamp can be released by 'thinking' the voice into the face and then out. Aim your voice at a point above eyeline and hum towards that target. Notice then how the voiced hum bypasses the clamped position and becomes free. Also 'thinking' the sound onto the lips starts to pull it away from the chest and head. A clamped sound has to be liberated from its traps.

C. The Glottal Attack

This trap is a potentially dangerous vocal tension. Instead of the breath starting to vibrate the vocal cords gently and smoothly, the glottal attack or shock bashes the cords together before the sound begins – usually on a word starting with a vowel. Air pressure has built up behind the cords just before the speaker vocalises. The telltale sign is a pronounced 'click' in the throat at the beginning of words like 'idiot' and 'apple'. The sound stays trapped in the throat and only jerks into action with a pop. The cords are not starting the sound smoothly but lashing it into action. The cause is usually some nervousness or a tightening in the throat which needs relief. Think how damaging this would be if magnified twenty times its strength into something like a vocal depth charge!

Does this sound like one of your habits? Say a series of words with short vowels like 'idiot', 'apple', 'at', 'obvious', 'under', 'education'. You should hear or sense something if you glottalise. Certain regional urban accents, like cockney and New York borough accents, have the glottal attack as a common feature.

In average conversation the attack is not problematical. But it is very worrisome if you speak loudly, shout or use a lot of vocal power and force. The glottal attack combined with a push is a deadly combination for the voice. The vocal cords can take a bruising. There is some evidence to suspect that within minutes of speaking loudly with the attack in full force the cords begin to redden in the first sign of rawness and damage. In acting, work on accents which use the glottal attack must be modified to protect the speaker's voice. I shall talk about this again in a later section on accents.

When I was teaching in a North London school, I usually noticed that on Mondays many of the children had husky or broken voices. I eventually realised that they had spent the weekend supporting their local football team – Arsenal. What better word screamed over and over could induce more vocal abuse! '*Arsenal! Arsenal!*' Imagine the glottal attack meeting that initial vowel. It would be interesting to study the voices of Millwall supporters. The 'm' safeguards the voice from assault.

The glottal attack and the connected build-up of air pressure in the throat are useful for humans to perform certain physical tasks. When we lift a heavy weight, for instance, we trap the air in our bodies and throat to maximise our central breath power. The vocal cords close as we lift and then let the air pass with a grunt when we finish. Here the glottal attack finds a real purpose and I have come across the sound in athletes who lift heavy weights or engage in physically violent sports like football and boxing. This natural use of closure and pressure has crept, however, into some people's everyday vocalisations. Children pick up the attack in their mother sound.

Speakers will use the glottal attack to feign aggressiveness: street pedlars in marketplaces and fruit stall owners use it in their calls to attract customers. When you hear it listen. Notice that the attack cuts down on the speaker's ability to move easily through range. This is not a 'sung' sound but a clacking sound. It is usually accompanied by the physical habit of thrusting the head forward with the release of sound, adding pressure to the neck and throat. The jerky quality of the sound resonates through and informs the whole body. Another of those domino effects. Nothing connected to the glottal attack is fluid.

Some contemporary musical styles like 'rapping' use the glottal attack. You can also hear it in the singing of James Brown and Michael Jackson. There is a perceivable loss of range and additional strain as the voice rises. After extensive use a voice full of glottal attacks must tire and even go to devoicing. The voice fragments.

The remedy for the attack is to stop the closure of the cords before the speaker vocalises. Speaking on the edge of a yawn helps keep the throat open as does speaking on a silent 'h' at the start of attack words like the ones above: 'hArsenal', 'hidiot' etc. Chanting problem phrases and words gently will also help. The fluidity and flow of a chant unplug tension and nervousness. Many speakers with glottal attack are amazed once they realise how easy speech can be without the bashing. They usually comment that 'nothing is happening' or that they 'won't be heard' with such a mild sensation in the throat.

For a healthy, lasting voice the glottal attack is a trap no professional speaker can afford to fall into. You cannot use the habit in heightened and extended speech. It might work over a microphone or in lowered naturalistic speech but not in huge spaces where sound must carry. The voice will only suffer in the end from the abuse.

D. Devoicing

We fall into this trap when our voice continually falls to a whisper and it is clear we are not being heard. It is a gentle unobtrusive sound. In space the sound is fuzzy and inaudible. Sometimes it seems as though a speaker is not speaking at all but only moving the lips. It reminds me of the vaseline-blurred lens that photographers use to get romantic pictures because I get the distinct feeling that the voice is coated in some way that dulls sound. Words and phrases lack all definition.

This position does no real damage to the voice but it tires the speaker and frustrates the listener. The voice cannot be expressive but signals futility and helplessness. All focus is lost along with resonance and energy. This is the voice of the caring professions: gentle, reassuring, clinical. Men and women share its use in the guise of doctors, nurses and therapists. Journalists use it to winkle a sob story or confession out of someone. It is sometimes described as 'being off the voice' or 'breathy'.

Devoicing is useful as a choice. We all devoice when we show shame or want to grovel. Don't let it stick as a habit. People who devoice tell of being loud as children. They learned to compensate by cutting down the energy in their voice rather than just the volume. Women show signs of this habit more than men. The sound signals a lack of intrusion.

In the devoiced position the vocal cord is not vibrating fully. It is only quivering and not fully engaged. The speaker is on low power. If the full potential of the cord is untapped no speaker will ever know what reserves of power he or she possesses. It is like a low-wattage lamp or an engine running on half its cylinders. Devoicing disconnects the speaker in the throat making it hard to express levels of emotion and sound truthful. Devoicing also sounds sentimental and undermines many speaking tasks. Imagine being defended by a lawyer who devoiced! I once taught a world-famous analyst. One of his patients had attacked him for being patronising and insincere. Those were not his real traits but simply how his devoicing portrayed him. Years of adopting a soothing tone had weakened the resolve of his voice. Sound could no longer shift to a more commanding range if he chose to be direct and commanding. It all got trapped inside the devoicing.

Physically, devoicers frequently look down or away, their shoulders rounded, spines slumped. They typically experience shock when they discover the other half of their whole and begin to speak hooked up to full power. They will says things like: 'Is that me?'; 'I sound so loud!'; 'Am I being too aggressive?' The awe and confusion comes from the encounter with a 'new' voice. Suddenly they can work less vocally. It is not such an effort to speak.

Intoning, chanting, or gently speaking will get the devoiced voice working better. To release the voice from this trap I get the speakers to intone a good solid text over and over, making sure that he or she is connected to the breath so that the complete system is in motion. Then I get them to suddenly speak the text before they have time to censure or analyse their voice. The power voice comes through always at this point. It is loud, clear and effortless. The individual must then speak on this position daily. Most people feel they have a new toy to play with. The difference is immediate.

E. The Pull Back

This trap can exist side by side with the other vocal tensions. 'Pull back' means that the sound or word makes its way into the mouth and then gets immediately pulled back onto itself.

We sometimes describe it as 'swallowing our words'. It also takes the form of 'spasmodic speech': the words come out in unsustained pulses, the voice sounds snatched. Half the words make their way out, but the end of the word or sentence falls back into the speaker. Stage directors will tell actors with this habit to 'watch the end of words' or 'finish the thought'. Sometimes the body of the 'puller back' will literally jerk back as though they are physically retrieving what they have just said.

The rest of the voice may be working fine but the 'pull back' often signals that a speaker lacks confidence and commitment, denying everything they say. Sometimes, though, they are just too confident and high-status to bother completing a statement. Nonetheless there is a betrayal of trust in words and sounds and the speech transaction itself.

The 'puller back' draws energy in rather than sends it out. Ascending breath is cut off at a crucial juncture just as something said is being completed. So the larynx is sandwiched between two opposing forces of going out and coming back in. It is like a vocal revolving door. The result can be vocal turbulence and friction.

What the 'puller back' must learn to do is to follow through on each and every sound, word and thought. They have to avoid traps and tangles. The breath must be relaxed and steady enough to sustain the forward and out sound. The speaker must remember to speak to the arc. Like water from a hosepipe the stream of language must travel away from you and towards an objective. The technique for freeing this habit is closely linked to the placing exercises I list later on. So if you pull back when you speak you may want to look at these pages (211–13). Often a speaker who feels neglected and unheard will pull back. They feel that what they say does not matter and so they trail off or halt the passage of ideas. The habit can be such an affliction that the speaker will actually retreat as they attempt to speak. We all pull back in the face of power so we all know the experience of the habit. 'Pullers back' may also bite their lips and exhibit lip and jaw tension. Speaking is not a happy experience. Sometimes this sort of speaker gets tongue-tied or bottled-up and needs time to sort out an utterance before speaking. So taking your time before speaking helps get through this trap.

8   The Voice Workout

What follows now is a series of exercises which I think work extremely well for both beginner and advanced voice users. If you work at them conscientiously and regularly, you should experience improvements in five to ten days. I stress the word 'conscientiously' because you must work by taking into account everything I have said about voice and breath up to this point, incorporating that knowledge into the practical exercises. At the start, work through the exercises in the sequence I have given. Most of them are quite short (even when the directions seem lengthy) and cover a growing awareness of vocal power. Afterwards, root around among the exercises, picking and doing ones that help you solve particular problems.

The average speaker may only want to work through the foundation exercises, but the practised and professional speakers – actors, teachers, lawyers, business people, politicians and commentators – should go further to master as many aspects of this twenty-two point workout as possible. I have included expansion exercises for these speakers. What I have done here is to consolidate what I would teach a professional voice student over two years of work.

I have tried to isolate here what I think are the best and simplest of the key exercises you can do on your own or in a small group. At various points along the way you will be encouraged to improvise and devise your own exercises using any principle I lay out here. These are really meant to be a guide to start you working. You may find during the process that working with a skilled voice teacher would be better for you.

Remember that no exercise is beneficial if done in a spirit of doom and gloom. You must always be convinced that you are helping yourself and that improvement will follow. You are working to please not a teacher but yourself.

Do the exercises, feel their effects, remember those effects and then forget the exercises entirely as you take the results inside yourself. You cannot go through life checking your voice, yet once you have both felt and remembered a squarely-struck sound it has a way of incorporating itself into the body's memory system. My advice is always to shed the teaching part of any technique as soon as it has proved itself. That effect should become a healthy new habit.

First digest the principle and application of an exercise and then do it. If you feel a beneficial effect, fine. If not, check the exercise against the instruction. Always work with ease. Never try to struggle with the work or work juggling the book! Very little will result if you do. Remember, too, to wear loose, comfortable, easy clothing and shoes without heels or even bare feet. Never stretch or stress yourself.

Reminder: These exercises are not meant to be cardiovascular aerobics but almost gentle, massaging techniques, so avoid any strain. Stop and rest if you begin to feel it. Check the later section on General Health and Care of the Voice (p 287) *if you experience any discomfort with your voice during any phase of the workout.*

Floor work

Trained actors and singers spend hours exercising their breath and voices while lying on the floor with their backs braced, their legs straight or knees lifted. This is what is called 'floor work': a safe and soothing position from which to work the voice. The benefits are immediate and manifold. On the floor the body is quickly aligned, supported and released. It ceases to fight itself, feels utterly safe and composed and surrenders to gravity. Once the body is calm and released, the regularity of breathing begins to address most habitual holds and useless tensions.

My main concern about floor work is that it may become too soothing and relaxing. It may become habit-forming as a way to work. So any exercise done on the floor should also be done standing, sitting or moving about. Floor work should be followed by upright work. Floor work can drain an inexperienced speaker of energy and the mental focus needed to produce a dynamic piece of vocal work. Voice work looks and feels easy but is also rigorous and demanding. Sometimes work done on the floor misses this latter toughness.

Use the floor to release and work the voice in the safest position possible but then move upright to carry on the work in a more centred way. I have found, in some particularly tense people, that floor work can fill them with panic rather than release. It can be a vulnerable position for some just as it is relaxing for others. So monitor what it does for you and always return to the floor position for deep relaxation exercises which are, I think, the best way to release useless tensions and physical anxieties. What you should try to do, therefore, is alternate positions for their relative strengths.

When you begin to work on the floor, follow these routine checks:

- Lie on your back with your legs straight out or your knees up with the soles of your feet planted firmly on the floor. For extra comfort and relaxation raise and support your lower legs and calf muscles on the seat of a chair.
- Always work in a warm environment. You feel chills more acutely on the floor. Cold is counter-productive to concentrated work.
- Check that your head is not tilting back, constricting the neck and throat. This will complicate the passage of breath. Align it. Many people need a thin book or cushion set under their head or neck. Do not use a bed pillow, however, as the head must roll easily from side to side.

- Check that the shoulders are released and the jaw unclamped. The teeth should not be clenched. Breathing should be steady and easy.
- Don't stiffen the thighs or buttocks together. Let them go. Relax!

This is a wonderfully relaxing position from which to begin. Many people fall sound asleep during initial floor work sessions. At last the body has a chance to relax and you have given yourself the right to relax. Stress radically diminishes. You are safe here.

1. Foundation Exercise

The first exercise is really a thought process to accompany you through any physical work you will do on your voice. You must bear these three crucial things in mind throughout your work and carry them into your basic thought process about the voice:

- physical release and alignment
- breath work and its support and connection
- the free, warmed and placed voice

If this thought process becomes a standard one for each type of speaker all further work you do on voice and speech becomes instantly possible. You will remove a whole series of blocks by beginning to 'think' your way past the blocks. Many problems you have in range, resonance and speech will now be on their way to finding a solution.

From this point to the very end of the book you must always remember to breathe. Keep reminding yourself to do it.

2. Relaxation

Relaxation is one of those key skills we search for throughout life. I have talked at length elsewhere about useful and useless tensions and how we must always be on guard against the former. Any work on the voice must begin and continue in a state of relaxation. The following sequence of exercises is the best way I know of achieving it.

The aim here is to build freedom and release in the body so that even under extreme pressure, stress and tension you can manage to keep your breath unheld and flexible and your voice completely open. You can feel nervousness (we all do) but you can also learn not to allow the nerves to stress the physical structure of the body.

The key areas of relaxation when we do voice work are: shoulders, upper chest, neck, jaw, tongue, spine and stomach. But all other areas of the body should be equally relaxed. So begin as follows:

- Lie down on the floor on your back. Make sure that the room is warm and you feel secure (i.e. don't lie in a draught or somewhere that a door might suddenly swing open and hit you). If you feel your head is tilting back you might need a thin cushion or book under it to stop stretching and tightening your neck.

- Mentally take a journey through your body from toe to head, checking for wherever you feel tension or holds. Start with your feet and move to your ankles, then to the knees and on up through the body. Concentrate on relaxing all the joints. By 'thinking' your way up through your body you will actually begin to notice and discover tension.

- When you happen upon a core of tension give a command to that part of your body to 'release it'. For instance tell yourself to release your stomach, let go of your shoulders, unclench your jaw, relax all fingers and toes. Just relax everywhere. All these are main problem areas for you to notice and check. Go everywhere in your body during this diagnostic sequence. Allow yourself a good three to five minutes to do this.

- Come back to a state of pure relaxation and give yourself the luxury of doing nothing else except breathing. Do this for one minute. Inhale and exhale. Find a natural breath and not a held one, one that you can do easily without the slightest feeling of self-consciousness.

- Now, in that relaxed state, take the breathing deeper inside yourself and begin to experience the breath support muscles. Breathe in through your nose, taking as much time as you need. Don't force it. On the inward breath feel all the muscles around the centre of the body open outwards, swinging the ribs wide like a gate. The swing need not be dramatic but aim for a fluid intake and release of breath. If the upper chest begins to lift place a hand on it to keep it still. Allow all the abdominal muscles to release along with the upper chest. Continue to breathe in and out. Take your time. Breathe outwards through your nose. You should feel all the muscles contract as the doors of the ribcage shut. Never force the breath but wait for your body to naturally ask for the *next* breath. Within five minutes of doing this concentrated breathing you will feel greater ease and calm.

- For an even greater feeling of physical release and relaxation – which takes more time to achieve but which also gives you a greater understanding of tension – try the following. Take the journey through your body again from toe to head but this time consciously *apply* tension to each part followed in turn by a release. The application of tension will give muscles and joints a greater sensation of release. Concentrate on your right foot. Tense just that foot and then release it. Do the same for each of your extremities and parts of the torso, shoulders, neck and face. By locating and placing tension you get a more knowledgeable awareness of where it lives, how it breeds and feels, and what relief from it can feel like. Spend about seven to ten minutes doing this tensing and relaxing.
- Finally, apply rigid tension overall to the entire body, almost as if you have been given an electric shock. The release after this feels wonderful. Now you will really begin to understand something about relaxation and the impediment of tension.
- Just stay on the floor without moving. Enjoy the overall sensation of complete relaxation for about ten minutes. What you should begin to notice is how tension invades every part of the body when we are unaware of it and how it exhausts us, but you should also begin to feel the calmness that replaces it once it has evaporated. At this point you might begin to enter a deep sleep or experience a physical lightness rather like floating, falling or drifting. Now you are relaxed.

Reserve this exercise for the right time and place. This particular relaxation exercise is not recommended if you are gearing up for high physical or mental activity within the coming hour. After doing it you might feel mentally unfocused or dissipated, so don't drive a car, work out vigorously or even attempt to read a book. This kind of relaxation slows down motor responses for a time but makes you feel calm and together. The chief benefit of this sort of relaxation technique is to teach you how to stop fighting your body and just learn to surrender and deplete yourself of tensions.

Getting Up

It is unwise to get up quickly from these floor exercises. If you rush up you will only feel dizzy and nauseous. So:

- Roll gently onto one side of your body. Rest there for thirty seconds.
- Keep your head connected to your body. Don't jerk it up or move it around.
- Slowly roll over onto your stomach and then up to your hands and knees.
- Kneel back and rest the weight of your upper body on your buttocks.
- Now return to a standing position by gently building up through your spine. Place the feet firmly on the floor and apart with your knees in front of you. Keep your weight down and imagine, as you rise, that each vertebra is building up, one by one, from the base of your spine with the head the final crowning piece coming into place. Watch how toddlers get up. They perform this routine naturally.
- Once on your feet, allow your shoulders to fall into natural place. Don't put them into an awkward position or brace them backwards or forwards. They will find their natural alignment if you let them, otherwise you will notice tension. Now, fully standing with feet apart and directly under your shoulders, you should feel that tension has been shed. Your mind, however, may still be slightly unfocused so give yourself time to settle back into the world.

3. Repeat Relaxation

Go through a complete repeat of Exercise 2 in the standing position. In fact you must learn to repeat any exercise done on the floor in the full upright position, as well as while sitting and walking, in order to make the most useful connections in all your work. You will also find that in the upright position you won't feel so light-headed because the blood is circulating more naturally and evenly. Plus this is the position from which you do most serious talking and so you must learn to identify tension while standing and how to resolve it. Just go through all the same steps once more. Take your time.

4. Centring

After getting up from the floor and going through a relaxation technique once more you are probably close to being physically 'centred' or balanced. A good deal of the tension that throws the body off-centre has probably been either dulled, reduced or displaced. Take advantage of this state to experience the natural state of feeling centred. We will be returning to the centre position again and again throughout the work.

- Stand with your feet directly under your hips. They should be neither too wide nor too narrow but should form a firm, sturdy base. Your body weight should rest slightly on the balls of your feet without you feeling like you are tilting forwards.
- *Un*lock your knees.
- Feel that your hips are being supported by your legs, almost as though they are pedestals.
- The spine should now be 'up', neither slumped forwards nor arched backwards but straight as if the floor were still bracing it.
- Shoulders are unheld and unpositioned. They fall into natural place, a sensation you will notice.
- The upper chest sits naturally without being hoisted up. Don't think you have to stand at either attention or parade rest. Like the shoulders the chest will fall naturally into place. It is a comfortable position.

- The head balances easily on the spine. Nothing about it is rigid. It should turn and rotate flexibly.
- The eyes look out at the world *not* under it, down at it or away from it. So look squarely ahead at a distant point just above the horizon.
- The jaw is released and should open easily. Although the lips are together the teeth are not clenched. The facial muscles are totally relaxed.
- A very simple way of testing whether you have achieved a centred position is to rock gently backwards and forwards, sensing the motion filter through your entire body. If you are centred you won't feel off-balanced. Repeat this rocking ten to twelve times until you achieve a confident fluidity. If you are centred your weight balance will naturally return to centre as you rock. You won't sense that you are about to topple over. Any tension in any of the areas you have relaxed so far, even tension in the jaw, will make you feel off-balance or too rigidly controlled. Just try placing tension in certain areas and you will definitely sense the lack of balance and the immobility that it brings with it.

By now you might have a clearer understanding of where your personal habitual tensions manifest themselves: Face? Shoulders? Stomach? Buttocks? Legs? Feet? This is a good point to sort one or two of these out so that a greater effort to relax can be focused on these areas in future repetitions of the exercise.

As your confidence to identify tensions and to centre grows with each repetition of these first four exercises, you will discover you have a much greater chance to control and monitor the whole of your voice. Any tension you have identified at this stage will most certainly manifest itself and return to haunt your voice at some stage. So begin wrestling with it and relaxing it at this point.

5. Releasing the Neck, Shoulders, Face and Spine

Having centred the whole body, you can now concentrate on all those areas where habits and useless tension are likely to reside. We first start with the head and shoulders. You be

the judge here about how much time to spend on each phase.
Let tension and the noticeable release of it guide you when
to stop.

A. Neck and Shoulders

- Just lift and drop the shoulders; a bit more than a shrug
  but neither a violent nor wrenching action. Lift them up
  to your ears and then try shifting them in various positions
  from there before dropping them down again. As you drop
  them don't predict their final position of rest. Let them
  just fall naturally. One might be higher than the other.
  One might be doing more work or carrying more weight
  in your life than the other. This is a good point to notice
  something like that. It may be causing a shift in balance.
  Keep breathing throughout all phases of the exercise.
- Now circle the shoulders in all directions. Let your shoulder
  sockets guide you in this so that the arms are taking
  direction from the shoulders rather than leading the way.
  Keep breathing throughout. Don't use force and don't be
  alarmed if they make a crunching sound or feel stiff. Work
  them gently. If they hurt severely, however, or you simply
  cannot perform this stage of the exercise, you may need a
  good massage or a visit to an osteopath. Shoulder tension
  can be crippling for some people and attempting to exercise
  this area will tell you how stiff and severe this part of the
  body has become. It does affect your voice.
- Now swing each arm in turn, in the direction of an under-
  arm pitch, letting the weight of the arm release the shoulder.
  Keep the swing of the arm fluid and guard against any
  action that might throw out your shoulder. Keep breathing
  throughout. Now windmill the arm in a 360° turn, taking
  the swing through your entire body, and allow it to come to
  rest. Don't place the arm but let it come to a natural rest.
- Stand back in the centred position with the knees unlocked.
  Now raise your arms above or in front of you and stretch the
  body in all directions (up, to the sides, towards front and
  back). Imagine climbing up a scaffold as you stretch above,
  for instance. Keep breathing throughout. After each stretch
  allow an uncensored release to happen and take note where
  that release leaves your body. For example, as you stretch
  in front of you allow the release to flop you over before

gently building back up through the spine to the centred
position. What you are repeatedly trying to do here is to
tense and then to release naturally, to notice tension and
ways of releasing it.

- With both arms crisscrossed in front of you, gently massage
the back of your neck and down into your shoulders. Keep
breathing throughout. It is amazing how much release you
can provide for yourself by doing this.
- Begin to experience the actual weight of your head by
letting it drop onto your chest. Don't forget to continue
breathing. Now swing the head gently and slowly from
side to side across the chest. You can take this into a full
circular head roll as long as you don't feel any wrenching
or uncomfortable pulling in the neck or spine. Avoid a full
head roll if you sense this will result. Just allow the head to
swing and sway like a pendulum. Many of us fail to realise
the head's weight and the pressure it exerts on the neck
and shoulders. Always as you release the neck remember
to keep the jaw relaxed and unclenched.
- Now with head centred allow it to fall naturally to the
chest. Centred again let it fall to the side, the back, and
the other side. Be very gentle and careful here with the
head's weight. Don't force it. Keep breathing throughout.
What you'll notice in the gentleness of this activity are the
various points where the tendons of the neck exert useful
tension up towards the head in order to control and prop
it up in place.
- Try rotating your shoulders and head simultaneously in one
continuous, gentle action. This will feel uncoordinated and
disorienting at first but it will free many of the muscles in
the neck and shoulders that bear tremendous weight and
strain when held in check. Keep breathing throughout.
Let this wriggling activity be free.
- Slowing yourself down, come back to centre and full
relaxation.

B. Face and Jaw

- First gently massage your face all over. Then move all of
your facial muscles – as many as you can experience – inde-
pendently. These are such areas as the cheeks, mouth, lips,
ears, nose, eyes, brow. We don't usually exercise these parts
except in natural reflexes so spend a few minutes at it.

- Stretch the mouth open wide, but gently, then release it. Repeat a few more times.
- Circulate the jaw in a continuous chewing motion. This may be a new experience for you. Be prepared for some crackling sounds so do go gently. Never pull on, roughly manipulate or swing the jaw. It is a tender mechanism. Keep breathing throughout.
- Stretch the tongue in and out. Go gently at first and gradually try to extend it without overdoing it. First try and touch your nose with your tongue and then your chin. The tongue is a muscle we rarely exercise and like any muscle it can become lazy and cause us to get tongue-tied. You feel its laziness, too, when you are tired or dulled by alcohol. Keep breathing throughout.

C. The Spine

- Gently shake and wriggle the spine, starting from behind your abdomen like a belly dancer. Work from the spine, allowing the head and shoulders to follow the motion and neither start nor lead it. Try for a continuous flow and not a jerky or distorted movement.
- Movement in the spine undulates the whole body and activates the nervous system. So spend a bit more time experimenting here.

Even a few minutes of neck, shoulder, face and spine routines will help settle nerves or tensions and get the voice ready to work. They actually restore energy and balance. Each can be done with minimum effort and most of them work even if you are seated, like behind a desk, in a dressing room or even behind the wheel of a car.

6. Expansion Release Exercises

Here are some more dramatic and vigorous releasing exercises that build on the foundations above. This is a key series of exercises to balance you and clear out any constrictions still left untouched.

- Stand in the centred position, looking straight out.
- Standing in place with your feet apart, shake and sway the

shoulders vigorously. This is almost like a dance routine. Release all excess tension and even make sounds if you want. Really let yourself go.

- Now bend the knees slightly and allow the hips to rotate in a circular motion, coordinating this movement with the shoulder movement above. Keep breathing. Eventually let your hips take over the control of all movement until it all becomes a free and easy motion. You should stay balanced as you do this. Then stop.

- Now raise your hands and arms above your head. Let your body and arms drop forward in one complete motion into a crouch-like swing as if you were getting ready to leap up, but stay put. Instead of leaping, break the momentum of your upswinging arm movement and return to a standing position. In this movement you are trying to attain the full flowing motion of a schoolyard swing. Take some time to experience the movement because this bit of the exercise gets you more into your body and makes you bolder with movement as you breathe.

- If you believe your spine is slumped or too weak, try sitting cross-legged on the floor or sitting upright on the edge of a sturdy chair. Move about gently so you can begin to experience your spine in motion. Gently rock so you can feel the base of your spine. Remember to keep breathing, if only gently, at this point.

- Now, keeping the shoulders and upper chest released, allow the spine to slump as if you've suddenly been deflated and then allow it to build up again as though inflated. Start doing this more *dramatically* so you can notice the slump weakening and then strengthening and then do it *slightly* so you can note the slump with the smallest of changes. The objective here is for you to feel when your spine is off-balance. While seated and planted you can sense better how the spine should be positioned for the greatest ease. These spinal 'press-ups' will also alert you to tensions in this area.

- Still seated, start to undulate your spine. Then begin to snake it. Begin to feel the strength and support you have there which can replace any weaknesses. Slumped spines are positions we often fall into out of habit.

Warning: Never allow this part of the exercise to last more than a few minutes because it can be tiring. Older people

should take a good deal of care with it and go very easily.
Do this as a gentle exploratory exercise and not as a vigorous
one.

- When you stand up and return back to centre you should
  feel stronger and more agile and aware of the spine as a
  backbone of support. Although this exercise can be done
  on the floor, I think you'll get a greater awareness of any
  habitual problems by sitting on a chair.
- Back now at centre and still breathing. Any physical activity which encourages the body to swing while remaining
  anchored to earth will release unwarranted tension. The
  aim here is to attain a rhythm that balances breathing and
  repetitive action with grace. Think of your use of the whole
  body as you do this. Here are some suggestions:
  - imagine throwing a ball or javelin or swinging a club or a
    bat while breathing and then vocalising
  - imagine you are punting with a pole or steering a gondola,
    mowing with a scythe or sweeping a large area while first
    humming and then singing a song
  - imagine yourself alone in a large temperate swimming pool,
    doing an easy breast stroke down a marked lane

Don't try to compete with yourself here or try to outdo
yourself either. Don't try to block or truncate any motion.
This will only produce frantic energy and the wrong sort of
effort. Get into the motion and rhythm of the action and let
the job you are performing take care of itself. Let the action
lead you forwards. Don't consciously push for an effect.
Follow-through in combination with appropriate breathing is
essential. Any kind of swinging movement, even skipping or
hop-scotching, encourages a fluidity of easy motion, breath
and vocal release.

- When working with the voice avoid the sort of exercises
  which deplete energy or encourage blocks and holds that
  contain it: weightlifting, aerobic workouts, running and
  jogging, intricate dance movements. Anything, in other

words, where a frenetic and concentrated amount of physical exertion rushes energy away from the breath and the voice towards the muscular movement. You cannot speak easily during a series of press-ups! By all means work out your body in this way for cardiovascular benefits and toning, but my main caution is that you should *never* combine it with voice work. There are no benefits involved in this sort of straining exercise for the breathing voice.

7. Deep Relaxation

The final group in this opening series of exercises uses one of the deepest relaxation techniques I know. It takes a bit of time to get it right and to feel its benefits so allow yourself about twenty minutes to do it properly. It is elegantly simple enough to be done by anyone.

- Lie on the floor (preferably in a warm, carpeted room, not on cold linoleum or wood) with your lower legs below the knees elevated and supported comfortably on a chair. Move about and nestle in until you are completely comfortable and breathing regularly.
- Shuffle your body close to the chair so that your thighs are straight up and perpendicular to the floor and your calves parallel to it. The chair is now fully taking the legs' weight and you need not tense to support them further. So release any excess tension here.
- You may need a thin cushion (not a pillow) or book under the back of your head if it is awkwardly tilting back, stretching or constricting your neck.
- Keep your legs open and apart. Don't tighten the lower abdominal muscles or groin area. Once in this position allow the neck, shoulders, spine, lower back and abdomen to release fully. The total effect should be serene. Within minutes you will find that your body just can't resist the full release and relaxation.
- Now all you need to do is breathe in and out, in and out. Allow the whole body to find its own breath rhythm. Don't try to force it, hold it or gasp for it. If at any point you find breathing difficult (perhaps a sudden thought, for instance,

interrupts it) try 'sighing' out ('ahhh') and then wait for the body to signal that it wants to breathe again.

- Next breathe out as far as the body needs, then wait before letting the full breath drop back in, opening the centre of the body and releasing the chest and then the lower abdomen.

- If the upper chest lifts and starts to block the easy coordination of breath, gently place your flat hand on the breastbone (sternum) or your fingertips on the lower edge of the breastbone to check this lift.

- Don't interfere with the breath release but let it go as low as possible into the nether regions of the body. Most people experience a hold nearest the groin. So just keep breathing over the allotted time, gradually letting the breath go lower and lower. The muscles need not be forced to do this activity. It should be easy and unforced. Sometimes your hand placed just above the groin will help you feel this release more confidently.

- If you manage to take the breath release this low into the body (it does take time) you'll begin to feel a tremendous sense of power. Some people experience a huge emotional release and may begin to weep uncontrollably. This emotional release, however, is not the aim of the exercise but only a by-product of it. Don't push yourself in this direction. Just let your breath lead you on this journey towards total relaxation. Take your time. Do it all gradually.

This exercise is excellent for voice work but also works whenever you need any kind of the deepest relaxation or emotional or physical release. I am always amazed how so many of us release through rage rather than relaxation. Use deep relaxation for whatever purpose you require. Some doctors I have worked with have suggested that thirty minutes of this kind of relaxation exercise is worth, physically, eight hours of sleep.

Many actors and singers use this relaxation technique between matinee and evening shows (but not, however, during short intervals within a show) and at nights to unwind before sleeping. The exercise seems to help to give you a more restful night's sleep and thoroughly rests the voice after any exertion.

Now that you have released and relaxed, you can start building up the breath.

Breathing Exercises

After the breath has been located naturally through relaxation you must begin to find flexibility and learn control, avoiding those unwanted holds and tensions that distract us from taking the breath we need for any thought and feeling.

The principles of breath for voice work are as follows:

- To place the breath and allow it to find its natural position.
- To open the entire ribcage around the centre of the body. The back area, in particular, is one of the most neglected areas and opening it produces a full breath capacity and draws tension away from the upper chest.
- To allow the diaphragm to freely move down and out, creating a release of muscles above the waist and down into the lower abdominal area.
- To activate all muscles that support the outward breath, creating a column of air that connects to and starts the voice.
- To build breath capacity.
- To control the breath capacity essential to any speaker who regularly encounters extended vocal work.

One of the main fears we all have as speakers is that we will run out of breath and lose control. These exercises will help to overcome that principal dread.

During all these exercises try breathing in and out through the nose rather than the mouth. Through the nose you can take a deeper, calmer and longer breath that keeps the voice moist. Air coming in through the mouth alone, especially if it rushes in, dries out the voice. Many constant mouth-breathers only allow themselves to take snatched, high breaths which can severely dry the voice and set off alarms in the body as it signals tension. Try both types of breathing to experience what I mean. The body will naturally alternate styles to achieve the right balance since each is essential in voice and speech work.

8. Foundation Exercises

It is crucial to breathe throughout all phases of the exercises.

A. Stretch I

- Start from a centred, standing position and then return to this position after each exercise, remembering to check that shoulders remain unbraced and the body stays aligned down the spine.
- You should be able to do all the breathing exercises without experiencing any unwonted tension in your shoulders, upper chest or stomach. If you do feel something there stop and troubleshoot the problem and wait until relaxation returns before proceeding.
- Make one last check to ensure that the head sits easily on top of the spine, the jaw is unclenched and the knees are unlocked. Feel the natural breath coming in and going out. Now you are ready to go further.
- Begin to breathe for a full minute and as you do so check where you sense movement in your torso: sides of the ribcage, back, front, stomach area? Where? Feel these areas, massage them with your hands. Actually get hold of these areas.
- Place one hand on one side of the ribcage and the other on the diaphragm at the front of the torso just above the waist (the ribcage at the front makes an upside down 'V'; feel in this area for movement). These are the first places where you want to feel movement and the areas that should remain open as you breathe.
- With your left arm above you, stretch over to the right side to expand the left side of your ribcage. Don't flop forwards when you do this, just gently to the side. As you arc the left arm over you notice the ribcage expanding

with the pressure. Now breathe. You should feel the ribs struggle to open on the stretched left side. Now come up and back to centre and check your breath again. You will feel a greater freedom in the left side than you do in the right. Now repeat the stretch but this time from right to left. The tightness in this side should now have loosened as well. Repeat this activity a few more times to experience the opening of breath to these parts.

B. Stretch II

- This second exercise is one of the most basic and freeing of all stretches. If this one works for you it is likely to end up as one of your key exercises. This is the opening-the-back stretch! (I call it the 'bear-hug'.) I developed this exercise after watching the way marathon runners naturally return their high running breath to a centred position after a race.
- Begin by hugging yourself with your arms crisscrossing your breast, with wrists and hands wrapped round the back. There's no need to clutch or grab yourself. Just hug; don't hold on for dear life.
- Now try and hug yourself without creating any shoulder tension whatsoever or raising your shoulders.
- Let your head drop the chin down onto your chest but stay as loose as possible and do not strain your neck.
- Once in this position flop forwards from the waist, keeping your knees slightly bent.
- While in this down, hugged position take your time to breathe in and out as fully as possible. Eventually you will feel the breath open the back area and travel right down to your bottom.
- After several breaths like this, release the hug and let your arms drop down towards the floor, coming up very slowly and back to centre. If you rush up you will get dizzy.
- Once centred again you may feel more activity, perhaps a tingle, around the back of the ribcage. The breath has reached a part of yourself which you don't typically feel.

This exercise both relaxes and stretches the whole breath system, preparing it to take on vocal work.

C. Stretch III

- Stand centred, breathing regularly and gently 'pant' on the diaphragm muscle sounding a light 'ha, ha, ha'.

In between each 'ha' allow the breath to move the muscle out. As you 'ha' the muscle will move slightly in. If you sense your breastbone (or sternum) is moving along with the diaphragm, place a hand there to still it consciously. This allows you the opportunity to experience the upper breath support.

- Now begin to open the lower breath support as follows: allow your knees to bend and loosen, assuming the low centred position found in most martial arts. Place your hands on either side of your pelvis above the groin and breathe, allowing the hands to monitor the movement in and out. Don't cheat by moving this area either by not opening the whole ribcage or by visibly pushing and pumping these muscles. The entire upper and lower breath system must work in tandem and should feel free, easy and unfraught. If the breath becomes frantic you will feel it in your stomach.
- Return to centre and see if you now notice more breathing activity in your abdomen area. Now sense both lower and upper areas working together.
- This next exercise I call the 'air pump'. Still working with the lower abdominal muscles, move your feet together. Flop over from the waist, keeping your neck and head as untensed as possible. Bend your knees, enabling yourself to place both fists on the floor just in front of your feet. As you breathe in you should simultaneously push down with your arms and try to straighten your legs on the intake of breath. The air will pump in and down low. Feel it? As you breathe out you release the pressure and feel your bottom lowering and your knees bending. Do these several times and then return slowly to centre. This should have stretched the lower breath area further.

Putting all of this together, here is a combined routine designed to stretch you in all areas most crucial to muscular breathing. Do this with ease and a sense of rhythmic flow and take as much time as you need to breathe. Breathe in each position about two minutes.

D. Combined Stretch

- Start in the prayer position. That is, get down on your hands and knees, then allow your bottom to collapse onto your feet with your arms relaxed along the sides of your body (or wherever they feel most comfortable).
- Let your forehead or a side of your face lean all the way forwards, resting on the floor in front of you. Feel comfortable and without any strain, breathing in and out. You should feel the intake of breath reaching and stimulating the muscles in your back, sides, diaphragm and abdomen.
- Next roll onto one side and curl into a foetal position and breathe. Straighten up to kneeling and roll onto the other side. Breathe again.
- Now lie on your back and hug your knees to your chest and breathe. Release your legs and return them to the floor and rest. When ready and rested return to your feet and back to centre. You should feel great!

Having stretched the abdominal, side and back muscles, you can next work on gaining flexibility.

9. Flexibility Exercises

These exercises can be done standing, lying, sitting or walking. Try all possibilities so you can test their full benefit. For this reason I won't stress one position over the other.

- Breathe out as far as you can *without* allowing the spine or head to collapse. It is crucial that both stay up and strong. Wait for the breath to come in and don't struggle as the breath pours in through the mouth, nose or both, reopening the whole system with a surge of air. Don't attempt too many of these exhalations at one time but I do want you to notice and feel a delightful sense of muscular elasticity as you do this exercise. Notice particularly how the breathing system understands exactly how to replenish itself. As the muscles of the body open to receive the air, you might feel more of a sensation of space inside you.

Be aware of keeping tension away from the upper torso, however, and follow the principle of the two movements of breath: breathe in, breathe out, continually in one complete motion; NOT breathe in – hold breath or top it up – then breathe out. That hesitation is counter-productive to gaining flexibility.

- Swing both arms up and out to the sides (creating a 'T') as you breathe in and then let them drop back to your sides as you breathe out.

- Sounding an 's' or 'f' or a gentle hum, breathe in and release on one of these sounds as far as it is comfortable to go without any tension or spinal collapse. Breathe in and repeat this sounding process three to five more times. With each repetition you are now taking a full 'recovery' of breath, one after the other, and getting more confident and flexible as you do it. You are fully engaging the breath system and operating from it. The particular breath you are using here is the one we naturally use to cover long thoughts or to deal with powerful emotions. So this is an important exercise for professional speakers in particular.

- Starting with this same breath now take it into speaking. For instance, count as far as you go on one breath but without making it seem like some sort of endurance test. Work with whatever comfortable intervals the breath provides. Recover breath and repeat the exercise, working towards flexibility and lengthier intervals. Carry on like this for two minutes. The breath should be swishing in and out like a water wheel, and you should find yourself counting or speaking as though an arc of sound, fluidly connected with the breath, were issuing forth. This is called the 'circulation' exercise. Again, pay careful attention to how you can maintain and lose power during one of these repetitions.

- Sigh out loud ('ahhh') using just the muscles in the dia-phragm and keeping the ribcage flexible. Next try playing with a series of sounds like 'hah', 'mah' or counting (i.e. 'one' – breathe – 'two' – breathe, etc. up to seven). Feel the action of the breath. This is the diaphragmatic or 'top-up' recovery breath used for short bursts of thought, retorts or sudden truncated feelings. There should be no dramatic movement in the upper chest region during this exercise. Place a hand there to steady yourself if necessary.

Naturally this diaphragmatic recovery as well as the full recovery above must bond together and be used interchangeably depending on the impulse of whatever we speak or vocalise. So I want you to take special note of the length and value of both sorts of breathing. Your breath can actually be geared quite accurately to both small and large units of thought. The next exercise is a means of bonding both sorts of recovery:

- Begin counting over a series of numbers from one to twenty. Mix the intervals into short and long (one to three; four to ten; eleven to thirteen; fourteen to twenty etc.) and then repeat the loop with a new mix of intervals. Over the shorter counts you will be using the more immediate diaphragmatic recovery, over the longer ones the full recovery from deeper down. Begin mixing and matching so you can experience the relative values of each and how one sort of recovery plays off the other. Always stay connected to the support which each recovery supplies.

10. Capacity and Control Exercises

This next series of exercises extends the capacity of the breath and enlarges your speaking endurance. Although the exercises seem repetitive and tedious, there is no doubt that capacity and control give any speaker real confidence in his or her vocal ability. Most speakers cite their main fear in public speaking as 'running out of breath' or 'losing control over breath'. These exercises are designed to overcome those fears and give you necessary confidence, so realise those are the benefits awaiting you.

When actors, in particular, return to the stage after doing prolonged work in television and film, their chief worry is 'Will I have enough breath to make the lines work for an audience?' These exercises help that problem and also any problem a public speaker has in delivering long thoughts or lengthy presentations or reports. Remember that sudden loss of breath and a deteriorating voice are instantly noticeable and mar an otherwise fine performance in front of listeners. So capacity and control make up a vital stage for serious speakers to attain.

If you earn your living by using your voice in a variety of ways then your breath must be flexible, strong and athletic otherwise the creativity of your voice will suffer. Such a heavy voice user cannot afford to bypass these exercises. Look upon them as a daily insurance premium you are paying to keep you healthy, undamaged and out of trouble.

These exercises can be done standing, sitting or lying. They should be done with complete freedom in the shoulders and upper chest region and without any collapse in the spine. If you work diligently with these exercises your capacity and control will improve within the space of a week.

- Centre yourself and breathe in gently without rushing. Release the air on an 's' or 'f' sound. As you release the air be aware of controlling the flow by means of the muscles around the centre of the body (the diaphragm, ribcage and abdomen). Don't try to control the outwards flow from the throat, jaw or mouth. Think of these muscles as being dormant or non-existent for the purposes of this work. Notice that the steadier the movement is from the ribcage and diaphragm, the steadier and stronger the sound becomes. Quite a difference in sound, in fact. If the sound you make is pulsating and not steady then your upper support muscles are probably too tight and you should troubleshoot these with some of the relaxation exercises from further above.
- Now begin covering longer intervals of time on these releases of breath and sound: first ten seconds, then fifteen, twenty, thirty and so forth. A practised speaker should be able to release to a count of twenty-five and a professional speaker up to a count of forty-five. But don't push to achieve these results with unnecessary tension. You'll get red in the face! Build up gradually and comfortably.
- Next try to take in *only* the air necessary to cover specific intervals or counts (ten, fifteen, twenty, thirty, forty-five) and begin to notice just how much you need in these instances. Naturally we take the air we need to serve and accommodate a thought or when we are happily chatting away to friends. Yet one of the reasons we become conscious

of and worry about our breath is that we never notice it until we are under threat and then suddenly have 'panic gasps'. This part of the exercise lets you consciously measure natural breath intervals. When you stop at the various intervals do it clearly with a full stop. Don't just run out of breath. If you can achieve this exercise you are now beginning to experience breath capacity and control plus how to release the natural breath consciously.

- Now try the very same phase of the interval part of the exercise with the sounds 'z' and 'v'. These sounds are 'voiced' and will require more breath control to keep them steady over lengthy counts. Don't despair if you initially sound like a bee that is buzzing all over the place. As the muscles around the jaw and mouth coordinate and accommodate themselves to the exercise, you will begin to control and regularise the sound by use of the breath muscles alone. This, together with the other three exercises above, has given you the chance to experience breath capacity and control on the full recovery of breath.

This next sequence of exercises is for diaphragmatic recovery of breath:

- Sounding the 'sh' sound, release in controlled pulses, gently forced, from the diaphragm and abdominal regions. Vary the length of each release and note that it will take more effort to cover an interval of counts. Try and work the muscles in the most economical way and don't force out the breath too strongly or loudly. Think of tapping off the sound and not pumping it out.
- Repeat this same exercise with the voiced 'z' sound as in leisure or 'measure for measure'. Keep the vibration here under control.
- Now take the full diaphragmatic recovery exercise into a continuous 'm' sound and play around with it at various pitches and intervals. As you feel the 'm' on your lips open the sound in a 'mah'. The 'ah', because it is so open a sound, is one of the hardest to control. It is tempting here to manipulate this sound in the throat or by closing the jaw and tightening the chest muscles. So fight those constricting temptations and 'think' the sound as coming from the breath muscles only. You'll instantly notice a much more certain and unconstrained sound emanating from you. Also notice

here the freedom in the chest, throat and jaw. That is the effect you are aiming for so remember it.

- Release on 'm' for a count of three and then open into 'mah' for a count seven. Now double and sustain the sounds for longer intervals, working with diaphragmatic breath only.
- Using the 'ah' sound, tap out various combinations of the sound, touching each interval off from the diaphragm only. For instance, on one breath touch off three 'ah's, then four, seven and up to as many as you can without suffering either discomfort or constrictions. Be as subtle and unforced with the diaphragmatic movement as possible.
- Now transforming the 'm' into 'hah' try and control a release of sound as you sit down and then stand up all in one breath. Next get more adventurous by walking around and releasing on 'm' into 'hah', trying to keep the sound steady. Then walk quickly. Finally break into a run. Coordinate sound and motion into one action.
- Do a physical activity that gets you slightly out of breath (like running on the spot). At the point you are beginning to get out of breath stop the activity, pick up a reading and then read as you try to 'think' the breath down to the diaphragm to get it under control.

These exercises (plus any variations you can devise yourself) will improve your extension of breath and make your voice bolder as you speak. Even just three to five minutes a day of conscious exercising begin to give the breath a new 'memory' of where it should come from – a place further down from its current source. Keep in mind that the source here is the diaphragm, ribcage and abdomen and *not* the throat, jaw or mouth. Something the practised and professional speaker will start to notice is that volume in the voice is controlled by the breath muscles. So sense the work here and not higher in the throat where volume only produces strain and further constriction.

11. Placing and Locating the Breath

The more muscular awareness you have of your whole breathing system, the more confident you will become at identifying problems or increasing your capacity. These exercises are designed to firm up your ability to draw on these muscles for placing and locating the amount of breath needed to perform a vocal act of different measures.

- Stand at centre and take a breath. Placing your hands on either side of your ribcage, gently but firmly make it move in as you breathe out. Sense but don't fight the upward swing as the air drops back in.

Move your hands further down and monitor carefully whether or not you are stopping the abdominal muscles from releasing as you breathe out. You may discover that you are doing quite the opposite – tightening rather than loosening the muscles. Right there is a big cause of control loss. The lower support is constricted and needs freeing to produce the proper stream of breath.

Reminder: The ribs and abdomen are two chief areas you must work to keep free of tightness.

- Next lift a chair above your head as though you are about to throw it. Don't strain with a weight heavier than you can handle. Keep the shoulders as relaxed as possible. Breathe in and out regularly as you perform the action. As you do this 'lift and throw' motion notice the added power you can now feel in the breath and its muscles. Also notice how loose those muscles become and how much more confident in the breath they are supplying you. Put the chair down. Breathe again. You should instantly feel more support and power. Test this by vocalising on a 'hum' or by speaking some text.
- Now breathe as you push substantial but moveable objects around in space. One singer I teach does this as she pushes her filled shopping trolley around a supermarket. Once again the breath muscles will rise to the challenge and enlarge capacity to fulfil the task. The breath always wants to help support you so let it engage in its natural capacity.

A. Separation

In certain heightened moments it is natural to separate two sets of breath muscles: the ribcage and the diaphragm/abdominal muscles. This separation works as follows: we breathe in

and all the muscles open to accommodate the breath. The
separation occurs as we breathe out. The diaphragm and
abdominal muscles contract first before the ribs join in and
overlap the action with one of their own. (*N.B.* This is not
the breath technique known as 'Rib Reserve' in which the
ribcage is locked and held rigidly in place.)

Exercising this separation is very useful for people who
have to use their breathing system to support a huge vocal
sound like screaming or shouting, or those who have to fill
a massive space. It is not a constant position but one that
allows an enormous sound through the body and gives extra
control to these heightened moments.

- Gently 'pant', supported by the diaphragm, trying to keep
  the ribcage slightly suspended and not bouncing around
  with the diaphragmatic movement. Don't do this for long.
  As you near the end of releasing all the breath allow
  the ribcage to join in the process naturally. Repeat the
  process with the voiced 'ha', allowing the movement of the
  diaphragm to increase its activity and change the volume.
  When the ribs join in let them do so with vigour and
  enthusiasm.
- Release on an 's' sound, again consciously separating the
  two muscular activities but keeping a fluid overlap of
  diaphragm first and then the ribcage. To help you feel
  the separation change the 's' to 'z' as the ribs join in.
  Do exactly the same separation on the voiced sounds 'oo'
  (on diaphragm) into 'ah' (as ribcage joins in). Never allow
  tension to exert itself in your shoulders or chest as you do
  these repetitions.

If these particular exercises in separation work for you then you
will notice a leap in capacity, control and vocal muscularity.
Daring, too. If the work confuses or panics you then leave it
be. This positioning of the breath is a useful technique for
professional speakers but not essential.

B. Strengthening

*Caution: This next group of exercises requires more physical
exertion and should not be done by anyone with a bad or*

injured back! It puts a great deal of pressure on the lower back but it also strengthens the breath muscles.

- Lie on the floor on your back, making sure your head is not tilting backwards. As you do these exercises concentrate your mind on only using the lower breath muscles, keeping the work clear of the muscles in the jaw, throat and upper chest.
- Breathe in and as you do so lift your legs easily in the air (without a struggle) so that they are at a right angle with the rest of your body.
- As you breathe out on an 's', 'z', 'sh', 'm', or 'ha' (or speaking a text) you should be returning your legs to the floor as slowly as possible with the legs remaining straight. Yes, this is a difficult one and really does test a certain amount of abdominal muscularity. You will feel it!
- As you get very fit and bold you can extend the routine by bringing the legs right over the body to touch the floor with your feet above the head, all this in one motion as you breathe in. This is an exhausting and extended routine so don't attempt too many repetitions.
- When you've finished, draw your knees up to your chest and hug them to release any back tension. Don't get up immediately. If you are going to use any voiced sounds during this routine then warm up the voice first (see p 209). Check that the throat is free. A yawn always helps free any constriction and opens the back of the throat.
- Now squat on the floor with your hands in front of you to balance yourself. Keep the shoulders and head as free as possible. Pant on the diaphragmatic recovery and then voice the sounds 'sh', 'ha', 'hay' and 'ma'. Vary the length of release and the volume.
- Repeat the sequence but this time on your hands and knees. Keep the head and shoulders free so look down as you pant and make the sounds.

12. Extended Flexibility

In order to speak in large daunting spaces, like the Olivier stage at Britain's Royal National Theatre or the London Barbican stage at the Royal Shakespeare Company, or with extended texts that address long thoughts or huge emotions, you must develop tremendous flexibility in order not to think or worry about your breath. Here are some exercises which allow you to build on what we did above.

- Using an 's' or a 'z', going into a 'ha' or simply speaking a large chunk of text, breathe in and release the breath and voice as far as you can without suffering spinal collapse and tension in the jaw, throat or upper chest. Feel the moment you are about to lose contact with the breath from a weakening of the breath muscles (a feeling often marked by a closure of the jaw or throat or a tightening of the shoulders). When that begins to happen recover the breath as fully as possible, starting to sound or speak again without any holds or blocks.

Build up so that you are able to do five to seven of these full recoveries, one after the other without loss of speaking momentum. Don't be shy about feeling the work in your breath muscles. You are supposed to work them! But keep the effort very fluid and don't stagger or gasp for air.

The equivalent in text work for this exercise is to recite four to five lines of iambic pentameter verse on a single capacity of breath, recover, recite another chunk of the same length, recover, etc. This is a very athletic way of speaking, often not needed, but a good way to build confidence with a lengthy text. It is perfect practice for the challenge of a long monologue or soliloquy.

- This next exercise is for fast, easy recovery from the diaphragm without feeling any tension in the upper chest. If tension is going to creep into the breathing system it will do so by this route. So keep monitoring the upper chest for signs of it. Most people believe that in order to take a fast breath you have to lift the upper chest as you draw it in. *This is not necessary.* A fast breath can and should be taken low into the body as follows: count one and recover low; one, two and recover low; one, two, three and recover low; and so on up to a count of ten. Repeat the ten count again and then reverse the process (i.e. one to nine; one to eight etc.), doing the low recoveries more quickly.

Now dare to do the exercise without thinking so it starts to take hold more naturally. The breath should begin to go low into automatic downshifts. Let the lower muscles do much of the work. Don't tighten them, just let them relax and respond. If the upper chest moves, place a hand there to steady and monitor it.

In order to gain complete flexibility through this exercise, you might have to put more concentrated effort into letting these muscles work and take over. Remember that the aim here is to feel that all the work is connected organically to the voice. Thrashing or pumping the abdomen muscles is not required ultimately but you find yourself going through a phase of this before you can let go totally! We really only need the pumping motion to vomit and expel toxic waste, not to breathe.

- Any physical activity that throws all the muscles into action will eventually aid breath flexibility if not done too strenuously. Running, for instance, until you are out of breath and then concentrating on a low easy recovery. Also: climbing stairs while speaking; speaking while pushing yourself off a wall; jumping up and down while humming. Experiment with finding your own version of these so you can experience the workings of breath and voice in *action*.

13. Extended Capacity and Control

There is a very simple equation you should always bear in mind: the larger the space and the more heightened the text (either emotionally or intellectually), then the more breath you will need to fill the challenge. Fine-tuned control means taking the breath you need to support the emotional, intellectual or spatial demands. Control means being able to measure and sense what you need. It can often be uneconomical to take too much and damaging to take too little. Aim for proportion. Learning how to start and stop the breath is another key requirement. I remember a comedian describing timing to me: 'It is easy to get a laugh, but stopping it is the important thing.' The same applies to breath control.

- Try to extend the release on the sound of a 'z' or 'v' over thirty to forty seconds. This should be done without experiencing any tension in the chest, shoulders, neck or jaw. Don't clamp the throat. Sense all the work coming from the centre breath muscles. Recover and try again for longer intervals, again monitoring for telltale tension. Doing this extends the control of breath capacity and makes you conscious of it. By releasing on 'z' or 'v' you can hear if the sound is steady or out of control. So aim for a strong, steady sound.

It takes about ten days for breath capacity to be worked into shape and it will disappear just as quickly, so this area of voice work needs constant attention. If you will be needing good capacity for a performance or speech, begin the process two weeks before the rehearsal or event.

- Sing or chant while swinging the body. When you are out of breath try and release as steadily as you can on 'ha'. The quieter the release, the greater the capacity for control. This is a good exercise for developing understatement rather than overstatement in the voice.

14. Support and Connection

'Support' is a name we give to the muscular action in the diaphragm and abdomen which creates the column of air that supports the flow of voice. While performing all the breathing and vocalising exercises here, constantly check that there is muscular support holding up the voice or existing beneath the sound. The action may be slight but it is one you should always be able to sense. Just by making a 'z' or 's' sound you can sense, down low, muscles instigating and carrying the sound aloft.

I have worked with numerous professional speakers who have religiously worked on extending their breath capacity and control, but have forgotten to connect it to sound! Until we can connect to a word with a properly controlled breath we cannot own it or sound real. This connection is what makes all voice work possible and productive. Owning our feelings and thoughts and being able to convey them by means of the breath is a necessary part of the release process.

It is a completely natural habit to support and connect, but many unsure speakers never tap into this wholesome habit of speaking that links thought, emotion, breath, support and sound together into one burst. So we always have to remind ourselves of the *ease* of this natural muscular position.

We've explored some of the locked doors that bar the passage of the unconnected voice. I would hazard a guess that at least eighty per cent of all vocal damage is caused by a misuse or mistrust of support. It is unhealthy and dangerous to disconnect the process, particularly if you make great demands on your voice. Forget support and connection at your peril!

As you go over all the above breath exercises, doing them at regular daily intervals, begin to remind yourself to 'connect' and 'support' to whatever sound you make.

- Sigh out ('ahhh'). As you vocalise that sound you will suddenly begin to notice and feel the breath muscles underneath it. That's support.
- Pant on a light 'hah', 'hah', 'hah' or 'mah', 'mah', 'mah', feeling the sound originating or starting from the diaphragm and *not* the throat or upper chest. That is also sensing support.
- Build up a vocal text, word by word, feeling that each word starts with and comes from support: 'To' (breathe); 'To be' (breathe); 'To be or' (breathe); 'To be or not' (breathe); 'To be or not to' (breathe); 'To be or not to be' (breathe), etc. Use the muscles as subtly as possible.

Don't rush or provoke them. Let the breath drop in easily and the support get underneath the words to float them out. It is a different sense of speaking, but a supported sense. Not at all difficult or technically complex.

- Count over various intervals, constantly noticing the support gathering underneath the sound (e.g. one, two, three; one, two, three, four, five, six, seven; one, two; etc.) and the greater or lesser support needed for differing intervals. Now take in only the breath you think you need to do these varied intervals once more. The more economic you are at taking only the breath the sounds require – and at learning when to stop and start breath – the more connected the system becomes to efficiency.
- It is useful and important to feel and begin to recognise the moments when you lose support or feel disconnected. This is crucial for a professional speaker.

The lungs, you must remember, never completely empty of air but there comes a point when you simply haven't got enough muscular energy to support the voice from the breath muscles alone. This can be a dangerous moment if you are in the midst of a vital speech. You have to get your body used to 'thinking' connection, support and recovery. Too many voices suffer damage because speakers don't. They simply push on without muscle support, trying to squeeze out air that won't come. Attempting to vocalise without support is akin to bashing your head against a brick wall. You might make a sound but it will hurt and you will not crack through. You'll crack your head open instead! Give the wall a mighty heave with support and you will breach it successfully.

The Tell-Tale Signs of Support Loss

At the point when you lose real support you will feel one, some or all of the following; take these as serious warnings:

- tightening in the throat
- jaw tension

- upper chest caving in
- spine collapsing
- voice being swallowed back down the throat

After a long period of inactivity or no support the voice will feel tired, sore, itchy or tickly. The voice might also feel stuck in a limited range. All of these signs represent the body trying to conserve air and pleading with you to breathe, begging for support. Obey the plea. We usually don't, taking the attitude: 'I'll get to the end of this line if it kills me!' A perilous thought process without justification or support!

- It is useful, however, if a bit perverse, to experience this fallacy in action. Try humming without support; in other words close off the breath muscles and feel the tension unique to a lack of support. The upper chest, throat and jaw are doing all the work and eventually a sort of panic and disconnection set in. Stop when that happens. That's working without support and is, in fact, the way many of us produce sounds daily. Referring to the list above, where are you most experiencing the tension or tightening? As I said, this is a perverse exercise but you've done it to demonstrate what a lack of support feels like.
- This time speak to the point of no support without recovering any breath. Again recognise and remember the tension caused in this process.

It is crucial to impose the idea of support to all daily speech transactions. Actively think about and use support. It is not just a professional tool or trick. It is vital to healthy, natural speaking. It may, at first, give your voice an odd sound, especially to loved ones who know you well. But bridging the gap between no support and full support involves a span of adjustment to all concerned. Eventually the voice will sound real and less put on. You will also feel less conscious effort in supporting and begin to enjoy a greater sense of ease. I guarantee you will be able to speak longer and with more variety once you have taken on board the idea of supporting your voice.

16. Freeing, Warming Up and Placing the Voice

We have been following separate stages of a whole process. As you become physically aligned, centred and relaxed and you have captured the freedom of breath support moving up and down the system, you can start moving even closer to liberating your voice.

The following exercises unblock the holds and constrictions in the throat, jaw or facial area. Just imagine the power of support, being pumped up and then suddenly being dammed in these areas. This is what we are setting out to liberate. During all these exercises it is again crucial that you remain both physically free and connected to breath support and that you perform all the vocalisations without effort or strain.

A. Freeing

- Breathe in and release the air on a *silent* 'h'. Not a rasping sound but just a silent one closer to a breath. This simple exercise begins to build up a sense of unforced vocal cord freedom.
- Now take the same sense of freedom into a 'hah' sound or an easy 'ahhh' sigh. The sound should become connected to and supported by the breath system, getting past the throat. Note when the passage of air becomes quite steady and unforced.
- Massage and work all the facial muscles gently with your hands just as we did in a previous relaxation exercise. Open and shut the eyes, tensing and relaxing them. Don't allow the released muscles to become tight again. Now gently chew the jaw around. Try to open the jaw to accommodate a two-finger height. If the mouth won't open at least that far, work gently until it feels possible. Smile and open the jaw. The action of smiling will also open the back of the throat. Feel it? You may yawn. Keep the jaw open on the smile and stretch out your tongue, placing it against the chin. Then release it, allowing it to retract of its own accord. All of these exercises free up the various muscles.
- Keeping the 'two-finger drop' opening, place the tongue tip behind the bottom row of teeth. Speak the sequence

'k, g, ng' as accurately and quickly as possible despite
the distortion. Now try to prevent the jaw from bouncing
around. This exercise will develop muscularity in the soft
palate. By this stage all the facial muscles, including the
tongue and soft palate, should be ready to allow the voice
to come through.

- Speak now on the edge of a yawn. Count or speak anything
  on a fully supported yawning vocal position. This will
  quickly open and free throat tension. From this extreme,
  open position shift into a more natural speaking mode,
  remembering the roominess the yawn offered to your throat.
- Gently slide from the top of your voice down to the bottom
  – not note by note but in one clean swoop, your voice like
  an air-raid siren in reverse. Start on the topmost note of
  your voice. But think 'up' as the voice drops down. It's
  a nice, bold sensation. If you fix your eyes at a point just
  above the horizon it helps to produce the sound, so let the
  voice glide down but 'think' it up to that point you see.
  This will produce an arc of sound as it leaves you.
- Now reverse the above process and glide from the bottom
  upwards. This is harder and slightly more stressful as you
  think up at the same time. It seems to double the intensity
  of the sound.

Both facets of this exercise free the 'push down' or 'clamp'
syndrome so common in Western voice production. A clamp
in the throat quite literally holds down the voice and prevents
the freedom you've just experienced.

- Now take this open sensation into actual speaking towards
  that point on the horizon. Any note can be made freely,
  up and out. Always think of the arc as the motion of
  release. I am not advocating high voices but I want you
  to realise that all voices move up and down rather than
  get stuck in one place. 'Pushing down' or 'clamping' the
  voice can seriously impede range or choice and lead to
  unsuspected abuse.
- If you experience a sharp glottal attack or shock as you
  speak (the sensation of a click or shove in the back of your
  throat as you start a sound) then try making short vowel
  ('o' or 'u') sounds or thinking of an 'h' or yawn preceding
  each vocal try. For example, with and in front of words

like 'idiot', 'education', 'obvious', 'apple', 'actual', 'it' or 'up' a glottal attack will be instantly softened by the 'h' or yawn without producing the effect of the glottal kick-start or head-butt that is habitual for so many speakers. If this fails to relieve the attack, try to sing the sounds or words gently before speaking them. This too helps to unclog the tension at the back of the throat.

- If you believe that you 'push' your voice out of your mouth then chant with an initial thought of a yawn. Next breathe and support. Once you feel the push has gone take yourself immediately into speaking. With an aggressive 'push' you have to think in reverse to light and easy.
- For any devoicing or whispered quality the move from intoning or chanting into speaking will help. On one interval of breath make the shift from intoning into speaking. By making that transition on the same breath you find yourself now speaking on a whole voice.
- If you find yourself pulling back on sound or hesitating, try speaking 'hah', 'mah' or 'may' while throwing an actual or imaginary ball. Take the throwing action into your entire body so that you hurl the sound from you towards a target or receiver. Now speak a piece of text in exactly the same way. Remember to breathe. Next return to a physical centre and reproduce the sounds followed by the words, trusting they can leave you.

B. Warming Up

The voice is a wonderful and extraordinary instrument that needs care and time every day to liven up before it begins to work at its best. Many speakers demand too much from the voice without giving it the grace of a warm-up. How can it work efficiently if it is not sufficiently oiled and warmed?

All voices are different. I don't pretend to understand the uniqueness of voices (I'm not sure anyone does) but I do know that some voices take more time to warm up than others, anywhere from five to twenty-five minutes. It often depends on the time of day. It is much harder first thing in the morning when the voice has been resting. It also depends on the weather, on how warm, cold, damp or humid the day is. Cold and dryness make it harder to warm up. Find out about your voice and use exercises that achieve the position of feeling warmed as efficiently as possible.

It is hard to describe how a 'warmed' voice should feel. It starts or vocalises without feeling tacky or sticky, particularly on a softer, smaller volume. A warmed voice moves easily through ranges. It flies.

I find that many professional speakers rush the warming process in an overeager attempt to place and produce the voice. Resist this temptation to get a quick start. Without a proper warm-up you are cutting corners and will only impede other areas of voice work. So the rule of thumb is to take as much time as you need. It might be a different amount every day. Work slowly, deliberately but enjoyably.

To follow the freeing exercises above, here is a simple routine to warm up the voice:

- Gently breathe in and then support outwards on a gentle hum. Keep your mouth closed and breathe out though your nose so that the hum stays internal. Humming a note slightly higher than your habitual one will probably warm the voice more rapidly. The higher vibration on the cord aids the warming process. When you run out of breath just breathe in and start again.

Now play with different notes rather than just a steady one. Hum a 'made-up' tune, thinking always of the sound arc we used above. Hum up and out without pushing. Now take the hum into an 'ah'. This whole part of the process could take from two to fifteen minutes.

- Hum or gently 'ah' into the top of your head. You should feel vibration in your cranium. Let the sound travel about, vocalising into the nose, then the face. Feel a buzz in the cheeks and on the lips. Hum down into the throat and chest. Awaken all these areas. Next gently speak in all these areas. Be neither too careful nor articulate. Just speak as it comes out. Gibberish will do.

- Hum throughout the entire range of your voice. Swoop and play. It is particularly important that you feel support within the limits of your range even as you venture outside them. As you move away from your range you will need to exercise more contact with the support.
- Laugh up and down your range: 'hah, hah, hah', 'hee, hee, hee', 'ho, ho, ho', 'mah, mah, mah'. Achieve equality of volume throughout.

At some point you should feel your voice starting without jerking or effort. Now it is warm.

- If all else fails, a good bout of well-supported intoning or chanting will normally do the trick. This intoning should be accompanied by an enormous sense of physical freedom. So swing, walk or run as you intone. Intoning is one of the healthiest and most connecting exercises but it is most effective after the simple humming routines above.

C. Placing the Voice

Now, once the voice is free and warm, you can work on placing sound. There are many words and phrases in voice work that confound the novice. 'Placing' is one such word. What is it and how does it work?

Imagine all the breath and support power we have been activating, now coming through a free and warmed instrument. All placing means is to release the power and sound to the world, to place sound outside yourself. Sound, like a word, must be placed as far forward in the mouth as possible in order to leave us and have an effect. Think of the image of a dart being launched, no longer part of us but finding its place on a target. With our voice, however, a part of us stays with the sound dart when we place it. We make our mark with sound when we release it. This is why placing a word is so difficult; we have to really commit to what we are saying without hesitation. If we place sound inappropriately, like a badly thrown dart, it could miss the target entirely.

So the sound must come up through us precisely, making its way towards the mouth and lips and escaping into the air as it voyages on an arc propelled by support. Then the voice can be said to be placed. Try the following:

- Stand centred. Flop over from the waist as in the early centring exercise. Once bowed over begin to hum with your mouth closed. Gravity will help place the sound on the lips. After several hums start to come up gradually through the spine, continuing to hum and keeping the sensation placed forwards on the lips. 'Think' the sound forwards to aid this process. You should feel vocal energy filling the mask of the face and the energy of the vibration should increase as the sound gets ready to be released.

- As you come up and feel this energy reaching a maximum level let the sound escape into a 'ha!' Most people have a huge problem with the 'ha', either closing it down, pulling it back, containing or denying it in some way. They won't just release it. This is partly because the 'ha' is one of the most open and revealing sounds we can make. How we release it says something about our sense of vulnerability or confidence. It is an open and honest sound so release it fully, place it, send it completely outside yourself. Don't hold back.

- Now back to standing centred, fix a point in the distance just above eye level. Breathe out to that point. Then send a vocalised 'oo' to that point, perhaps even extending your lips a bit more than is habitual. Feel the 'oo' sound reaching forward and, in your mind and heart, really reach out to that point on the horizon. 'Touch' the point with the sound. Feel the flow of the support and the open sound leave you and transfer to that point. Once you feel certain that the 'oo' sound has left you and is travelling on its way, open up into the 'ah' sound. Be very careful here not to close down or pull back on your energy and placement. Let the sound flow from you, let the energy go. Once you are certain it has begin to count out loud: count 'one' (breathe); 'one, two' (breathe); 'one, two, three' (breathe) and so on up to twelve. Feel all the words and syllables leave you completely on each count. Sustain and place them outside yourself. Again, don't deny the sound or pull it back. Remember the spoken arc.

- A useful exercise to help you sense an outward flow of

energy and sound is to place a hand on a wall. As you speak any text, push against the wall, feeling the connecting support but also feeling the vocal energy releasing and leaving you as you push. This is forcing you to activate and place the sounds or words.

- Many people live in overcrowded urban spaces that lack privacy and inhibit the voice, making the vigorous placing of sound a real problem. Once you find yourself in a genuinely open place where no one can hear or judge you then send your voice to a distant tree, hill, mountain or across an ocean.

- The pulling back of a sound or hesitating on a word can be a denial of an act, sound itself or belief in what we have to say. So you literally have to throw the energy around in space. Use balls, paper cups, rolled-up socks, anything that will help you to generate and fling sound. In this instance, you really have to work hard and playfully to place sound and word as though a physical object.

17. Putting It All Together

We have been working on lots of different aspects of a total process so let's take some time to put it all together and see how and if your voice has progressed. These exercises combine freeing, warming and placing all in one:

- Release and sustain an open and supported sound for a count of ten: perhaps breathe in, begin to hum on the sound of 'm' for a count of three and then open the sound into 'ha' for seven counts. The 'm' will place the sound forward to the lips and the 'ha' provide the release it needs to escape. Always try to sustain a strong sound. Don't let it trail off, fade or fall back. Finish the sound outside yourself.

- Next you can sustain this release over a count of fifteen and then twenty. Play with different notes and levels of volume. Become daring. Remember, the louder the sound, the more breath and support you will need.

- See if you can do the same sort of release as above but without starting with 'm'. Go straight into the 'ha' without pushing or activating the sound with a glottal attack. If you sense you are pushing rather than placing the sound think of the silent 'h' or begin with a yawn.

- Control a crescendo of sound over a count of ten or fifteen on either 'oo' or 'ha'. Then diminuendo the sound. This will take tremendous control from your support. 'Think' the control as coming from there and not in the throat or jaw. Always place the sound forward, letting it escape.
- If at any time you feel that the placing goes wrong try releasing, going from 'm' into 'ha' rapidly. For instance an 'm' for a count of three going into 'ah' for three counts, returning to 'm' for three etc. Try and stretch over seven alternating changes for a total count of twenty-one. The 'm' is your continual reference point to ensure that the sound is placed forward.
- Play around with the diaphragmatic breath by releasing on a series of 'ah's and 'mah's. Think forward and open.
- Intone as freely and as loudly as possible without pushing and feeling the strength of support.

After this combined exercise the breath, voice and support should be oiled enough to handle further work and exploration. The body, breath and support are housing and releasing a free, placed voice. This whole process might take as little as ten minutes. However, if you are a professional speaker you will need to judge the particular demands on your voice and stretch accordingly. In doing this kind of work you have already begun to stretch the range and resonance of the voice. Your placing is moving forwards and preparing you for more defined speech work.

As you work you should never be feeling a discomfort in the throat, although you might experience a stretch or widening. This is perfectly fine. The more playful, silly and unjudgemental you are about the work the better off you are. Don't be hindered by thinking you should be making a certain 'good' sound or be frightened if you hear unpleasant sounds. All sounds are useful as long as they are supported and free. This lack of self-censoring will liberate the voice as much as any of the actual physical exercises.

At this point in our work on the voice I think only extended practical and professional voice users need to go on to the next series of exercises (Range, Centre of the Voice and Resonance). *Everyone, however, should pick up the work again when we get to the sections on* Speech *in Chapter 13.*

18. Range

'Range' is the natural expression of feeling in the voice. The more we feel, expressively, the greater the movement of notes in the voice. As our feelings change and are moved, so should our vocal range. Anyone experiencing an emotional shock will shift the range of their voice ten to fifteen notes. Remember the times in your life when you felt waves of extreme emotions – fear, joy, anger. These would have been accompanied by dramatic vocal shifts.

The average Western speaker tends to use only three to five different notes for everyday communication. That is a very limited range. Any speaker who has to communicate words or texts full of heightened emotions should creatively have two and a half to three octaves at their disposal in order to serve the emotional intensity of the work. For everyday communication a range of some eight notes should be sufficient and easily accomplished. That gives us a greater latitude of expression.

There are several main difficulties we face when exercising our vocal range:

- Underuse makes the whole potential range rusty. It needs steady oiling in order to respond for the speaker.
- The range can never be stretched or freed if there is neck or jaw tension or if the support is underpowered. Note that it is important to draw on support in order to extend the range.
- Breaks, jumps or holes in the range can be caused by lazy muscles that cannot respond quickly enough to a speaker's emotional needs or by the belief that you have different compartments of the voice (i.e. head voice, chest voice etc.) or unclear, unenergised placing. Always think

that you have *one* voice and not a series of different
voices. Whether consciously or unconsciously, speakers
with breaks will avoid speaking near a break or confronting
it, entrenching the break even further. At some point you
must work through a break. Remember, however, that
the voice is finite and will not stretch endlessly. You will
always have breaks near the top or bottom end of your
own particular range.

- However marvellous your physical range – and it may be
quite wide as well as deep – it will be useless without some
emotional connection as you speak.

Work on range has had a 'bad press' because speakers gifted
with this capacity will often use it to show off. Think of some
of the vocal caricatures we retain of pre-war actors: all range
with neither intellectual nor emotional worth. We are back
here to the 'beautiful voice' syndrome. Underneath the range
there is a complete lack of emotional integrity. The ultimate
sound we hear is dead and hollow. Many young actors, for
instance, fight the stretching of their range because they fear
they will start to sound phoney.

I don't agree with that thinking, even though I can understand where it comes from. I believe you can develop a huge
range and still sound completely real if you are organically
connected to genuine feelings and those feelings urge you to
explore a different range. The two are linked and result in a
perfectly acceptable technique. If we are free, uninhibited and
unashamed of taking the right to feel, then it is false *not* to
explore the range of expressions available to us. We wouldn't
wail on three notes if we really needed to purge pain. That is the
difference between an effect and a need. So I am all for stretching range as a part of stretching the speaker's capacity.

19. Stretching the Range

Throughout these exercises, stay connected to the breath and
support. You might notice that the higher notes require a
slightly higher position of support than the lower ones. Also

keep as physically free as possible. The use of body swings as you work helps.

- Keeping physically centred and with no accompanying head movements, come down through the range of your voice first on 'm' followed by 'ah'. Count down through the voice. Begin quietly and as the voice perks up, start adding more volume and daring, eventually sweeping through the voice up and down. As you do the exercises 'think' your energy up.

- Speak as high as you can without feeling tension. Now speak as low as you can, still getting the voice placed forward. You might feel a stretch in the neck muscles which is fine but if you feel any strain 'think' of a yawn or rest from the exercise.

- Quickly count to twenty, the odd numbers sounded at the top of the voice and the even at the bottom. Keep the head still and place the voice forward.

- Intone on different notes. Work on those particular notes that sound or feel more alien and less habitual than the rest.

- Release on a 'ha' supported from a diaphragmatic breath. Let each 'ha' be on a different note and play all through the range. Experience the different support needs for higher and lower notes.

- If you have access to a piano, strike notes and try to sing them. Next play sequences of notes and repeat them on 'lah' or 'mah'. Don't worry if you sound off-key. Play and have fun. Try and cover the two octaves spanning from middle C. Again, don't mind bum notes. If you can stretch further without strain do so. Now hit certain notes and try to speak around that range.

- Take a piece of text and speak it as you would imagine a very hammy Victorian or Edwardian actor might speak it. Enjoy doing it and use the lengthening of vowel sounds to help you experiment. Now match this extravagance with a physical freedom and make it as dramatic as the sound. Then return to speaking the text normally and the chances are that your whole range will have perked up enormously as a result of this bit of parody-acting.

- Speak very slowly, stretching each word through several notes. Be as extravagant as possible with this process. You don't have to make sense of the words but merely enjoy the exploration with them.

Working through the Breaks

- If you discover a break in the range as you glide down it, stop and pitch just above the break and hum or 'ah' through it, thinking very forward as you enter the break. Now repeat this rapidly several times and keep breathing throughout the work. Within minutes the break should feel smoother or actually vanish.
- As you move through the voice don't change gear or separate placing into the head or chest area. Think of a whole voice and an energy of forward release that is available throughout the range. Speak into the head thinking that the chest sound is also there and speak into the chest thinking head.
- If you discover a break (if you haven't got any don't worry, not all voices do) begin to hum and intone into and through the break area trying to sustain and control the note. If the voice wobbles or jumps don't be frightened off. Stay at it. Speak across a break. Oil and work it.

20. The Centre of the Voice – Optimum Pitch

Many voice teachers talk of the necessity of finding the 'centre' of the voice as the means to attaining an 'optimum pitch'. Both notions are based on the supposition that each of us has a comfortable ideal centre and pitch all our own. The concept varies from teacher to teacher as well as the means of achieving results.

What I take to mean the centre note or optimum pitch of a voice is the note achieved when everything (breathing, control, support and placing) is effortless but energised; when we show minimum signs of work throughout all the instrument's processes.

There are scientific instruments that can identify and objectively measure this note as an optimum pitch but this never takes into account emotional and intellectual responses of the individual speaker, both of which can change from moment to moment and create a new centre. So optimum pitch, you see, can fluctuate and alter.

In my experience it does, however, seem to be useful to

discover something close to this centre in order to gauge what a speaker's range might possibly be: in theory the centre is the centre and you should have an equal number of notes around it which you can strike.

No one will discover their centre if they cannot first physically centre themselves and feel secure breath support or if they contain and trap their voices in any way whatsoever. Generally speaking, I never attempt to help someone locate the centre of their voice until they are securely into a second year of training, but play with this notion if it intrigues you. I don't think it is crucial to actually identify this note because when you speak with total freedom and have taken all your rights as a speaker you will invariably be speaking organically around a centre. It is something you don't need to be trained to perfect.

Here are some exercises you can try as a step towards discovering your optimum pitch or centre:

- Many people actually discover their centre by tricking themselves. If you stand at centre and allow the breath and support to drop clearly into you at the same time, if you feel your vocal instrument open unimpeded by constrictions or habits, you can probably hit centre on the first note you sound. Try it sounding an 'ah'. The combination of freedom and readiness will allow the voice to scan through a range and rest on centre. Now speak around the note you have sounded to test the range above and below it. How does that feel? If you have hit centre you will experience a state of ease and minimum noticeable support.
- After extensively stretching your range in some of the exercises further above, now go to the topmost note you have been able to sound easily. Count the notes down to the base of this range and simply divide in half. That could be the centre. I say 'could' because this simple test requires a voice that has been well-tempered, supported and balanced as well as one which has become familiar with all the ranges it can reach. So the voice will need to be experienced in order to take this test seriously.
- Probably the best and simplest test is to sit at a piano humming various notes and finding four to five notes that feel most comfortable to sound. Take your time. Sense that

each has a clear support and that there is no blockage in your throat. After isolating these notes gently hum one after the other. You will begin to feel that two or three are the easiest to make. Gradually choose and eliminate notes until only one remaining sound soars out of you. Speak around this note. It may not be the note you actually use to speak on normally, so this test may inform you of a bad placing habit. That is, are you speaking in a position that is more difficult for you than comfortable? Alternate between this position and the one you have chosen as centre to test for degree of comfort. Which do you like best?

Reminder: Please remember when doing these explorations that any undue tension will demolish the advantages of the whole process. The main benefit in finding a centre is that it will give you a chance to search the whole range and scope of your voice. It can also be a wonderful illustration to you of how bold and easy speaking can be.

21. Resonance or Vocal Tone

Very few people use their full vocal resonance. Most of us run our voices on half power. By only using half or fewer of our resonating areas we are cutting down on the sound possibilities we have at our disposal. The resonating cavities reinforce whatever note we make. The more we can use our resonances the easier our vocal life becomes because we allow ourselves to cut back on effort and tension. It is a bit like giving the voice a chance to echo rather than pumping it for power.

Nowadays we mostly use only the chest and throat resonances. We neglect resonances in areas like the head, face and nose that carry the voice extremely well. Many modern theatres and lecture halls, for instance, are designed with dead areas where the voice does not easily carry. So the only way it can survive in these padded spaces is by using the more piercing resonances in our head that cut through the dullness. Sound from the throat and chest only comes across as muffled and adds to the problem. Many speakers who use microphones tend to place their voices in the throat and chest to create a particular laid back sound. DJs and 'belt' singers are other obvious examples. And that has an influence on the way many of us speak when we do it in public. My main concern is that the voice usually gets stuck in this position and relies too heavily on those resonances. It could eventually suffer damage as well.

In exercising for resonance and tone there are two objectives to keep in mind. Both are simple:

1. To wake up the underused resonators and play with them so that you can familiarise yourself with the sound possibilities.
2. To learn how to balance and focus these sounds.

Here I should warn the less traditionally-trained speaker that there might be moments when you begin to sound 'beautiful'. The old definition of a 'beautiful voice' was one that emanated a fully balanced, resonant sound. The well-modulated 'actor' sound was produced by balancing all the resonators together. This was the key focus of traditional voice training up to the 1960s. Then it went out of fashion as a technique. By learning to ridicule and devalue this sound, many younger actors have never been allowed to discover a vocal richness and variety in their voices. Bear with this process to hear what you can uncover. It is another stage in voice work. Action and the motivated need to speak must be part of the process in order to make the voice *real* and to protect you from making sound for its own sake. But dare to sound the whole voice and test its potential for resonance.

- *The waking-up process.* Hum into the head, breathing and connecting to the support system and keeping the throat open. Now speak in the head. It may sound odd. The vibration should be felt right up to the crown.
- Repeat this same sequence for the nose (nasal sound) and then the front of the face (a reedy sound).

- Next take the sound down to the throat and finally the chest. These last two are universal resonators which are always working and the easiest to activate. Yet be careful not to lock or push down in these areas, putting a lid on the sound.

If one or more resonators feels alien, take note. These are probably underused resonators and might require more attention to activate them. Be as frivolous and unjudgemental as possible with this work.

- Next, to balance and equalise these areas intone by using any text or counting. Keep the breath fluid and the support connected and open the entire voice including the jaw. Intone and in the same breath move into speaking, trying to keep the voice placed well forward as you speak.
- Now intone higher than you normally speak or at the centre of your voice. Speak and as you move into speaking you might have the pleasing sensation of your voice dropping into place. As this happens you often experience a fully resonant voice as the result: all resonators are working together. Enjoy the sound and don't let its largeness, richness or fullness frighten you.
- As the voice locates its resonant potential and the resulting power, you might need to stop and give yourself notes: 'I am supporting too much'; 'I sound too loud.' The sound can suddenly be enormous and echoing. Don't cut down on your resonances but simply adjust the support you are providing. This way you can actually work with less effort!
- At this point the 'figure of eight' exercise can enter your vocal work. This wonderful old exercise has been balancing actors' voices for ages. It helps to touch off the whole voice in one looped and continuous process:

$$\text{'OO'} \quad \overset{\nearrow\ \text{'OR'}\ \searrow}{\underset{\searrow\ \text{'OR'}\ \nearrow}{}} \quad \text{'AH'} \quad \overset{\nwarrow\ \text{'AY'}\ \nwarrow}{\underset{\searrow\ \text{'AY'}\ \nearrow}{}} \quad \text{'EE'}$$

Make a journey intoning or chanting through the path of this sequence, starting and stopping at the centre 'ah': '*ah, ay, ee, ay, ah, or, oo, or, ah*'. An 'm' or 'h' can be placed before the sounds (i.e. 'mah' or 'hah'), opening the sounds and placing them forwards more easily. All nine sounds are comforting to chant and gradually the whole voice opens to them and resonates from all sources. Don't rush or push this exercise. Do it with ease and rhythm. First try each sound on a single breath, keeping the sound placed forward, connected and the jaw free. Gradually perform the whole sequence on a single breath. Finally speed up the sequence so that you can comfortably cover the loop three times on a single breath. From this go to intoning through the figure once, on the second journey make a transition midway into regular speech, and on the third time through just speak rather than intone.

- At this point you should be more and more aware of what a balanced, placed voice sounds like. Staying with this 'figure of eight' exercise, experiment with different notes and levels of volume. *Remember, though, always to take the exercises immediately into speaking before you have time to think or control what you are doing.* The exercises are of little value unless you can test immediate results in a normal speaking voice.

22. Volume Control, Level and Projection

Gaining control over the voice means gaining control over volume and level of sound and being able to project the nuances of sound out and over a space. Any actor, singer or public speaker has to be able to adapt to any size of theatre or auditorium or microphone position. The vocal aim is to allow an audience to hear comfortably and concentrate listening without strain or distortion, without having to lean forwards in their seats or draw back from too much volume. Audibility can vary in order to achieve effects but what we are searching for here is a general level that can be altered up or down at will.

Level also depends largely on the acoustics of a space. Without even being an expert in these matters you can gauge how the acoustics will suit your voice by checking the materials and furnishings in a room. Wood is an excellent conductor of sound, it helps balance the voice and provides resonance. Cement, glass, tiles and brick will create a lively sound likely to echo and reverberate, requiring you to use specially good articulation and lower resonances. Carpets, curtains, felt and padded seats will cushion and deaden sound, requiring the need for the upper resonances of the voice. Any speaker who enters a new and, for them, untested environment or space needs to change vocal level to suit circumstances and acoustics. The process of projection itself is really quite natural and not at all a mystery. Once you have adopted a right to speak fully and forcefully, space suddenly shrinks to accommodate what you have to say.

Just try walking and talking through a variety of spaces. You automatically adapt and find the right vocal level to match the change in environment. You can experience this by having a conversation with someone as you move from room to room. Or call across an empty field or a traffic-choked street. Call though a closed door and then open it and call again. We make an instant adjustment in volume and projection for any spatial instance. Professional speakers must continually engage in this kind of experimentation. At the Guildhall School of Music and Drama the second-year students do a play that tours to ten different schools. They all return from the experience affirming what I mean about experimenting with levels in differing spaces.

A. Outside Noise and Acoustics

The volume and level must also change when you compete with either noise or silence. An actor has to change level dramatically when speaking through or over a sound cue. Naturally we change levels when we enter a quiet space, a church or library. If we speak while combating the wind, loud music, a crowd, other speakers or inside an aircraft with all its noise we automatically change volume and level. We can do it even more effortlessly if the body, breath and voice are free and supported. If we are aware and sensitive to a space we will also organically adapt to these acoustics.

Some spaces are 'live', meaning that the sound echoes and returns to the speaker. In these spaces, like a large stone cathedral, you can hear your voice come back to you a fraction of a second after speaking. In any well-designed theatre a slight acoustical return is good and helps the actor to judge whether the voice is filling the space. Problems arise when the space is too alive in which case less volume is required alongside more articulation and a lower vocal harmonic.

Dead spaces, like small conference rooms and meeting rooms, absorb sound rather than returning it and need fierce focus and higher vocal harmonics found in the head resonators. A speaker who is really adaptable will also realise that bodies (i.e. an audience) also absorb sound. The more packed the audience, the deader the space.

B. Levels within an Emotion

Still taking all the environmental and spatial requirements of sound into account, the other side of the volume equation concerns human feelings. The higher our emotional tension, the louder our voices become. When we clamp down on our voices it is often in an attempt to cap a 'loud' emotion bubbling to the surface and ready to escape. We learn to stifle the sound in order to stifle the feeling. As I have said elsewhere, the greater the pain or passion, the bigger the sound needed to purge it. The bigger the conflict, the more clamorous the voice.

There are three factors that govern vocal volume:

1. Always work from support. The louder the sound then the more support you need. In only rare cases of screaming do you actually need to pump the abdominal muscles. A large and difficult space, however, will need considerable muscular capacity and work as does a large emotion.
2. The vowels in any word are the main body of the voice. The louder we become, the more lengthened and weighty the vowels in our speech become so that the support has

something to work with and through. In order for the voice to be effective and clear at different levels of volume, we have to allow the vowels room to escape. Vowels must have their full capacity so the jaw opens wide to let them through.

3. For many people the fear of being too loud or too emotionally committed creates a common habit of pulling the vowel back in moments when volume is required. The vowel starts on its natural pattern of release but then is denied and trapped by either swallowing the sound or clenching the jaw. This is grossly inefficient because the support has not been allowed to work through the whole sound or word, connecting vowel to consonants, but it can also be dangerous as two forces of energy collide in the throat: the greater support needed for the emotion wants to release through the word, but the speaker's denial suppresses it midway. All the energy stays bottled in the throat.

Bearing all the above in mind, here are some exercises to help release a more sure sense of levels:

- Whatever the size of a space or emotion, you must remain physically open to it. Don't pretend it isn't there either or else it will plug and bottle you. Instead breathe with it. Unclamp any growing vocal tension. You will take the breath needed to fill any space if you breathe with the space, using your imagination to target every corner of the room or theatre. Make actual eye contact with the perimeters of the space. Don't limit yourself just to the parts where the audience is sitting. Many studio-size theatres fool actors because they don't take in the *entire* space and breathe within the whole. Always be sure to compensate for the height as well as the width and depth of space. Breathe the entire volume.
- Notice how the breath changes, becoming shallower as you limit your awareness. Hold your hand close to your face and breathe towards it, move it further away breathing to reach it. Look at your feet and breathe. Each focal distance requires a different breath. Look at a seat close to you and breathe. Now at one further back and further back still. The breath and support needed to touch a close point will not be enough to fill the whole. Once you embrace the whole space in your imagination and breathe accordingly,

you will be taking sufficient breath to fill the space and find the right vocal level. Do try this space and breath exercise in natural surroundings too: overlooking the sea, on a hill, in the woods or parkland.

- Face, head on, any anxious emotion in order to help tame it for the voice and you will begin to take in the breath needed to cope with the feeling. This wilful acceptance of and desire to liberate emotion mean you will naturally take sufficient breath in order to release the feeling. Remember the times you suppressed laughter or tears? The body suffers from that restriction of breath and feels like bursting.

- Find a spot at the furthest point in a space. Find that point and hum or 'oo' to it. Imagine boring into that spot with supported sound, not vocally pushed sound.

- Now, remembering that intensity, shift focus and embrace the whole space. So you might be shifting from a seat in the first row of a theatre to the whole auditorium, balcony and boxes included.

- It is crucial to remember here that you can have an intimate, focused conversation with someone but still be filling an entire space with your imagination and breath. This is a technique basic to actors who have to address some-one on-stage but be heard throughout a theatre. Equally important to remember is the fact that you can turn completely away from an audience and be heard by one and all. This will naturally require more breath support and word definition.

- Throw sounds, words, phrases to different points in the space while still being aware of the whole. You will sense the word reaching out. You will sound the space and feel the sound returning to you. Make the sound into something shared with the space and the audience.

- Talk to a spot close to you and gradually radiate your focus outwards until the whole space is held within your vocal control and focus. Breathe as you do this and volume will naturally follow the process of radiation.

- It is often an efficient idea to find a bigger level than the space requires before experimenting with how little you need.

- The greater the space, the more you need to sustain the energy through the word or thought, plus the more you must think through a thought to its conclusion, ending every word clearly.

- The simplest way to find a level on a microphone is to find a physical position where you can talk to it and not around it. Imagine speaking to a hand puppet. Don't fear the instrument or make it into something threatening. Adjust breathing and focus accordingly.

When using body microphones in conversations and television interviews just speak as you would in normal conversation, neither raising nor lowering the voice. The instrument is geared to pick up a normal level. In musicals sing and speak as you would to support your voice in the space without a band or orchestra. The microphone is only there to boost you. You still have to work, but work as normal. Do remember that the microphone is not a God-given gift to the voice. It can distract you from a decent level of vocal work and at its worst expose your speech flaws!

- If there are several of you working in a space then do the obvious yet rarely done exercise. As one of you speaks from the stage or presentation area, the rest should scatter about in the space to offer feedback: 'Can't hear'; 'Too loud'; 'More support'; 'I can hear the sounds but not the words'; 'Finish the end of words'; 'Start the words'; 'Don't skid'; 'Look up, think out more'; 'Sustain the energy to the ends of thoughts'; 'Too muffled – think into your head'; 'Too ringing – don't support so much'; 'When you turn up stage you need more support'; 'You're not breathing!'

What always interests me about these basic exercises is how much the listener learns about the space and the voice. Clarity in space requires a listening commitment on the part of a speaker. The actor or public speaker who bothers to listen to others in his or her company coping with the demands of a difficult space always has a better understanding of what he or she needs to do with the voice in order to deliver words in space. These are good habits of work and we need to exercise them all.

9   Speech and Phonetics

After earnest work begins on the voice then all the work involving speech becomes possible. Breath comes first, voice and all its components follow and speech is the third element and end result of the vocal chain of events. The process of speech is really nothing more than breaking up the voice into recognisably defined units called words. As sound enters the mouth we use the lips, tongue, teeth, hard palate, soft palate and facial muscles to break it up into a series of phonetic structures that are recognisable to the ear – language that is simple and clear.

Words have intellectual and cultural connections as well as emotional and sensual ones. The voice cues words in crucial and dramatic ways. If the words we speak are dead it might be the sign of an undeveloped voice. The sound quality and physical make-up of a word can affect us well beyond its purely intellectual meaning: 'onomatopoeia', for instance, is a term we use to describe the effect when a word's sound mirrors its sense as in 'the cat *purrs*' or in Robert Browning's more descriptive moment: 'A tap at the pane, the quick sharp scratch / And blue spurt of a lighted match.' Quite simply and effectively the sound and word melt into a perfect image that by-passes purely rational thought processes. These connections between intellect and emotion are what give our speech colour, variety and impact in both normal and heightened conversations, but do notice in the above examples the primary role that vocal sounds play in the utterance.

Since not every person has precisely the same emotional and

sensual attachment to words then speaking a text (particularly heightened poetic language like Browning's or Shakespeare's) will never sound exactly the same. It is both comforting and overwhelming to think that every rendition by every speaker is and will be unique.

Sounds into Words

Sounds become words through a series of complex muscular actions performed by the lips, tongue, facial muscles, jaw and soft palate. These moveable parts – all of which must manoeuvre with great ease – form, stop or partially stop and mould the voice through contact with the teeth, hard palate, roof of the mouth or alveolar ridge. To discover these areas consciously take a quick tour of the inside of your mouth with your tongue. Touch your top teeth and then move your tongue upwards above the teeth until you reach the gum. You'll encounter a ridge there (the alveolar ridge). Continue running the tongue back towards the throat. That hard bony roof of the mouth with a seam is the hard palate. Further back at the throat is a moister, fleshier area or the soft palate. By now your tongue is curling back towards your tonsils.

Aim of Speech

The aim in achieving clear speech is economy, efficiency and an effortlessness in articulation. Yet no listener should become absorbed or intrigued by superb articulation in action. It should, in fact, be unnoticeable. In other words the speech muscles should work so well that the production of the word does not get in the way of its meaning. These speech muscles are prone to laziness and flabbiness just like any other muscle in the body. They have to be exercised regularly to articulate well but they can be sharpened up dramatically if given concentrated exercise over a couple of weeks.

Throughout the exercises that follow please remember to keep the breath moving throughout every phase and remain centred. Try to keep connecting breath to voice to speech as links in one chain of events. Remember, too, to keep on your natural voice. Don't whisper or devoice. The sound you make must be centred and solid. Always place the voice forward and not trapped in the back of the mouth. Keep the jaw free and unclenched, teeth slightly parted and ready for work.

If at any point the facial muscles become fatigued then stop. Terrible tension can result if the muscles are thrashed unreasonably. Muscular work is required but do it gently. All types of speakers should do all the exercises with practised and professional speakers moving on to the extended work with consonants and vowels.

1. Foundation Exercises

Articulation muscles can easily become lazy and need oiling to lubricate themselves. When we are tired or frustrated we tend to slur speech or try to speak faster than the muscles will allow. Within two or three days of inactivity the facial muscles feel the rust setting in just like the Tin Man in *The Wizard of Oz*. One of the facts of articulation work is that the harder you work the muscles to get them to perform, the harder you must work to keep them at peak level. Dancers understand this when it comes to other parts of the body: one day without work, they know; two days, the company knows; three days, the audience knows. So take these flexing and strengthening exercises to heart.

A. The Face

- Using both hands massage all facial muscles and details of the face. Don't be too rough. Just wake up the face with a brisk massage like we sometimes do after getting

out of bed. Then end by just stroking the face all over
to give it a good foundation.
- Now just move the forehead alone. Do press-ups with
your eyebrows. Keep other areas of the face still. By
moving areas in isolation you will build up an awareness
of the muscles that can get lazy or tense.
- Move the eyes and eyelids in isolation.
- Move the cheek muscles. Other parts of the face will move
with them but only in response to the cheek movement.
- Move the lips, purse and push them forward, baring the
teeth. Thicken and thin them. Make interesting shapes to
break your habitual setting of the muscles. Blow through
the lips as in the snorting, sputtering action of a horse.

After these exercises the face should feel more alive and ready
to work.

B. The Jaw

Release here is of the utmost importance but should always be
done with complete respect for a tender, sensitive instrument.
In other words, don't swing the jaw, pull or roughly handle it.
The jaw is not designed to be treated in an aggressive way.

- Gently massage the hinges beneath the ears.
- Begin to feel the jaw drop naturally and comfortably. You
are aiming for a 'two-finger drop', the opening you get
when inserting the index and middle finger. Smile and
keep the smile alive in the face as you open and close
the jaw gently. This exercise not only opens the jaw but
the back of the throat, plus it is the safest and most
economic way to open the jaw without straining the
facial muscles and throat. You might want to yawn. This
is a good sign. It shows the throat is opening.
- Chew around in a circular motion. Start in a small way
and gradually enlarge the action. Don't do this roughly
however.
- Think of biting into an apple and open the jaw to its
widest, most comfortable position with this in mind.
- Rest now in a neutral position, teeth slightly parted and

unclenched but the lips joined together. Appreciate the
jaw's freedom.
- Bunch up the entire facial area into one tight squeeze
and then release without placing the muscles. Let them
just drop back into place and find their own position.
Do this three to four times.
- Finally, spring the mouth open – without force – then
release and allow it to return to centre without you
controlling it.

C. The Tongue

Unless the tip, blade and back of the tongue receive exercise
and work, all consonant 'placing' work becomes problematic.

- Smile and open the jaw as wide as you can get to a
two-finger drop. Stretch out the tongue as far as it
will go when flattened against the chin. This stretches
the back of the tongue and you will feel it. Release
the stretch and allow the muscles to place themselves
naturally. Don't force the tongue back into place or the
muscles back into habitual positions. The tongue sliding
back into the mouth will feel odd but go with it. You
may have to wipe your chin! Repeat three times.
- Flick the tongue, lizard-like, in and out of the mouth
keeping firm tension in the muscles right down to
the tip.
- Stick out the tongue as far as possible parallel to the
ground. This may ache but it is a nice sensation.
- Hold out the tongue with tension and just wag the tip
up and down. Another slightly painful but enjoyable
exercise!
- Keeping the jaw free and released and as wide open as
comfortably possible, begin to slowly flick the tongue
from the top alveolar ridge (behind the upper front
teeth) to the gums (behind the lower front teeth). Then
into the cheeks from side to side. Repeat the action with
more speed: top to bottom, side to side. Always keep
the jaw free and still. Don't let the jaw bounce around.
- Twist the tongue around in all possible ways. Bunch
and then release it. Make a clear 'l' sound as in 'lily',

followed by a dark 'l' sound as in 'wall'. Move between the two sounds very quickly to give the tongue more spring (i.e. 'lily / wall', 'lily / wall', etc.). This action activates the back of the tongue as well as the tip. You should be able to feel the difference and sense the different muscle qualities in the tongue as you do this.

D. The Soft Palate

If this is not well exercised the voice can sound too nasal. The soft palate separates the nasal cavity from the mouth. If it is loose then air escapes down the nose at the wrong time. A loose soft palate can also create a slight rattle in the voice as the air shifts between nose and face.

- The jaw should be free and open at a two-finger drop. Place the tongue behind the bottom teeth. Repeat the sounds 'k', 'g', 'ng'. There will naturally be distortion. Repeat with speed. Now repeat with words ending in the suffix 'ing': 'singing', 'laughing', 'crying', 'talking', 'walking', etc.
- Place a hand under your nose to monitor the air flow. Speak 'm' into 'b'. Air should be felt on the 'm' but not the 'b'. Do the same with 'n' (air felt) into 'd' (no air felt).

At this point you will have worked all the major areas of articulation. Remember to keep breathing throughout. Don't become constricted or held in the breath or throat. Keep the head and neck as free as possible. The effort here should be to gain coordination of breathing and articulation. These exercises can seem silly, especially when you begin to make faces and strange sounds. So do these in private and not on a bus or tube! I remember warming up while driving to work and getting the strangest looks while stopped at traffic lights.

2. Placing Consonants

Working with consonants – those speech sounds in which the breath is at least partly obstructed and which form syllables when combined with vowels – is the real physical contact work of voice and speech. It can be muscular, thrilling and very sensual work.

Consonants fall into two categories: 'voiced' or 'voiceless', depending on whether or not they vibrate the vocal cords. The voiced consonants literally have full-throated voice behind them as you say 'b' or 'd', for instance. You can hear the voice reverberating on those sounds and feel it vibrating as well if you place your hand on your neck. The voiceless consonants, such as 'p' or 't', have no vibration in the neck or vocal cords. The sound is being made by air stopped or trapped in the mouth by the organs of articulation. Physically 'b' and 'p' are formed in the same place and way but separate on their voiced and voiceless qualities. Many other consonants can be differentiated in this same way: 'v' and 'f'; 'g' and 'k'; 'z' and 's'; even 'th' can be sounded either voiced or voiceless.

Now let's do some exercises with consonants so you can explore their potential. Remember to breathe throughout. Try every sound as I describe it. Although you are making these sounds all the time, I think you will derive considerable enjoyment from feeling how they are made and then by making further connections with your everyday speech. This kind of thought transfer is crucial.

Remember to follow a principle of efficiency and clarity: sounds should be made effortlessly and, if required, quickly without too much thought or comment. It is as important to stop a sound clearly as it is to start it. Keep the jaw free throughout. All the sounds I am describing are Received Pronunciation (RP) sounds:

- *b* and *p*: These sounds start and are created by the lips. Consequently both are described as 'bilabial'. Concentrate on the complete closure, stopping or partial interference of the voice on these sounds. Notice how each consonant is formed in the same way but 'b' has more voice than 'p'. The lips come together but are neither pursed, pulled back nor unnaturally contorted.

Repeat a series of 'b's and 'p's. Go quickly from 'bah, bah, bah' to 'pah, pah, pah'. Notice the air pressure is built up for a fraction of a second and then released in a 'plosive' sound (the air explodes). Say: 'boy', 'bother', 'beep'. The 'p' has more subtlety and less voice but it is equally plosive. Say: 'pour', 'pother', 'peep'. Place your hand in front of your mouth, sounding these 'b' and 'p' words and you will feel short, clean bursts of plosive air hitting it. The air should feel focused and not dissipated. Strive to be clear, light and clean with these sounds and neither too defined nor aggressive. Both these sounds can come across as too muscular and play havoc with microphones and frequently 'pop' electronically.

- *m*: This sound is voiced, bilabial and 'nasal' (i.e. the soft palate lowers allowing air to escape through the nose; one of three sounds that do this in English RP). The lips close on the sound but there is no plosive escape of air since it comes through the nose. In theory the 'm' can be sustained as long as there is breath as in a 'hum'. As you 'm' or 'hum' you should place the sound forwards in the mouth to feel a buzz on the lips. The jaw remains unclenched and released, the teeth are parted. The 'm' takes on qualities in spoken language when released into a vowel. Try: 'm, m, mah', 'm, m, may', 'm, m, mee', 'm, m, moo'. Now repeat many 'm's with a variety of vowels as quickly as possible: 'many men, many men, many men', 'mummy, mummy, mummy'. Keep the sound clean and don't distort the sound by tightening the mouth. The lips should bounce easily and efficiently together and apart.

- *w*: This consonant is voiced and partially closes the voice by the two lips moving forward like a gentle beak. It can be classified as a semi-vowel since it has the body of the voice moving through it. The first part of the sound is made in this position, the second is formed as the lips release and part. Try a series of 'w's followed by vowels to lengthen it: 'w, w, wah', 'w, w, way', 'w, w, wee'. Then try: 'weeping willows, weeping willows, weeping willows'. This sound becomes unclear only when speakers fail to push their lips forward enough to form the first part of the sound. You cannot do it with tightened, closed lips which you'll discover if you try it.

- At this point repeat 'b, p, m, w'. Do it rapidly as

possible. Then take these consonants into the first words that enter your mind. Be as silly as you can. You are doing light muscular work.

- *th*: This sound can be either voiced ('that', 'the', 'then') or voiceless ('breath', 'death', 'earth'). The lips part and the tongue tip makes a partial closure and contact with the back of the top front teeth (as in the word 'teeth'). Too many people make this sound by sticking the tongue too far forwards past and between top and bottom teeth and then drawing it back, which is unsightly and also makes it harder for the tongue to recover enough to make the next consonant or vowel sound. It is an inefficient way to produce the 'th' sound and mars the look of your speech when done in public or on camera. The sound should be neatly contained in the mouth, the tongue behind the teeth.

  This is another continuous sound that can be made as long as you have breath. Try a voiceless 'th' (just a release of air) and continue the sound. You should feel air passing between and around the tongue tip and teeth. Now move into voicing the 'th'. The sounds you have just made are described as voiceless or voiced, 'dental' (due to contact with the teeth), 'fricative' (because of the escaping air that causes friction). Putting the sounds you can make together say: 'Three free thugs set three thugs free.' Say this tongue-twister until it sounds smooth without excessive hissing. By keeping the tongue tucked *behind* the teeth you will cut back on excessive friction.

- *f* (voiceless) and *v* (voiced): Both these sounds are best described as labiodental and fricative since articulation combines lower lip, top teeth and air friction. The top teeth should touch the most convenient position on the lower lip without resulting in the sort of facial contortion some people get when making these sounds. One of the most common faults with these sounds is to start the sound with the top teeth overhanging the lower lip and then scraping the teeth over it as the sound is made. Try it. Very inefficient and overdone. Lighten rather than tighten the pressure to make the sounds. Keep the tongue free, alive and centred, not lazy. As a test of the latter just let your tongue lie inert at the bottom of your mouth and try to produce either sound 'f' or 'v'. It will be muffled and distorted. Equally unclear is the quality of sound that results when the tongue makes too much contact with the alveolar ridge (behind the top teeth), distorting and blocking the free passage of air.

- *t* or *d*: The first is voiceless and the second voiced. Both are alveolar and plosive. To make either sound accurately the tongue tip is placed on the alveolar ridge just behind the top teeth with the air and sound exploding out as the tongue flips it forth. The sound is quick, clean and sharp. If you cannot produce it in this manner the tongue is probably too lazy, inert or placed too far in the back of the mouth. Maybe it is too thickly up against the teeth or the ridge, muffling the passage of air. The lips should not remain closed. The sound will click clearly if made correctly. Sound 't, t, t' and 'd, d, d' quickly and you will become aware of how rapidly and flexibly the tongue muscle must respond and recover. If made loosely or too plosively both sounds will be cruelly picked up by a microphone. If the sound produced is released too slowly then a hiss will be the result. Try both sounds in combination to discover the right way: 'tittle tattle, tittle tattle', 'daddy dormouse, daddy dormouse'. Make the sound 'trippingly on the tongue'.

- *n*: This sound is voiced, alveolar and nasal. It is made with the tongue in the same position as for 't' and 'd', up against the alveolar ridge, but the sound produced is nasal due to the air escaping past the soft palate and out the nose. Go quickly from sounding 'd' to 'n' several times. Then 'done, done, done' to 'none, none none'.

- *s* and *z*: The first is voiceless and the second voiced. Both are alveolar fricatives. The tongue rests on the alveolar ridge with the sides of the tongue touching the top teeth. The jaw should not be taut or the mouth pulled back. Air passes over the tongue and through the partial closure created by the tongue and ridge. The tongue should not touch the teeth. That creates a lisp. Try that position so you can hear it. If the tongue butts too tightly up against the ridge you create a whistle or 'sibilant s' sound. Experiment a bit to find the right and wrong adjustments. Air should be gently released and not pushed out.

I suppose the 's' sound is a speech teacher's misery and the single cause of paranoia for so many people.

Let's put the problem in perspective. People who live
in fear of the sound usually compound the problem by
pushing on it or tightening the voice or mouth around
it. The 's' is one of the highest frequency sounds we
make. Consequently it is heard more clearly than other
consonants and so more frequently commented about
than other speech sounds. Quite often the 's' sound
is placed correctly by us but because the voice and
breathing are underused, or the speaker devoices to
a whisper, the 's' quality is out of balance. Students
are forever weeping about their 's' sounds, fearing the
reactions they get from lay people.

Before you plunge into further despair or overwork or
push to get a better result on the 's', first check to make
sure you are on a full or centred voice. If you only draw
breath from the upper chest and throat that can produce
the hiss or whistle, so breathe from further down. Intone
words with the 's' sound. Most of all, avoid pushing and
tightening around the sound.

The 's' sound needs a light touch. Do a series of
light 't's and move fluidly into the 's': 't, t, t, t, s, s,
s, s'. Touch the sound lightly at the ends of words and
cut away quickly to reduce the hiss as in: 'yes', 'puss',
'fuss', 'lass'. You should notice a difference already.
Try to make the sound as minimal as possible without
losing it altogether or making believe it does not exist.
This sound is also affected by dental work, mouth injury
or braces on the top teeth. If you have a gap between
the top teeth you can make a clear 's' by allowing the
tip of the tongue to touch the gum behind the bottom
teeth. Some speakers use both positions. A misplaced
or too heavy a position on 's' will be exposed over
a microphone, the high frequency of the sound being
amplified into a piercing shrill. When making the 's'
sound delicacy is a key word.

The 'z' is far less problematic since we are forced to
use more voice to make the sound. Pronounce it and you
will feel the sound starting from further within you. We
often don't use 'z' properly. In RP, for instance, the 's'
should be replaced by a 'z' at the ends of words when
the 's' follows a vowel or a voiced consonant: 'words',
'birds', 'scrubs', sings', coos'. These 'z' positions are
often devoiced into an 's'.

• *r*: This sound is voiced, 'continuant', made without

friction and 'post-alveolar'. To best make the 'r' clear, the main body of the tongue has to arch up behind the alveolar ridge and create a narrow passage between tongue and hard palate. The lips purse slightly forwards. It is termed 'continuant' because it will go on as long as you have breath. When you stop the sound, do it cleanly. Lazy lips can transform the 'r' into a 'w': 'rabbit' becomes 'wabbit', 'roar' becomes 'war'. A tight jaw and tongue can distort the sound into a growl: 'right' goes to 'rrright'. If you can roll the 'r' then you can quickly sharpen up the sound by moving from the rolled position to an 'r'. The rolling has the advantage of getting the tongue to make contact with the hard palate so that as you move into the 'r' the necessary closure can be found. The same exercise can be done by replacing the rolled 'r' with the trapped 'r'. Move this into the English 'r': 'very', 'broom', 'three'. A very subtle sound. The narrowness of the closure has to be precisely found and this then has to be coupled with the pursing of the lips.

- *sh* and *zh*: These sounds are either voiceless (she or shoe) or voiced (measure or leisure), fricative and palato-alveolar. The lips are forward and the tongue makes gentle contact with the palate just behind the alveolar ridge.

- *ch* and *j*: These sounds are either voiceless (church) or voiced (judge), palato-alveolar and 'affricative'. The lips move slightly forward and the sound starts with a closure, then a strong, slow explosion followed by a release of air. The voiceless sound starts on a 't' which is then released: 'chew', 'chirp', 'cheddar'; the voiced on a 'd': 'genuine', 'gypsy', 'Jewish'. More tongue contact is made as the release begins.

- *l*: This sound is voiced, lateral, light and dark. It is made without friction. The light 'l' (as in 'lily', 'lady', 'low') is made with the tongue tip touching the alveolar ridge, followed by an easy, frictionless release. The tongue should rapidly be able to make a series of 'l's. The dark 'l' is more problematic. It is a heavy sound with a full syllabic weight as in 'full', 'wall', 'cold', 'bottle', or 'boil'. It is all too common to short-change this consonant sound by swallowing it, and since the dark 'l' is found midway or at the end of a word it can make words sound unfinished. The tongue still makes

contact with the alveolar ridge but its back is pulled
back and up. Keep the back of the tongue slightly
suppressed but alive. Try going quickly from the light
to dark 'l' words with this in mind. You will discover
immediately that to make the dark 'l' successfully you do
need to have a working back of tongue.

- *k* and *g*: These sounds are voiceless ('kind') and voiced
  ('good'), plosive and 'velar'. The sounds are made by the
  sudden release of held air through the closure between
  the back of the tongue and velum, the area behind
  the soft palate at the back of the mouth and top of the
  throat.
- *h*: This sound is voiceless and 'glottal fricative'. Its
  quality is produced by the coming together of vocal
  cords and glottis to create a minor friction of air as in:
  'halt', 'how', 'hearty', 'hurricane'.
- *ng*: This sound is voiceless, nasal and velar. The air
  flow used to make it is impeded in the same way as in
  the 'k' and 'g' except that there is not a complete closure
  and no plosion occurs. The soft palate is released and
  sound vibrates in the nose to make the sound nasal. It
  takes a flexible back of the tongue to finish the sound
  well. Try sounding: 'laughing', 'singing', 'dancing',
  'talking', 'walking', 'jumping', 'thinking'.
- *y*: This sound is voiced, palatal and a semi-vowel
  because it nearly becomes a vowel except for a slight
  interference. The tongue and hard palate make slight
  contact as in: 'yes', 'year', 'yellow'.

Things to bear in mind when working on consonants for clear
and defined speech are:

- Always stay connected to the breath.
- Always keep the jaw and muscles of articulation as free
  as possible.
- If you have trouble making a particular sound or word
  then work at it until it becomes free. As with the voice,
  nothing in speech work comes quickly and easily. It
  is all rather like learning a new dance step. You start
  slowly, learn to coordinate the movements and gradually
  build up speed. Tongue-twisters (many of which have
  been collected) help some people and confound others.
  Nursery rhymes and clapping sounds can be useful:

> *Pat-a-cake, pat-a-cake, baker's man*
> *Bake me a cake as fast as you can.*
> *Pat it and prick it and mark it with 'B'*
> *And put it in the oven for baby and me.*

- You can also try mouthing or whispering text. The lack of voice will make you more aware of the physical nature of each sound and will alert the muscles to the work needed for forming the various consonants.
- Remember to finish every word clearly and cleanly. Economy and efficiency are desirable.
- Looking in a mirror can be useful when placing sound. But you may need to feel it more than watch yourself produce it.
- Articulation muscles, if worked too much, can get tired and tighten the whole voice. After a session of articulation I always free the voice again by gentle humming and intoning. Also beware of neck and shoulder tension.

3. Vowels

Vowels are the 'voice' in the words that usually release and express our emotions. They are interrupted by the consonants and must be coordinated with them: as in 'wood', 'dead', 'care', 'big' and 'sword'.

Pure vowels are one kind of sound. Their sound identification is clear, unmistakable and uncorrupted by another vowel. These break down into long ('bee', 'far', 'door', 'blue) or short ('bad', 'beg', 'big', 'sob', 'bud', 'good').

Vowels are always voiced and in English RP should be sounded openly and without constriction or glottal attack. The glottal attack – a spasm in the glottis that interferes with sound – is that click we sometimes feel in the throat before a vowel sound begins. The cords bash together as we vocalise. Glottal attacks can be chronic but are also the result of nervousness when we speak. The short pure vowels, in particular, are prone to glottal attack when sounded. Watch this carefully by 'thinking' the throat open as you sound words like 'at', 'it', 'education' or 'under'. You can also 'think' an 'h' before these words to soften the passage of sound through the cords and glottis.

Diphthongs are composed of two pure vowels married together and articulation moves forward from one to the other without any break in sound as in 'coin', 'boy', 'loud', 'die', 'day', 'care', 'steer', 'no'. As you speak these words, notice how your muscles of articulation follow through to create a second sound.

Triphthongs marry three vowel letters or sounds together into one continuous movement of sound as in 'beau', 'admire', 'royal'. Although these are almost redundant in English RP, I have included them for practice in the charts which follow.

The positions for all these vowel sounds are approximate and depend on the individual facial and oral structure and regional and national character of the speaker. When working on making RP sounds, however, we tend to bypass these obstacles to produce a sound that is clear, open and placed or focused as far forward in the mouth as possible for the sake of clarity. Vowels, like some consonants, can get trapped and clogged in the back of the mouth and throat, yet pure vowels are also moveable, depending on the emotional content of the word spoken. Never aim for any sort of 'perfect sound'.

The Neutral Vowel

The neutral vowel is neither pure nor impure but a stress device we use constantly in spoken speech. We don't usually say 'tooday' but rather 'terday', taking the stress of 'too' and neutralising it to 'ter'. Whenever a word has an unstressed vowel position it will be reflected in the use of the neutral vowel.

The same is true of the way we move between stressed and neutral positions as we stress or neutralise words in any utterance. When we need to specify a word and its meaning we give it its full sound weight and don't neutralise the vowel. Take a simple sentence:

My sister is coming for supper today.

If I stress *my* the meaning of the sentence would eliminate the possibility of *your* sister coming today. If I stress *sister* I am eliminating my *brother* or *mother*. Stressing *supper*, I eliminate *breakfast*, *tea* or *lunch*. Emphasising *today*, I eliminate *tomorrow*.

All this is obvious and the important thing to remember is that we naturally stress vowels and give them full weight only to single out words for emphasis. We move toward neutralising the sound in others where meaning is not so particular and crucial, hence the formation of neutral vowels.

4. Phonetics

Phonetics is the term given to the symbols that precisely record the speech sounds we make. In a good dictionary these are the oddly spelled words in italics that usually follow a main entry for an individual word. The actual spelling of a word does not accurately approximate its sound. The system of phonetic symbols does and can be used to record every uttered sound a speaker makes. With phonetics it is possible to write down the slightest shift in vowels, consonants, stress or inflection. Remember Henry Higgins in George Bernard Shaw's play *Pygmalion* writing down all that Eliza Doolittle said and then reading it back to her? He was reproducing her sounds phonetically.

Phonetics is a method of recording sounds so that they can be codified and repeated with some degree of certainty. Its use, however, should not become dictatorial or allow us to become cut off from the deeper organic and emotional parts of sound and language.

All of us have heard people who speak a form of English so phonetically correct that we know they are not native speakers.

Speaking phonetically can sound robotic and the artificial results of phonetics training are what I resist the most. I admire it, however, as a tool that guides us in the placing of sounds and checking sounds when they go off-balance, though you can train your voice and speak without knowing a thing about phonetics, just as you can learn to sing without knowing a note of music. So here are some useful ways to think of phonetics whether or not you intend to learn more about the subject:

- If you have even the most basic grasp of English RP phonetics then you can look up a word in a good dictionary and derive its standard pronunciation. You need never fear that you are saying a word 'incorrectly'. Do realise that the pattern of pronunciation changes over time and between dictionary and dictionary. It also changes between British and American spoken English.
- There is no doubt that ear training and being attuned to spoken speech are vastly improved by learning to notice the shifts between vowels and consonants as understood through phonetic charts.
- The neutral, standard descriptions of vowels and consonants create clear reference points of sound which can be charted individually as an accent shifts from one to another, allowing us to grasp more clearly how different accents vary and are produced.
- If your mind works well with the notion of sound as a sign you can rapidly pick up accents through phonetics. Many actors, for instance, do not find this easy. I suspect their imaginative response to a word, their need to make language come alive in some part of their being, is greater than their rational skill to think in terms of phonetics.
- I have taught British pop groups who have used phonetics to record their hit songs in Japanese or German without the slightest knowledge of either language. Opera singers use the technique as well, so there may be commercial reasons for learning the system.
- For voice teachers, phonetics can often help identify a student's speech problem and aid in analysing the correct adjustment for a bad habit.

- It can be useful to see, clearly represented, how a word
  is to be physically formed through a combination of
  sounds.

In the end, use phonetics purely as a tool and never divorce
sound from the whole voice and physical act of speaking.

Phonetic Symbols
For Standard English / Received Pronunciation (RP) Sounds

Consonants

Plosives. These have a complete closure of two organs of articulation, behind which air pressure builds up and is released suddenly.

p	voiceless bilabial plosive	push, pact, parity, limp
b	voiced bilabial plosive	bar, baby, beat, rub, cab
t	voiceless alveolar plosive	tea, tart, table, hit, blot
d	voiced alveolar plosive	did, damn, duck, had, plod
k	voiceless velar plosive	car, kick, cram, lock, thick
g	voiced velar plosive	go, grab, giggle, hug, pig

Remember – consonants are described according to whether they are voiced or voiceless, which part of the speech mechanism is involved in the articulation, and how it is made. They not only sound different, they feel different, and evoke different feelings in listeners: The Sensuality of Sound.

Fricatives. Two organs of articulation are brought together close enough for the escaping air-stream to make audible friction.

f	voiceless labio-dental fricative	far, fish, flimsy, roof
v	voiced dental fricative	van, verve, have, of
θ	voiceless dental fricative	thin, thursday, both
ð	voiced dental fricative	this, the, there, breathe
s	voiceless alveolar fricative	sea, sob, ceiling, kiss
z	voiced alveolar fricative	zoo, zest, has, crabs
ʃ	voiceless palato-alveolar fricative	shove, she, wash, hush
ʒ	voiced palato-alveolar fricative	measure, leisure, agincourt
h	voiceless glottal fricative	he, heat, humble, who, happy

Affricates. These have a plosive closure and a slow release with friction.

tʃ	voiceless palato-alveolar affricate	church, chew, chap, much
dʒ	voiced palato-alveolar affricate	judge, jab, ridge, frigid

Nasals. There is closure of two organs of articulation in the mouth, but the soft palate (velum) is lowered, so air is released through the nose.

m	voiced bilabial nasal	me, mum, meet, hum, limb
n	voiced alveolar nasal	nine, nothing, no, phone
ŋ	voiced velar nasal	ring, gong, singing

Frictionless Continuants. A narrowing in the mouth without friction.

r voiced post-alveolar frictionless continuant	read, rub, hurry, very
lɬ voiced lateral: light or dark	low, lady, lovely, jelly, wall, toil, wail
j voiced palatal semi-vowel	year, yes, yellow, yawn
w voiced labio-velar semi-vowel	we, warm, where, why

Vowels

Long vowels	i:	bee, feed, leaned, feel, meal, wheat, eager, healer Please eat the peaches and cream. We need to clean these green heaters.
	ɜ:	fir, curve, heard, curl, turned, murder, murmur, word They searched for her purse in the ferns. It's the early bird that hurts the worm.
	ɑ:	are, large, arm, barn, calmed, martyr, sarcastic Charles' heart was far harder than Mark's. The car was parked in the farmyard.
	ɔ:	door, sword, roared, warm, yawned, order, daughter Walk to the door in the north porch. Draw the stork with the chalk on the board.
	u:	do, mood, moon, cool, loser, boot, useful Do choose the soup and then goose for two. Hugh was well-groomed but moody and aloof.
Short vowels	ɪ	big, sin, still, mirror, miss, dinner, city, wishes This is an interesting index system. Bill-sticking is prohibited in this English city.
	e	bed, spell, feather, fled, treasure, many, letter Fetch ten eggs from the red hen's nest. Mend the fence when the weather is better.
	æ	bad, man, shall, fatter, hammer, valley, wrap, had Harry was standing by the back taxi rank. Grab the ladder and hang up the banned banners.

ʌ bud, gun, dumb, result, love, other, onion, rubber
The sunflowers were covered in butterflies.
Don't rush under the hut unless you love slugs.

ɒ bog, sob, shone, holly, knowledge, sombre, profit
He got a lot of copies of the longer song.
The hot dog wandered through the foggy docks.

ʊ good, pull, wooden, bullring, would, shouldn't
He took the cushion and shook it.
Have a good look at this cookery book.

ə butter, father, a cupboard, sugar, harbour, sofa
The best of the players was injured.
Her hands were as cold as a block of ice.

Diphthongs ai buy, rise, climb, wise, smile, life, lighter, cider
For mile after mile the ice was piled high.
The bright white was shining in my eyes.

ei day, plate, spade, feigned, game, claimed, rate
Take the name of the place where we stayed.
Jane can explain this strange mistake.

ɔi boy, annoyed, enjoy, coin, boil, poignant, oyster
The employees were boisterous and annoyed.
The oil has spoilt the embroidery.

aʊ bough, louder, house, owl, astound, drowsy, mouth
Some sounds are pronounced with a round mouth.
Brown owls were prowling round the grounds.

əʊ go, no, road, bone, soul, stolen, ocean, odour, hope
They don't own their own home, you know.
Joe was notorious for showing off his oboe.

iə dear, appear, fierce, curious, exterior, serious
We're not interfering with the gears, dear.
These really appear to be superior here.

eə bare, chair, repaired, careful, wary, scarce
She can barely spare the money for her fare.
Where do we dare to care for that affair?

	ʊə	tour, pure, mature, fluency, cruelty, jewel, steward
		Stuart used his influence to stop the duel.
		He secured the renewal of the insurance.
	ju	duke, tune, tube

Triphthongs	aiə	admire, fire, liar, buyer, squire
	aʊə	our, hour, flower, devour, shower
	eiə	greyer, player, layer, prayer
	əʊə	blower, slower, grower
	ɔiə	royal, employer, buoyant

Working Further with
the Voice

Dialects and Accents

This is not a book about learning an accent or dialect but
here are a few voice and speech hints which can help with
these processes:

- The sound we finally produce from our mouth is only the
  end result of a process. Actors, for instance, who sound
  as if they are 'putting on' an accent or imitating it, have
  learnt it generally from a mechanical shifting of sound.
  So begin to think about where the accent comes from
  and always connect any sound you make to the breath.
  Sound, whether real or imitated, has to breathe, and by
  breathing with it any sound aspires to being genuine.
- List all the influences that might have affected the formation
  of a given sound. Is it urban or rural? Does the geography,
  climate or environment affect the accent or dialect? What
  status has the speaker of the accent: high or low? Generally,
  the higher the status, the more confident the sound and the
  easier it is to flow through the body of the breath; the lower
  the status, the slower and more hesitant or constrained the
  speech might become. There can also be varying strata of
  status within various classes of speakers.
- Listen to the rhythm of the accent. How is it stressed and
  inflected in terms of vowels and consonants? Does it rise
  and then fall, fall and suddenly rise? What kind of energy
  is put into key words? Here, too, does the energy in specific
  words rise and fall, fall and rise? Just hum the tune of the
  accent. That will tell you a lot about its musicality.
- *Look* and *listen* to the way a native speaker produces
  sound. Discover where the accent is mostly placed: nose,
  throat, face, head, etc. Look at the movement required in

the facial mask in order to produce the sounds. How far forward does it come into the face? Is it at the back of the mouth or in the throat? Do speakers of the accent open their mouth when they speak or are they 'tight-lipped'?

- Is the pace of the accent generally faster or slower than yours? Is it spoken with more words per minute or fewer? Are pauses a common event in the accent? Does it proceed without any halts whatsoever?

- How physical is the accent? Are words pronounced clearly or are they less well defined? There might be a mixture: some consonants could be heavier and more defined than others. Are there non-verbal sounds in the accent, an 'um' or a click?

- Is there a particular body language used in combination with speaking a dialect or accent?

If you have done this kind of work on an accent you have probably captured the quality of sound it produces. Without even beginning to shift lists of vowels around you have discovered the 'colour' of the accent and can begin to work more specifically.

By doing all this noting of breath, rhythm, placing, duration, etc. you have radically changed the muscular positions in your own organs of articulation in order to make newly changed sounds. You have already begun to shift phonetic qualities into a new accent. At this stage you might need to clear up certain vowel sounds and the means of producing them but usually eighty per cent of these sounds are by now placed authentically. I could also go out on a limb and say that a grasp of the organic quality of an accent is more dramatically real than a phonetically accurate but disconnected accent, unrelated to the voice behind it.

Remember, though, that all accents are related to the language that produces them. Different segments of the same language are explored accentually in quite various ways. To discover what I mean trying reading a text by G B Shaw in accents other than standard or one by Tennessee Williams in a standard accent. The readings will sound peculiar. The way a good writer uses language is geared to its sound and accent.

If you are going to sound convincing with an accent you should be able to read it 'off the text', that is, converse in it. Most actors make the mistake of being accurate only with the text they speak. They can sound frigid because they have not genuinely warmed to the accent.

Compromising an Accent

This is a debate that falls into two parts:

1. If an accent is so authentic that an audience cannot understand it then adjustments might have to be made in order to reproduce it in public. This happens repeatedly in North America with British accents. The American ear cannot usually differentiate between, say, Northern Irish and Northumberland accents so the manner of the speaker is quite generalised. American friends of mine cannot differentiate between some of the regional UK soap operas like *Coronation Street*. You need time to listen to and understand an accent. This need to adjust might happen, too, in a play when a new accent is introduced. The audience cannot follow what is being said because it needs time to adjust to the sound.

   Some accents have qualities that make them difficult to project within a large space. This is especially true if an accent is vocally contained, if it has falling qualities in either the line or the word or if the sounds lack clear articulation, particularly at the end of words. In these cases some cleaning-up of the accent will be necessary.

   I believe that all accents 'clean' and 'clarify' themselves when the speaker is speaking about important issues, is expressing real needs and is heightened. Since most theatre calls upon the actor to do all these as part of the communication through words, this underlies how we should produce accents on-stage. The freedom and flow of the issues must come through the accent, even one that has been phonetically perfected.

   Sometimes there is the mistaken belief that lower-status accents are less clear and more mumbled than higher-status ones. Yet the oral freedom of some so-called lower-status speakers, their ability to be garrulous story-tellers, for instance, should help correct this false impression. If you enjoy and use language, in whatever accent, you are always clear. London cockney is a street-selling accent. When you are selling something you have got to be clear.

2. The second category is much simpler. Some accents have vocal qualities that would damage a voice if used with the large amount of support needed to fill a sizeable theatre. The sharp glottal attacks of either cockney or the New York Bronx accent are good examples of this. Both can be damaging if used extensively and with too much volume. The clenched jaw of the Australian or New England accent has to be released in order to work extensively in prolonged speaking.

   Generally speaking, if you have worked for a clear, free position in your voice these adjustments can be made very subtly and quickly. The sound of the glottal attack can be produced without the actual attack if you know what a free throat feels like. The push down in the throat can be released by 'thinking up' to allow the larynx its freedom. A tight jaw can be used without clenching the back of the throat. The quality of sound produced can be similar and the voice kept safe and damage-free, without producing tension and constriction.

Listening

With some very simple listening exercises anyone can make radical improvements on their aural capacity. I think that good voice and good speech come as much from listening as from anywhere else. How many of us, however, actually listen? In order to survive urban life and all its noise we have learnt to filter out noise and stop listening. As a consequence our hearing has been dulled. Here are a series of exercises that might help to encourage us to listen and hear again. Each of the individual exercises can be done in a group as well.

A. Individual Exercises

- Take time to sit still and listen. You might want to close your eyes to help shut out distractions. Sit very still and just listen for a full three minutes. Count the number of sounds you can hear. Then try peeling away the layers of specific sounds. Actually listen *through* sounds to try and hear sounds behind them. Listen to your own breathing and to other sounds you make.

- Tap out the rhythms in either music or other people's speech patterns. Compare the way people sound to other types of sound so you can cross-reference and catalogue sounds in general.
- If you have access to a musical instrument like a piano, play out separate notes or a sequence of notes and then sing them.
- Take several sentences and speak each one with different stresses and inflections. Then try to repeat them accurately, using the stresses that make most sense to you. The use of a tape recorder might be helpful.
- In conversation take time to listen to the other person or persons without worrying about what you are going to say next and without anticipating or interrupting them. Stay with the speaker and his or her thought process rather than just your own.

B. Group Exercises

- Sit in a circle. One member of the group claps out a rhythm. The group picks it up and echoes it. The instigator looks at someone who then changes the rhythm as the group does likewise. Then try to follow the exercise with your eyes closed, working off the shifting rhythm as a tap on the shoulder selects someone to change rhythm.
- Each member of a group says one sentence three times: first as neutrally as possible, the second and third times with variations and new stresses on different words. The speaker then repeats what he or she has done. The group tries to analyse the differences they hear in terms of stress, inflection and meaning.
- Perform the same exercise as the one directly above but this time stress three different accents. The group tries to spot and specify the differences.
- Any group exercise in breathing, humming, intoning or singing will require acute listening skills if the group is to stay together and harmonise well. The objective here is to

get the group breathing as one unit rather than as a series of separate breaths.

- Build sound pictures or improvise rhythms. One member starts with a sound: the sea, for instance. Then each member joins in to construct the picture with another appropriate sound: the wind, the fog horn, the pebbles, waves upon the shore, etc. Sympathy with other sounds should be encouraged and the sounds must have a consistency. A police siren, for example, would be inappropriate. The group can do the same sort of exercise with clapped, tapped or vocalised rhythms. Let no one individual dominate or steer the group. Keep the sounds in concord.
- Spend periods of any voice class in silence. This improves a group's awareness of sound. It also clears the air and improves concentration.
- As a group first goes on to the stage of a large theatre after leaving a rehearsal space, each individual should take the stage in turn while the rest of the group fans out through the 'house', listening to the speaker and telling him or her what they hear. This will tell everyone something about the challenge of speaking in a large space.

Vocal Warm-Ups

Any voice about to be used in acting, lecturing, teaching or above normal conversation needs to warm up. The voice works infinitely better afterwards. I have been doing group warm-ups with actors and students on average four times a week for the past twelve years and I still find it the hardest part of the job of working with the voice. It seems to me a delicate balancing act. Every professional speaker or singer must warm up before any extended use of the voice.

In principle a warm-up is simple. The aim is to stretch, flex, oil and warm all the working parts of the voice and speech apparatus. However, there are many potential difficulties and situations that might require adjustments and adaptations to the warm-up process. Here are some general points to cover most situations. They build on the warm-up we did earlier on p 209, so use them in combination with those specific exercises.

A. Preparation

- Some voices take five minutes to warm up while other take twenty-five. Get to know the right amount of time necessary for you. It might have to do with the time of day. Students usually work in the morning when the voice is still underused and most professional actors later in the day before a performance and after the voice has been in use all day. It is harder to warm up in cold weather than it is in hot. Air-conditioning is harsh on the voice as are dryness and lack of humidity. Even the group dynamic, whether it is focused or if just one person is a disturbance, can affect the work.
- *A warm-up is not a voice class.* Never confuse the two. It is a preparation for a performance challenge and not a start-and-stop process in which you are trying to learn technique. It must be continuous and have a momentum from start to finish. With a good warm-up you keep enlarging the voice's potential for a specific challenge and specific space. Its effectiveness relies on a clear routine that does not have to be taught or require tremendous thought but can be quickly absorbed and understood. The security of the warm-up routine should concentrate the mind and vocal energies. If you are taking a company warm-up don't be frightened of a repetition of exercises. The aim is not to provide entertainment but a gradual widening and enlarging of potential and focus. If the group is new to voice work then make the exercises as simple and direct as possible.
- During a warm-up monitor the group carefully, sensing needs and individual difficulties, not progressing to the next stage until the exercise has fulfilled its function for everyone.
- If the group is nervous – over dress rehearsal, first preview, press night, understudies going on – be prepared to do a lot of calming and centring exercises. Realise that you, as leader of the warm-up, will absorb a lot of the nerves released by the group and possibly leave the warm-up more frazzled and anxious than the participants.
- Ideally, any warm-up should take place in the performance space. If this is not possible try and do it in a room with a similar air supply. In the London Barbican Theatre, for

instance, the theatre is air-conditioned but the rehearsal rooms are not. So you have to perform the warm-up calculating for this variance.

- Assess the demands of the text and performance space to structure the warm-up accordingly. For instance, the bigger the space or the larger the emotional content of the text, the greater the support capacity needed. If the acoustics are padded or dead then upper harmonic work is needed to open the head resonances and focus the voice on this challenge so that every word and line is sustained. Restoration and Georgian texts, for instance, require masterful articulation so that sort of work must be built in together with attention to the beginnings and ends of words.

- In the end, try to find key exercises that work for the group and the challenge ahead. If one exercise works you probably don't need to do another along similar lines. If something just isn't working, move on to something else rather than pounding on with something useless. Keep thinking ahead of the group to keep the warm-up moving in a fruitful direction. No one warm-up is the same. A twenty-five minute warm-up is more exhausting for the voice coach than a four hour class!

B. Basic Routine

This routine covers all the basic areas of work and can be adapted for all speakers – individual and group – and occasions. Throughout the warm-up keep breathing, allowing the breath to be as fluid as possible. Any breath holds experienced during a warm-up will slow down the process.

- Find centre physically. The most immediate means is to flop over at the waist, shake out the shoulders, head and spine and slowly come up through the spine – vertebra by vertebra – letting first the shoulders and finally the head just drop into place.
- Release neck and shoulder tensions. Massage the neck and shoulders, do a gentle head roll and lift and drop the shoulders, letting them fall without placing them.
- Swing the arms while breathing. Gently stretch the arms and spine in all directions.

- Open the breath muscles. Use the bear-hug to open the back by hugging yourself and flopping over from the waist. Breathe. Don't rush the intake. Flop over to each side. Breathe to open the sides of the ribcage. Pant on the diaphragm. Sigh out, feeling all the support muscles underneath the sound. Do two or three full breath recoveries (inhales and exhales) fluently, one after the other, releasing on an 's'.
- Work on the lower abdominal release: count 'one' – breathe; 'one, two' – breathe; 'one, two, three' – breathe; and so on up to twelve. All this connects the support to the voice. Breathing and connecting the breath to the sound begin to warm up the voice.
- Awaken all the facial muscles by moving and stretching them. Gently chew around with the jaw. Stretch the lips and the tongue. Work the soft palate on 'k', 'n', 'ng'. Begin to hum on a comfortable note; the process can be faster if the note struck is higher than your speaking voice. When you run out of breath start again. Take your time and never rush the warming of the vocal cord. Keeping your head still, find a point above eyeline and focus on it. Hum down through your voice and think the sound 'up' and out towards that point. You will know as soon as the voice is warmed because it will feel neither tacky nor sticky when it makes sound.
- When the voice is warmed, place it forwards in the mouth with an 'oo'. Move the sound into an 'ah' keeping it forward. Sustain the sound on the breath. Move from an 'm' into an 'ah'.
- Warm up the resonances by humming into the head, nose, face, throat and chest. Intone, taking the intoning into speaking.
- Swoop around your range. Count over twenty using the whole range.
- Exercise consonants and vowels, using a series of rapid sounds. Sometimes tongue-twisters help. Take note here on articulation exercises: always do a simple centring release after each one. If people are nervous, articulation exercises can work them into a frenzied state and tighten the voice. It took me years to learn this.

Use variety in each area of work. You can work on text throughout the warm-up but some actors don't like to use the same text as they will be performing. This framework should take fifteen to twenty-five minutes to complete.

C. Some Adaptations

Different circumstances may require adaptations to the basic routine:

- *Large spaces and heightened texts* need more work on breath support, so use stronger swings, more vigorous recoveries, greater capacity, deeper lower support work. The voice will need to be very open and the range stretched to project further, the placing of the full voice sustained without the sound falling or pulling back on a word. Concentrate on clear articulation at the ends of words.
- *Small, dead studio spaces and intimate texts* can seduce speakers into feeling they don't have to work hard. This is not true. Breath control and subtlety of volume are more important. You might have to speak quietly but always on your voice, never drifting off it. Don't resort to devoicing. Work on subtle but clear articulation and intensity of speaking. Watch the ends of words and a lazy dropping-off.
- *Language-based plays* require an ease and effortlessness with a difficult text. Work on vowel and consonant work that is connected to the breath. Do exercises that explore an imaginative response to words. These can include the ability to connect one word to the next, see images in the words or speak only the vowels or consonants; any exercise that will free the text emotionally and intellectually.
- *Musicals* always require a basic warm-up before specific singing exercises but after any dance call. So the order of work is: dance warm-up, voice warm-up, singing warm-up.
- *Television and film* need only the basic warm-up finished off with a simple exercise to focus speaking in a direct and intimate way. One way to get on the right level of voice is to tell a story conversationally.
- *Extreme nervousness* suggests that the warm-up might work best with about ten minutes of relaxation, lying down on the floor, at the start of the warm-up.

All of these are suggested appendages to the basic routine. As I keep stressing, don't be too rigid in application. The whole principle of a warm-up is to cater to an individual's or group's specific needs in any given moment of preparation. Flexibility is far more useful than going by the book. You never know what problem will materialise so be prepared to shift course rapidly and adapt.

Vocalising Heightened Emotions

Crying, shouting, cursing, screaming and laughing are the most extended vocal actions we can perform. They release powerful and intense feelings through the voice. If the release of each is free and pure then the actions of the breath and sound unblock the feeling and ease the passage of pain or joy. These are purging sounds: we laugh ourselves out, we cry ourselves to sleep. The free release helps to finish the business of the emotion and relax or centre us again. If we use words in these heightened states, they tend to be words that we use onomatopoeically; that is, words containing sounds that help launch the feeling: 'howl', 'wail', 'woe', 'heave a sigh of relief'. Swear- or curse-words, when selectively used, are extraordinarily physical as expressions of violence, rage and aggression.

In this rather emotionally repressed Western society we find it difficult to express heightened emotions in public. Some of us only manage them when drunk. As drink breaks down barriers the feelings flow. This repression can lead to severe vocal abuse and damage when passions are forced and strained through constrictions and denial in the throat. At some point we all need to cry, shout or curse but we hurt ourselves in the process. For most people the sudden release of an enormous sound is immediately accompanied by a pulling-back into the throat. At this point we feel the push or strain on the vocal cords as breath tries to battle its way past throat tensions.

I believe that these emotional releases can be painless and completely free if done naturally without fear of judgement or self-censoring. Infants don't get sore throats from intense crying. In societies where public wailing is acceptable you rarely find cases of vocal abuse from this kind of emotional release. Under the influence of alcohol we can shout without tension. We may not be able to produce the pure emotional sounds of some cultures but we can start to work on unblocking the constrictions that prevent the attempt and cause damage.

The breath support and vocal functions of laughing, screaming, crying, shouting and cursing are fundamentally the same. Similar muscles and vocal techniques are used in each action although the quality of the separate feelings, the need behind each and its weight will radically change the sound produced. Turn the sound off a video recording of someone crying or laughing hysterically and you cannot visually tell the difference. Just as in work on vocal range, feeling will alter notes in the voice to the different pitches of hilarity and sorrow, even though both have the same physical roots.

No actor can perform any of these heightened emotions on-stage without first knowing why, but actors will frequently explore the whys without knowing how to technically produce the freedom of the how. Many actors speak about being completely in character and in the moment of a play and only then being able to effectively produce a shout or curse. Others have repeatedly hurt their voices trying to achieve these moments before they naturally arrive or else carry such a clutch of tensions within themselves that these moments never come. They can destroy their voices after just barely getting into a run. Here are a few guidelines and exercises to freely release these feelings. This is wholly practical work so you must enable emotions and freedom to get underneath the technique in order to fill the sound and make it truthful.

Begin by ensuring that you have all the following under control, including a variety of 'no's that might be harmless in everyday vocalisation or speech but become very dangerous if denied when huge amounts of air surge through the throat and face. At this point in the work all your technical know-how and freedom must come into play:

- strong and confident support
- a completely open throat and jaw
- no physical denial or closing down through the spine, head or shoulders
- no pulling back on sound or word (this will result in a headlong crash in the throat)
- no shame at whatever sound comes out
- no pushing down on the voice
- no glottal attack

Caution. You can just about get away without supporting your voice in everyday speech situations but just try screaming without proper low breath support and you will push and damage the vocal cords. I freely admit to being a coward where daring work is concerned so the technical skills required for this kind of work mean I will rarely do any of these exercises until an individual or class has a fine and natural yet controlled vocal apparatus in place. The individual or class is usually at an advanced stage of training (the second year) but even then some people who are not yet centred with sufficient support or open enough throats cannot do this work. I will never do these exercises during a short workshop (under three weeks) and where I have not been able to judge a vocal capacity fully. Please remember that one second of abrasive, undersupported or incorrectly supported sound can damage the voice.

A. Basic Exercise

Many of the steps in this exercise build on routines established throughout Part Two. Be sure you are familiar with each technical phase before moving through the steps. Keep a constant check on vital areas as you move into the body of the exercise. These steps are numbered so you can follow the routine precisely and not miss a stage:

1. Complete breath support underneath the sound.
2. An open throat. 'Thinking' of a yawn or 'h' before making any sound or word will help you here.
3. No physical pulling back in the head or shoulders, no caving in of the chest or collapsing of the spine. Be strong, open and centred.
4. No pulling off the sound into you or down on you. Always think up, out and through the sound in an arc.
5. If using words, invest weight in the vowel sounds.
6. Warm up the breath and voice thoroughly in advance.
7. Do a great deal of deep support work and exercise a wide, full rib swing.
8. Further warm up the voice with an open throat and very full sound.
9. Keep the tongue out of the back of the throat so no sound is blocked.
10. Exercise the upper-cheek-lift smile. This will be used to place the sound onto the hard palate – a natural position for a scream – and creates the 'hard' penetrating sound heard in screaming and shouting.
11. Stand centred with your arms stretched out above you.
12. Reach out without tensing the shoulders.
13. Breathe in and out just feeling the breath's potential power.
14. Think of a yawn and silently work to feel a surge of air from the lower support freely course through your body.
15. Open the jaw with the smile and repeat it. You will feel an emotional 'reaching out' and begin to appreciate the breath power and openness required for the work.
16. Lie on your back on the floor with your legs dangling – infantlike – and your arms flung out to open and release your shoulders.
17. Allow yourself to take the breath low and connect to a sigh, a moan, a groan and move into a howl. If you keep the throat open and the breath strong you will begin to move into a wail.
18. *Warning. Although these exercises are purely technical, you might at this point feel the stirrings of deep emotions. The breath and connections with other sound memories*

can jolt a technical wail into a real one, making it very hard to stop.

19. Return to standing position and apply the vocalisations in step 17 to the physical motions in steps 11 to 16. Be free with your body. Swing the arms if necessary. Rock and sway but keep open and reach up and out with your imagination. (If you get embarrassed or feel any shame the process will not work. It might be advisable to do the exercise in private since by now you may be wailing.)

20. Try taking the wailing quality into some text you know or improvise on the spot. This will help to define and specify the exact nature of the feeling (e.g. sections of Shakespeare like *King Lear* – 'Howl, howl, howl' or 'Blow winds'; *Richard III* – 'O my tender babes'; *The Winter's Tale* – 'Woe the while, cut my lace'; *King John* – 'This hair I tear is mine'; *Othello* – 'It is the cause'). Always imagine that you are freely vomiting the sound and that the sound, in turn, is going into the word.

21. To curse or swear will have the same technical principles, with different intentions behind the words. Greek tragedy will be helpful here for text work or simply supply your own tirade of curses. This should make you feel terrifically purged. Never deny, tighten or pull back on any words. Let them fly and use the wonderful muscularity in the sounds to translate into the words. What you might realise is that words released in this way need not go on for very long before you have sufficiently expiated yourself, are relaxed and can now go on to other things. If the sound is muffled, contained or misdirected and has not reached a level of physicality, continue to work towards a release.

22. Call out to the gods and goddesses with the same intensity as the wail, but flow. Reach out with the invocations: 'O Juno'; 'O Jupiter'; 'Thou, Nature, art my goddess.'

23. Using the same breath and vocal freedom, imagine calling and addressing someone across a vast distance. Breathe, thinking of the arc. Using 'bah' or 'mah' throw the sound across the distance with strong, connected bursts of support. Start on a lower volume level and gradually increase it as your confidence and breath build support and volume.

24. Play with a series of 'bah's and 'mah's and mix them with longer releases. 'Think' the smile which will elevate

the sound onto the hard palate and harden it. Begin to speak with the same level of intensity. You should now be shouting and as long as you keep the energy flowing through the throat without feeling a push or pull, it ought to be effortless.

25. *More Warnings:*

- *We never do any of these activities for long periods naturally, which is why it is totally ridiculous and unreal when actors shout and scream their way through parts. The shout, curse or scream ought to be selective and have a powerful effect when used.*
- *If you have performed the exercise well you will feel muscular exhaustion in the lower support area. Never exercise or rehearse in this way for longer than ten minutes. Steer clear of any person or any piece of direction that pushes you to perform longer. It can be damaging.*
- *Drink lots of water since the amount of air being pumped through your voice will dry it out more rapidly than normal.*
- *Stop the exercise if you feel even the slightest hint of push, strain, tickling or catching in the throat.*
- *Check on the cord for any damage by gently humming. Damage is not felt immediately but this quiet, gentle release will reveal anything amiss like faltering, shuddering or the presence of extra mucus. If this happens stop working immediately.*

B. Screaming

- This is really the PhD of voice work. Do all the phases of the Basic Exercise above without strain and with all manner of support before venturing into this area!
- Lie or stand in a tiger-like position ready to pounce. Feel muscular connection throughout the whole body. Breathe with that sense of connection.
- Smile to open the jaw and throat.
- Begin to calmly tap off a 'hah, hah, hah' from the deep abdominal support muscles. Let the sound gradually build in intensity and volume. Begin to pitch the sound higher and higher. Then repeat this part of the exercise, making sure you feel very secure with the support and vocal openness.

- Once you feel supremely confident about the whole support and apparatus built up behind the sound, through the rising 'hah' – keeping the smile, the head and spine up, the sound open and out – go for the scream. It should come out without any effort.

C. Laughing

- Follow all the stages of the Basic Exercise above, adding these routines to explore the range of your potential repertoire of laughs. Many of us laugh, not just to express unbidden joy, but to communicate less wholesome desires or even resentments. So laughter has different motives and intentions. Do these routines either lying or standing.
- Start by tapping out with the breath: 'ha, ha, ha / he, he, he / ho, ho, ho'. These sounds loosen the support muscles. The very action might cause you to break into genuine laughter.
- A useful group exercise is to lie on the floor in a circle with each person's head resting on another person's diaphragm. It creates something of a labyrinth but people usually work it out! One of the group then starts to 'ha'. The movement and sound transfer around the group and become infectious, selling to real mirth. The trouble is how to stop the laughter once it has been unleashed and the result is a lot of aching ribs.
- Once you feel loosened up begin to think of different situations where a laugh is the chief mode of communication. Activate a laugh that best fills the action. Use any of your own invention but here are some to set you off:

  - mock with laughter
  - show embarrassment with laughter
  - be sarcastic with laughter
  - seduce with a laugh
  - flirt with a giggle
  - try to suppress a giggle: hold it, let it slip, hold it, then release
  - think of a filthy joke and laugh
  - speak an insult and then laugh
  - use a knowing laugh based on an 'in joke' that excludes others
  - say something stupid, then titter to cover it
  - laugh with pure joy, delight or happiness

Provided that the breath and voice are completely open each situation will produce a different quality of laughter. Experiment and play with endless possibilities.

Singing

This is not a singing book. I am not a singing teacher. The vocal principles between singing and speaking are exactly the same, however, with only minor exceptions. All the exercises throughout Part Two can be used to good effect by singers in their work. I have taught many operatic, musical comedy and pop stars using the very same routines.

One of the delights of being a voice teacher is that I can teach in any language – from Japanese to Italian to Dutch to Hindi to Russian to Portuguese – anywhere in the world. The anatomical principles of the voice are the same in each place, the main body of sound the same. Only speech principles tend to differ just like musical principles. Many singers do have physical peculiarities that help to produce required sounds: long or short necks, large mouths and wide jaws, extensive chests and diaphragms, an extraordinary ear for deciphering musical pitch. They may also just have a God-given need to sing rather than speak as their means of creative expression. I should say that a good musical ear does not mean a good speech ear. To be able to sing does not give one clear hegemony over the voice either.

Over the years a barrier has been constructed between speaking and singing. Many excellent technical singers will say they cannot speak and wonderful actors will never try to sing. It usually comes from the fear of trying. What differences in attitudes there are between the two processes should be discussed along with the nature of training for each activity. Maybe that will lead to some conclusions about why the activities are so separate. We may not all be *great* singers – few of us are – but we can all sing just as much as we can all speak.

- One very wrong notion is the way we stop thinking about a 'whole' voice but segment it into a 'singing voice' or 'speaking voice'. The voice is whole and it has multiple uses.
- You could argue that singing comes from a much freer position than the technical starts and stops required in speaking. Stammerers can usually sing more easily than they speak. They don't hesitate because the vocal system is in constant fluid motion. Persons with mental difficulties are more likely to fall into song or sing-song speech because it frees them from anxieties. Children seem happiest when they are singing. As a result most vocal exercises to free the voice are based on the liberating effects of chanting and intoning. You should always use both. The whole vocal system settles into flexibility and effortlessness as we sing.
- So what goes wrong? Maybe the 'bum note' or 'bad voice' syndrome or some other embarrassment along the way. The art of singing has been rigidly codified according to the 'right note' idea. A singer will usually be judged on the quality and prowess of his or her top notes rather than on expressiveness or the need to sing. Notes are frequently learnt, not felt.
- The non-singer's greatest fear is that of not hitting the note correctly or going flat. So what! A bit of free ear training will soon diminish that fear. Being told as a child that you can't sing or are tone deaf is usually one of the unfounded and unclinical notions imposed on us.
- Ask anyone to mimic or parody an opera singer and they will start singing. The vocal system usually engages quite easily with the process until self-consciousness forces us to stop.
- To sing does require great breath capacity, support and control to sustain notes and phrases, but no more than it takes to speak classical verse from the stage of a theatre. The vocal challenge is about equal.
- You do need muscular support when you sing. You couldn't last or survive very long without it. Many singers who turn to speaking never equate that the support should be approximately the same. At concerts we have all been surprised when a strong singer stops and then introduces his or her next selection in a weak voice. Conversely, some Wagnerian singers try to take that same support work into speaking, with deafening results. The support always has to match the challenge, material and space. Most singers

should be able to find a happy equilibrium between singing and speaking voices as they harness both into a single voice. You can always tell the singers who have discovered this for themselves. They sound so much more real and human. There is little difference in the way Frank Sinatra speaks and sings. He does both on the same voice.

- Most singers only develop and extend a particular range of their voice (i.e. soprano or tenor). Classical speakers must have access to different speaking ranges and so pay less attention to perfecting the limited range. Singers can go further in this direction as well without fear of reducing the 'soprano' or 'tenor' in themselves but few try, staying locked into a specific range.

- As we can vary range, we can also vary the resonators we use. Singers may only develop one resonator, in, say, the head or chest, keeping the two quite separate and in danger of suffering breaks in the voice if placement slips from one to the other. Free access to all the resonators allows us to place the voice more widely throughout the body as well as to keep it placed forward in the mouth. The more you know your voice and can experiment with it, the less paranoid you become about placing and resonance and the easier it becomes to place specifically with greater security and flexibility.

- Both singers and speakers have to learn repeatedly how to equate what happens in the body with what happens in the voice. Both camps are full of ignorance on this point. Members of both groups will approach their chores by sitting or standing rigidly: 'I can't both move *and* hope to make that sound!' Singers refuse to move on stage in fear that they will disturb the voice. Speakers will not venture away from a podium or microphone. Their movements look disconnected and puppet-like. They think of the voice as a precious and settled object. Obviously the sound they make is very precise but it is often experienced best on a high quality CD rather than visually on-stage. Only in the last decade have we begun to see younger opera singers who dare to use themselves physically to act on-stage as they sing. The best musical comedy performers have learned to sing as they act. 'Performing' a song means that its sound has entered your body fully so that the physical, oral and aural are one complete communication. It really can be the most thrilling and daring kind of performance.

- Essential to both singing and speaking is the direction of communication. You give to an audience. You must focus the work to a specific place and address it to someone in particular. There must be an awareness of the outside world. So many singers and speakers close their eyes when they perform, cutting off themselves and us. Only a vain and indulgent singer or speaker does it for themselves. A love song is addressed to someone special. A ballad is a thrilling piece of shared storytelling. An aria is the expression of an enormous feeling begging to be released and purged in the world.

- A prime problem that both groups suffer together is the lack of attention given to a spoken or sung text. Observe any operatic master-class and most attention will be given to the phrasing of text and not the production of sound. After years of acquiring technical skills many singers, like speakers, will forget to control or colour the words of a text. Speakers begin with the text first, singers arrive to it last of all. Singers have to be reminded repeatedly of its worth: 'Tell the story in the song'; 'What are you saying?'; 'What does it mean?'; 'What are you feeling?' As speakers work on a text and get to know and own it, it becomes much easier to sing it and phrase it through song. Singers have to go somewhat in reverse by bringing their expressive musicality into the speaking of the word. Both need to remember that each strains to be on the same heightened plane where feeling has attained the quality of song.

Working as I do in a building in London that houses two disciplines in one – the Guildhall School of Music and Drama – a rather poignant thought occurs to me daily which may explain the lack of communicating skills in so many singers. Actors can only work by speaking to or with someone. They must listen to one another if they are ever going to be any good as performers, so they train and operate together as an ensemble, often getting tangled up in one another's lives and problems. The most incredible social skills are required if you aim to survive as a professional actor. Singers, however, spend hours alone in isolation. The practice is confining and often done in cell-like enclosures. They can become imprisoned in their voice. Even as part of a huge chorus they can *seem* alone. They get settled into a range and become prone to typecasting as a specific vocal personality. Singing takes on aspects of private life. It has the quality of reverie rather than direct address. In order to perfect their voices singers spend a lot of time listening to themselves, not others, and are in frequent danger of getting cut off.

What is needed between speaking and singing is a balance and a trade-off of skills. I often wish my drama students would spend more time with the musicians learning about technique and less time in pubs. But I also would love to see the singers released from rehearsal halls and flourishing as social animals. There is a balance of sorts to be shared by all.

Chorus Speaking

I have many distant memories of myself as a schoolgirl standing in tastefully positioned, toga-clad groups speaking in unison profound yet, to a child's sense, obscure choruses of verse. These choral chores were rehearsed for concerts and recitations to entertain our parents or for special events. We murdered many poets in our time: Belloc, Masefield and T S Eliot to name a few of the prime targets. Or, speaking with pace and diction, standing on plinth-like forms (I was always placed at the rear), 'comic' poems. All this kind of activity was lumped together and called 'chorus speaking'.

I remember you had to wrestle with your classmates for the right to speak solo words and passages. If you were really lucky (I never was) you might get to perform a whispered or intoned section on your own rather than just being a part of the droning 'hum' beneath the main speakers. We were literally drilled for hours. We hummed for a certain number of counted crescendos, dropping to diminuendos for certain other phrases, then paused dramatically for three seconds – finally saying the key word before screeching to a halt. We were ruthlessly conducted and disciplined on how to speak it down to the last detail.

I'm sure the teacher had great fun. The overall effect was probably interesting because voices in unison always are. But even then I wondered 'Why speak in this unnatural way?' The content and meaning of the passages were never explained, learning was by measure and rote, we all spoke in a vacuum. There was never any improvisation. The result was the same as that of an actor sounding good but making no sense at all of the text. Chanting for our hockey or lacrosse teams as they competed against other schools seemed far more creative.

As you can see I have a problem with chorus speaking. The whole notion of it only began to make sense to me when years later I read that the ancient Greeks had the idea of a chorus as being the 'voice of the people'. It represented all voices in one. A chanting crowd, be it at a football match or a lynching, becomes one. The members of the crowd breathe, feel, think and express as one organism. At least that is how I think choral speaking ought to function. It must start not as a drill but from a deep-seated need to speak together, to support one another throughout the process. Transferring that idea, it must serve and support a text and ultimately point an audience in the direction of what is being urged and amplified. It is not about vocal fireworks for their own sake but about being inflamed by the voice and a need to open up.

As a younger, inexperienced teacher I indulged myself in the pleasures of choral speaking and like my teachers from childhood I found it fun to play with a variety of voices. Gradually, however, I began to take in the glazed expressions in my students' eyes and register audience comments: 'It sounded interesting.' Never did they ask about the ideas being debated, they only heard sounds. No one, least of all the students or the writer whose work we spoke, was being served. I finally developed for myself a series of guidelines to justify chorus speaking. Here they are:

- The group must breathe together as one breath, one heart-beat. All group members must think together as one mind and experience together one text. Unity is essential on both the superficial and the deepest level.
- The journey through the choral passage or poem must be taken by all the speakers. Everyone must experience a beginning, middle and end. They all have to surrender individuality to a collective will. They must be active in the whole process even if they are silent for certain sections. Their silence must ride the moment together with any other speaker. As a result, the concentration of the whole group is essential and exhausting. Short potent rehearsal periods are more productive than long loose ones. The concentration for this kind of work diminishes after an hour.
- If words or phrases are portioned out to one voice or section of the chorus, the sense must be that one is speaking for the whole. Everyone must feel represented by whoever is speaking. We must be induced to feel that any sentence could be dropped and picked up and continued by anyone else. A text separates for dialogue and links back together for monologue.
- The speaking must always start from and return to the text. Every vocal effect must serve and illuminate it. Ask yourselves all the basic text questions: 'Why are we humming through this bit or "ah-ing" through that bit?' 'What does sound or silence add to the text?' 'Are we supporting the words?'
- Sound effects or images can be most evocative if they provide the text with colour and sudden illumination. Chorus speaking is a bit like mural painting. Once disconnected from the text such effects become boring, predictable and clichéd and sound 'painted' as if by numbers. Why settle for just a second dimension when you can arrive at a third?
- If a chorus becomes very connected as a group then no specific plan or approach is necessary. The chorus members will speak as one and improvise in the moment. This is an ideal but a reachable one. I recently did a workshop at the National Theatre Studio on Euripides' *The Trojan Women* and this particular kind of expressive unity was found by twenty actors after just an hour of work.

- Extra clarity of articulation is always necessary when many voices speak together.
- The excitement and energy produced by speaking together may mean that individuals don't monitor their voices sufficiently and begin to push too hard and hurt their voices. Be careful of this.
- Style and structure of the verse must be agreed upon and practised by the group. There are different ways to speak verse and any group must choose a premise to work from or divine one of their own invention and then stick to it as they create their own laws. The chorus speaks by democratic rule.
- The process of chorus speaking simplifies and eases as the rehearsals progress.

Sight-Readings or Cold Readings

The skill of being able to pick up any kind of text and begin reading it on sight or 'cold' is an essential one for any actor and many professional speakers. In fact it is a useful skill for anyone who ever has to speak in public. One of the hardest events to sit through is a halting reading, speech or report. Many public professions demand excellent sight-reading skills from relevant individuals: lawyers, television presenters, bankers, politicians, teachers, lecturers, doctors, publicists, sales people, consultants and others.

Actors' auditions frequently require this technique. More and more the cold reading is replacing the prepared audition speech as a component of the casting session. Most directors of theatre, film and television report dismal standards on the part of actors doing sight-readings. I have sat in on many first-day rehearsals on a company-based play where narrative lines were handed out on the spot by directors to actors who were better sight-readers but not necessarily the best actors. Worse readers, though better actors, were cut short during this allocation process.

How do you improve on this essential skill? There is no easy short cut but there are stages to a preparation:

- Many people are convinced they can easily sight-read because they read to themselves so rapidly and convincingly. But the two processes are quite different. Reading aloud engages all the muscles of the voice and speech. The physical is suddenly as relevant as the intellectual, so when practising any text out loud bond the physical to the intellect. This may sound simple and obvious but you would be surprised by how many public speakers never practise out loud before delivering a major address. Once delivering the speech they are mystified as to how certain phrases should sound, suddenly they stumble over passages that seemed perfectly fine when silently read. If that happens with so-called 'prepared texts' you can imagine the problems that arise with cold readings. So read aloud at least twice a week. If you have a live audience so much the better. Children make excellent audiences . . . and critics.

- Begin to read all types and styles of writing aloud. After a while it becomes too easy to sight-read selections that are all in one style. Search for and challenge yourself with variety. Experiment with all sorts of writers and writing in newspapers, journals, essays, letters, poetry, fiction, plays, etc. Look at texts both good and bad; usually the bad will be harder to sight-read easily while the good is easier to speak aloud.

- An unprepared reading is always more physically difficult and therefore more vocally stressful than a prepared one. You tend to forget everything you have been taught about voice and speech in order to concentrate on the text. Good habits suddenly become sloppy; bad posture, breath and speech habits tend to manifest themselves most readily in sight-reading, not to mention poor eyesight. But this can also be an opportunity to uncover just how bad your habits are because they come so sharply into focus. Watch particularly for signs of withdrawal: head tucking in constricting the neck, hunched shoulders, eyes staying glued to the page, faltering breath capacity, collapsing spine, shuffling feet and shifting weight off centre. Mumbling to the text rather than speaking to an audience is a frequent habit. Fiddling with an object or piece of clothing becomes a distraction for the listener. All these are the moments when you must give yourself notes: to breathe, to slow down the pace (a sight-reading is usually done too rapidly so the reader can get through it quickly), to make eye contact (draw the listener in to the reading), to unglue your eyes from the text.

All these techniques will improve quickly with practice but only regular work will make the improvements permanent habits.

- Take a few minutes to scan any piece of text before starting. Look at the end to see where you are going in terms of length and content but also to see how it ends. That may instruct you on how to begin. Judge the length and weight of sentences: are they short and declarative or lengthy and filled with complex words and clauses? Many sight-reading situations are less cruel than cold readings but if you think of the worst scenario then the grace of a five to ten minute look at a piece will be a glorious gift. Don't gallop through a piece. Work through a sentence carefully, looking ahead to the end of it and even to the end of a paragraph, but staying very much 'in the moment' of the thought. This last note is a crucial one.

- It is always better to stay clear and simple rather than to dramatise inappropriately and miss the overall sense. Many people try to 'push' or impose sense during a sight-reading rather than to just let the words and ideas do the work for them. Once you are certain that you are making sense then, by all means, feel free to let your responses to the text flow through you.

- Making initial eye contact with a listener *before* starting to read is an old but effective technique. Don't be too aggressive or coy on this point. I have sat through interviews and auditions where the sight-reader has glared at his listeners in an attempt to make contact. It only takes the emphasis off what is being read.

- Never hide behind a piece of paper or book or be drawn into it through the course of the reading. Stand or sit in a centred manner, holding the text about the height of your middle chest and well below your face. Eyesight (or lack of it) may certainly be a consideration so do wear your spectacles if necessary. Some actors are so vain that I have seen at least one individual fall off the edge of a stage during an audition because she refused to wear her spectacles! Eye glasses, however, do pull the head down and may cause breath or speech problems. Don't let the note on being 'centred' prevent you from shifting position and moving about. Do it so long as it is released movement and helps the text. Nervous twitching is only a distraction.

- So many people talk about their knees, hands and consequently the paper shaking as they sight-read. My only

word of advice here is that you are probably feeling the
shake more than we are observing it. On the practical side,
breathing always helps, as does wearing clothing and shoes
that are comfortable. Formal clothing and high heeled shoes
– as I have said before – are highly restrictive when it comes
to speaking so do practise in them at a 'dress rehearsal'.
Your legs will wobble if your shoes prevent solid contact
with the ground and you are already racked with nerves.

- Never apologise if you make a mistake. Any further comments will only underscore the mistake. Either go back over
the sentence or venture ahead. Make this judgement in the
moment and assess whether or not the meaning is clear.
But in your initial read-through try to pick out difficult or
tricky passages over which you may stumble as a reader.

- Pronunciation and general vocabulary work are also relevant
to this kind of sight-reading challenge. Look up any words
in the text you don't immediately understand and also
check on the pronunciation of unfamiliar or technical terms
(having a familiarity with phonetics will help to uncover
the RP of any word). I do realise this makes me sound
school-marmish but here is the practical reason: directors
and writers, in particular, and educated listeners, in general,
tend to get infuriated by actors and readers who don't know
the meaning and pronunciation of relatively common words.
After one particularly bad reading I heard a director say:
'It's not my job to give him a basic education.' Speakers
should be wordmongers. Words are your stock-in-trade.
Relish them, connect with them. The other practical point
here is that most speakers who are apprehensive of cold or
sight-readings have confided to me that their sense of having
a limited personal vocabulary is high on their list of fears.

- The last note is a comment on attitude. Remember that
most listeners – unless they are hostile or perverse – want
any speaker or sight-reader to sound interesting and to do
well. They have put aside time to listen to you. So take
that on board as permission to do well. Perhaps thinking of
a reading as some sort of linguistic mystery tour will engage
your energy and enjoyment. You can be sure of one thing:
if you morbidly dread the event your audience will too.

Tape Recorders

I must admit to having a suspicion of using tape recorders at the start of any voice or speech training. Let me say why. Tape recordings are used early to provide a 'before and after' sense of an individual's sound. But it is often a bleak and shocking experience for a student to hear himself or herself on tape. The shock, I have found, can be severe and off-putting. Very few people like or know the sound of their own voice. Unless they are hearing themselves on a fine, expensive machine their voice will sound much thinner and less resonant than it really is. Most cheap cassette recorders cannot capture the voice's fullness and resonance. More importantly, none of us hear ourselves as the world does. Our ears are inside our head, so our perceptions are of inner sound and not the outer sound heard by everyone else.

The most destructive act I can think of doing as a teacher is to reveal to an individual all of the voice and speech flaws at once. If I did that he or she would never open their mouth again. Yet this is a fairly common tactic with which I don't agree. I usually deal with the most immediate problems at once, trying to pinpoint the root of a vocal block so it is quickly freed and so that the individual has the confidence to carry the work further into the system. I like to give someone instant control over their own voice and not leave them with a sense that I have control over it. The connected nature of voice work means that righting one problem will lead to correcting others in turn. However, if an individual begins to work with a negative fear of how they sound on a recording the work may get immediately blocked and resistance will set in. I have seen too many students become depressed and be on the point of giving up work after hearing themselves on these tapes. Just recently a student hearing himself on tape said: 'No wonder no one listens to me, I sound so dead!'

As a teacher and voice coach I am all too aware that once a speaker begins to listen to himself or herself speak he or she has sealed all effective communication with the kiss of death. If you are listening to yourself in the act of speaking you hear little else. Most of us have been at gatherings where a 'professional' speaker might witter on happily listening to the sound of their own voice but not listening to anyone else in the room. Talk to any actor who has had to work on-stage opposite an obsessive self-listener and you will quickly hear a litany of criticisms and complaints. I think the use of tape recorders in voice and speech work helps spawn this habit. It certainly does for radio actors who frequently come to me for help in breaking the habit. It is easy to fall into this habit if you work with headphones on, listening to yourself simultaneously as you speak. Equally true are the tape recordings that frequently accompany speech and voice manuals and leave the impression that there is only one right way to sound.

But putting aside my own suspicions, the tape recorder, the telephone answering machine, film, radio, television and video are facts of communication in life nowadays. We use them often to record our voices. So here are some tips for areas of work that may help you use them more effectively. Recording may uncover habits that deny positive communication:

- *Pace*: Many fast or slow speakers are positively startled when they first hear the pace of their speech on tape. A fair amount of recording can be necessary to convince someone that the pace is out of sync. The person then begins to realise how hard it is for listeners to follow them. In this instance a tape can uncover a correctable habit. Most of us can cope with about forty-five seconds to one minute of listening to unvarying pace. But if you are made to sit through five whole minutes of listening to your own pace it might shock you. Think of what it does to a listener. This is one area where you can make decisive alterations once the habit of 'ceaseless pace' is revealed.
- *Articulation*: Just to hear either the absence or dropping of consonants or vowels, or over-articulated speech is enough to make anyone realise how these habits block and divert the listener from what we have to say. Certain consonants suffer especially on tape recordings: 's', 'sh', 'p', 't', 'k'. Vowels frequently get swallowed or overwhelm the utterance. Tapes

exaggerate these distortions because these habits become electronically amplified. So you must be careful about testing the severity of the habit by this means.

- *The Falling Line*: The missed beginnings or ends of words are frequently obvious on tape. The falling line will be heard as the energy of a sentence drops towards its end or we run out of breath before we are finished. Volume and notes will diminish. If a speaker is not starting or finishing a word with the proper articulation this will also be evident.

- *Range*: The lack or overuse of range – the note changes in the voice – is something a good tape recorder can catch. The lack of range is another shock for most individuals who frequently react: 'I sound so boring!' Too much range might excite someone more into believing they have a fascinating voice but we must be careful to link it to meaning and sense. Are both being made as we switch from note to note?

- *Repetition*: Many professional speakers have no idea how often they repeat themselves or clutter their speech with useless phrases or sounds. All of us rely on stock phrases or sounds to use as interjections, plugs for pauses and fillers for thinking time. The 'mmm', 'um', 'ah' and 'uh-huh' sounds are some of these, but also the phrases, 'actually'; 'you know what I mean'; 'as a matter of fact'; 'well'; 'you see'; 'okay'; 'rather'; 'but in point of fact'; 'hopefully'. The list really can stretch on and on no matter what language you speak. Hearing them on tape can tell a speaker just how distracting these repetitions and useless interjections can be. Be careful about discarding them altogether, however. Some of these can be charming and effective if used selectively.

- *Energy and Interest*: Sometimes a student is so vocally contained that they cannot believe that their energy and passion is not coming through in what they say. Nothing vocally reveals the colour of their imagination. This is a problem area which is difficult to trap on tape early on and probably best identified more positively once an individual has begun to free and place the voice effectively and show some liveliness. It is a useful technique to stimulate speakers who refuse to move away from a 'cool' and laid-back habit and must confront the tedium of their delivery. It also uncovers other habits. Through this means at the Central School I was forced to confront how arrogant and uncaring I sounded. I believed that a listener should come to me but was forced to realise that I put listeners off by sounding

dismissive. From that lesson I could start to work on
focusing and freeing my voice.

- *Stress, Pronunciation and Inflection*: All these are usefully
  tackled on tape, as is the learning of any accent, dialect or
  foreign language. You should not be encouraged to mimic
  the sound but to capture the musical stress, rhythm, placing
  and inflection of it. To learn any accent you must be
  constantly exposed to its sound. This is particularly true of
  English RP where there is not a sufficient number of speakers of it in a group. We lose the flow and sense of the accent
  when the sound of it is absent or speakers stop speaking it.
  Listening to fine verse speakers on tape will also help you
  to feel the pulse of iambic pentameter in vocal action.
- *Sight-Reading*: You can improve your sight-reading by
  doing it into a tape recorder and playing back the results.
  Don't censor yourself as you speak; do it for a listener, not
  the machine. Allow the flow of the reading to develop fully
  before stopping and listening to the results. Go for the sense
  of what you are saying rather than the manner of speaking it.
- *Rehearsal*: Many singers will use tape recorders for ear
  training and learning songs. Speakers will use them to
  learn speeches. This seems helpful enough although I am
  wary about settling in to a strict and unvarying repetition
  of a sound or text. This method can tamper with a singer's
  or speaker's creativity by pre-setting an interpretation that
  is in danger of becoming fixed. I do know of dyslexic actors
  who learn parts from hearing them on tape recorders. For
  them to struggle word for word from a script disturbs and
  confuses the flow of their thought. So in this instance, tape
  recorders are a valuable rehearsal tool, but be careful to
  learn the text as neutrally as possible, avoiding the influence
  of another speaker's inflection, rhythm or stresses that
  might hinder your own 'reading' of the part.
- *Breath*: To hear yourself breathe on tape can sometimes
  uncover rushed, snatched, high or unfulfilled breaths. This
  kind of breathing may work for normal conversation and
  sometimes on-stage but will be an impediment on radio,
  film and television where the sensitivity of the recording
  equipment will pick up every breath you take. Always
  remember that the microphone is cruel rather than kind
  to speakers, amplifying and exposing every restrictive habit
  in your voice, breath and speech. So, as a final piece of
  advice, be careful about how, when, why and where you
  work on electronic recordings of the voice in action.

Assessing Vocal Demands and Preparing for Them

If you have already assessed a vocal demand looming up in front of you and are worried or apprehensive about how you will handle the challenge, you have already begun to prepare. Perhaps you have to deliver a crucial speech or play King Lear on the stage of the Olivier Theatre. Perhaps the demand involves shifting an accent or singing a song, speaking in different size spaces or to new crowds, going from an electronic medium – television or film – back to the stage. Whatever the situation confronting you, start by recognising you are worried and begin to assess why and which parts of you will require work to get the job done. It is best to make your own check-list of things to troubleshoot, but here are some things to keep in mind as you prepare:

- Even a well-trained and well-conditioned voice begins to lose its flexibility and muscularity two weeks after its last stretching. It can take up to ten days to get it back on form. The two main areas of work that suffer immediately from lack of exercise are: 1) breath support and capacity and 2) clarity of articulation. Just notice, for instance, how sloppy your articulation becomes after only one day of not speaking. Search through the exercises above to isolate those which can be useful to overcome these handicaps.
- Are you worried about whether your nerves will be out of control? Make a list of those parts of the body where you are likely to suffer from tension: jaw, neck, shoulders, breath, pace of speech, projection, being either too loud or too soft, etc. Use the exercises above to construct a workout that will tackle the specific tension and relieve it. Do deep breath work and much floor work to release any potential problems, always reminding yourself to breathe.
- If your voice is moving from work in a small, confined studio to a large stage or from intimate work on radio, television or film to the theatre, breath capacity and vocal strength must be built up. Use placing exercises to focus the voice within a new volume of space. Your articulation may also need sharpening in relation to the new vocal demand even if your speech is quite clear. Heading your list of needs may be the phrase 'Will they hear me?' Voice and speech take quite a bit of honing, especially for events like

important board meetings where every word counts and the time to put across a crucial point is limited.

- If you will be expected to read a text out loud – for an audition or public recitation, for instance – make yourself sight-read once or twice a day during the week leading up to the event. You cannot prepare for reading out loud by reading silently. See the section above on Sight-Readings or Cold Readings (p 275) for further tips.

- If you are going to rehearse a difficult text by a writer who intimidates you, get hold of other plays by that playwright and read chunks of them out loud. The language centre of the brain sometimes needs oiling with difficult and particular sorts of texts in order to operate efficiently.

- If you are frightened of singing you must sing, even if it just means humming along with the radio. Sing anything you like in order to liberate the singing imagination. You will then have to do all the extended voice exercises to sharpen up the strength of your technique.

- Start listening in detail to any accent you might be required to learn. See if you can equate the way voice, speech and accent work together. Hum the tune of the accent. Recruit speakers of the accent, talk to them, tape the way they talk.

- If the part you are about to play demands huge emotional commitment or is about sustaining a role over a stretch of three hours on-stage in a large space, go into training several weeks in advance. Do all the exercises outlined earlier – from basic through to extended – in order to start work vocally fit. Be honest with yourself about problems and habits. Some actors don't work their voices before they tackle a challenging part almost as an excuse for not succeeding. That way they can always blame their voice for the failure.

- If you have been ill or are fatigued, rest the voice and then begin to work up your capacity gradually. Never underestimate the debilitating effects of an illness on the voice.

- If the part you are going to play is emotionally demanding then work your way through all the extended exercises where heightened emotions are accounted for.

Marking and Saving the Voice

'Mark' or 'marking' is the term given to the way in which singers save their voices from tiring, usually in rehearsals or technical preparations before an actual performance. Marking helps to contain and preserve vocal energy. Professional singers have strict trade union safeguards to protect them from overextending their voices but many still use a technique of marking as further insurance. Actors, who have no similar union safeguards to protect their voices, will rehearse all day and perform all evening on a full voice. So they have either learnt by instinct to mark their voices or must learn how to do it. Even the most skilled and trained voices will tire if worked constantly. Problems most often arise when a speaker has to repeat a vocally heightened moment again and again in rehearsals of different sorts.

There is always a danger that actors and singers can become too precious about their voices. Concentrating on saving a voice too much can create tension and panic. Of course one has to be very careful here, yet I do think there are times when to mark can be selfish to others and useless to yourself. It can hamper the work of other on-stage performers, technicians setting sound levels and cues which a marked voice can throw off (particularly if you are wearing a body mike) or stage managers directing other business on-stage. Marking does not help you to feel an unknown space or auditorium during a final dress rehearsal or preparation unless you can move up to full voice.

Unfortunately there are many basic misconceptions about saving the voice which can actually tire it further and even damage it:

- *Whispering*: This is really deadly for the voice. It tires it out, strains it and produces phlegm. Not quite as bad, but moving in the same direction, is any level of devoicing. So many people with sore throats or infections whisper and devoice, thinking they are saving their voices. It only aggravates the voice.
- *Not Supporting*: Another popular misconception is that by going off support we will save the voice from tiring. We avoid putting power into the voice, thinking it a relief.

However, you *always need to support*. It is precisely when you go off support that you invite calamity.

- *Mumbling*: People will frequently mumble into their throat as a form of marking, thinking that the abrasive containment of sound is protecting them. Apart from imploding energy in the throat you also make it very hard for others to hear you. Frequently you just have to repeat what you said, only louder and more frequently.

- *Over-Relaxing*: Many of us have the idea that by physically surrendering, slumping or falling off-centre we will preserve energy, but I maintain that we have to work harder to get the energy to speak when we over-relax. Many actors will flop or collapse in a chair or on the floor when not working in a scene, falling into a habitual slump that carries over into speaking. You have to use more energy to rise from the slump than you would use sustaining yourself in a centred position. Remember that you can be relaxed *and* centred at the same time.

Bearing these in mind, here are some more positive habits to think about as marking or saving techniques:

- Stay on the whole voice all of the time.
- Support gently but firmly, not using a large volume. Use just the breath and support needed to be clear.
- Stay up, physically centred and strong, particularly in the spine, chest, shoulders and neck.
- Put more of your energy into articulation so you remain clear. Transfer vocal energy into speaking energy.
- Place the voice very lightly into the head resonator so that you 'think' the voice right up through the skull. This will relieve pressure in the throat. You will discover the correct note to pitch the voice around because you will sense relief in the throat as you bypass the centre of a tiring voice. The position should be clear, light and easy.

Finally, the best advice I can give on saving the voice is don't vocalise fully unless you have to. Mark with the above principles in mind.

Also learn to relax the voice and give it time off. Even

forty-five minutes of relaxation and short periods of deep breathing done silently will rest the voice.

The situations that do not help a sick or tiring voice are perhaps obvious, but even professional performers and speakers don't always make the connections: smoking, drinking alcohol, speaking in dry, smoky atmospheres, conversing over loud sounds and music, shouting at sports matches, etc. All of these harm a well-tempered voice and are ludicrous activities for you if you are worried about keeping your voice safe and strong.

General Health and Care of the Voice

I do realise that this section might seem pedantic, fussy and occasionally alarmist. I don't want to seem that way about a process which, when working naturally, is robust, powerful, resilient and healthy. So these notes are really for consulting when something goes amiss, a 'do' and 'don't' list of what to avoid and what remedies might be available for a sick or lost voice.

When people have vocal complaints they usually include one of the following:

- a hoarse, scratchy voice not associated with a cold or illness but which lasts
- changes in vocal quality that are noticeable to family, friends and associates
- a radical change in vocal pitch
- breaks in the voice, like sudden shifts in pitch while speaking
- vocal fatigue for no apparent reason or the inability to speak as usual
- tremors in the voice
- pain while speaking
- loss of voice

Most problems related to the voice can now be treated more successfully than ever. Otolaryngologists, a recently created subspecies of voice physician, have made remarkable strides in both diagnosing and providing treatment for severe vocal problems. Through the use of special instruments they can actually watch the voice in action to see how it is peforming, going wrong and can be corrected through physiotherapy or medicine. That should come as a comfort to any chronic sufferer of vocal problems. Places like the Voice Clinic at London's Middlesex Hospital and other similar clinics around the world provide treatment which a decade ago was unavailable to the same extent. Physicians generally agree that most difficult voice problems can be corrected without surgery. Thinking about the voice and knowing it can suffer will help prevent much future pain.

A. List of Critical Warnings

- Never try to vocalise through pain, soreness or discomfort in the throat. Pain is usually a warning that you are doing potential damage to your system. If you continue trying to use your voice while it hurts you may lose it permanently or irreparably diminish its range and flexibility. You can also develop blisters or nodes on the vocal cords which diminish the voice's potential forever. Let pain stop you cold and silence you rather than push you on. Never scream till it hurts.

- A loose but useful check as to whether or not you have hurt your voice is to vocalise very gently on a 'ha' sound. But keep the sound as quiet as possible. You will notice, if the cord is swollen, that the voice wavers more than usual. Many people do not feel vocal damage for several hours. The adrenalin and excitement felt during and immediately after a performance or speaking engagement can mean you won't notice the pain until hours afterwards. I usually get panic calls the morning after the voice has gone.

- Always try to speak 'above' any soreness or pain. This also applies to speaking through a cold. If you hum down through your voice you will find the holes or gaps any abuse or infection has caused. Place the voice just above a gap, closest to centre. Keep the voice placed in the

facial mask so you pick up maximum resonance, placing
so that a 'smaller' voice carries the relief rather than the
main load-bearing weight of a full voice.

- Never whisper to save your voice. This is the one remedy
most lay people frequently resort to as relief for an ailing
voice. *It does not help*. It fact it tires the voice and leads
to further damage. Whispering is a ragged use of the vocal
cords that will only irritate an infection and produce more
damage.

- Some vocal problems are related to indigestion. The cords
become infected by belched gas. Stomach problems, heart-
burn, ulcers and chronic indigestion can be a sore point.
If you cannot home in on any other problem this may be
one you have missed.

- Prevent the voice from drying out. Drink water but avoid
iced water; as many as ten to twelve glasses a day. Like
any piece of machinery with working parts, the vocal
system needs lots of lubrication. Dryness in the throat
produces a much frailer voice that is more vulnerable to
abuse. Many air-conditioned and air-filtered buildings and
aeroplanes seem to be engineered to prevent the voice from
working properly. You need an extra amount of water to
keep the voice working in these arid environments. This
is equally true if you have to speak under hot lights in a
theatre or studio. You can always tell if your body, and
consequently your voice, is adequately hydrated with fluid
by the colour of your urine – the paler the better! Water
– not tea or coffee – hydrates the voice best.

- Alcohol does not help the voice. Unlike water it dehydrates
the system, drying out the voice even further. The myth of
port does not work either. Alcohol may relax you enough to
take the pressure of a habit off the voice, it may leave you
freer physically, but it then adds a problem. I am anxious
about any substance that prevents a speaker from feeling
pain in the voice. Pain alerts us and alcohol dulls the early
warning alert system. Alcohol also dulls and numbs the
intricate workings of the speech muscles, leading to that
familiar slurring of words.

- Smoking eventually harms the voice, too. Breath capacity
suffers first. Many smokers – some excellent, well-spoken
actors – manage to get away with the habit for decades
and stay in fine voice before the wearing effects begin to
show. Some smokers even enjoy the husky, phlegmy sound
that smoking induces. Often it is the passive smokers in

the dressing room who suffer most. If you are a smoker and intend to quit the habit, allow your voice six to eight weeks to adjust without taking on too demanding a vocal task. You will experience some changes, like the coughing of phlegm, and will need the time to get the voice back in balance. The rewards will be a much clearer, more flexible voice and particularly breath.

- Marijuana – like smog and air pollution – is dangerous to the voice because it burns at such a high temperature that the voice suffers from the heat and toxicity. Gusts of hot air waft over the vocal cords in a quite disastrous way. It also deadens any awareness of pain in the throat. I have worked with several rock stars with excellent musical ability who swear that marijuana has ruined their voices. If you must have it then drink lots of water during and after or use a hookah. None of this advice, however, is an endorsement of the habit!

- Other drugs, like cocaine, will cause the nasal membranes to deteriorate and quickly destroy the voice. They are deadly. Your nose will drip constantly and you will find yourself resorting to a fast, tight, snorting breath that limits range. Altogether, drugs simply abuse the voice and offer no enhancements.

- If you are a chronic cougher be careful. Avoid clearing your throat too often when speaking. It does not help but only creates more tension and mucus. Try swallowing or thinking of a yawn instead of coughing and clearing.

- Mucus is often a sign of vocal abuse as the body secretes a lubricant to ward off danger. Restricting dairy products or red wine will help reduce it to some degree. Avoid all dairy products, especially milk, six to eight hours before extended speaking or singing; they generate the flow of mucus. Garlic will help clear mucus.

- I don't like using drugs on the voice to get a speaker through pain. All painkillers and sleeping pills cut you off from monitoring damage that might be created. Cold tablets, antihistamines and decongestants often dry the voice so much that it is frail and susceptible to push and strain. Drink plenty of water if you are taking these. I believe it is generally agreed by physicians that common aspirin makes the vocal cords rawer and for this reason laryngologists never prescribe it for sore throats. If you take penicillin, tranquillisers or any kind of drug, increase your intake of water. Keep the system flushed and lubricated.

- Gargles and throat pastilles are sometime useful for *temporary* relief but not if they dull the throat to the extent of not feeling pain as you speak in performance. Gargling, in fact, can aggravate the throat to further pain. A steaming drink of lemon and honey is probably the safest relaxant before or while using your voice, also onion soup and raw garlic. Steer clear of iced drinks.
- Inhale steam – either natural steam from a kettle or induced steam from a vaporiser – for five minutes every three to four hours. Steam always frees the voice which is one of the reasons we sound good when we sing in the shower. Inhaling herbal remedies like Olbas Oil or Friar's Balsam or rubbing them on the throat and chest is good but drink plenty of water if the remedy contains menthol or peppermint which will dry the throat. Always check the contents and warnings on any inhalant.
- You should also know that throat disorders and diseases like thyroiditis, cancer, pulmonary disorders, diabetes, even neuromuscular disorders like multiple sclerosis can work against the voice. Whiplash and neck injuries plus traumas in other parts of the body infect the voice as well. All this last group contains very serious warnings indeed.

B. Loss of Voice

In extreme cases of vocal pain, infection or loss of voice you must give your voice a total rest of two to five days. By that I mean not speaking, and definitely not whispering.

The voice needs time to heal. If not fully recovered within a week then seek medical advice from a physician or specialist like a laryngologist. Don't keep resorting to home remedies but take the loss seriously. Loss of voice without pain can also be very alarming. The body has probably taken action to prevent the voice being used to protect it from further abuse. Again, seek medical attention if this kind of condition persists for more than a few days.

Common vocal loss while working extensively as an actor or speaker may be caused by your vocal production being blocked or disconnected. It is not necessarily a chronic but merely a habitual loss. Check for signs of this as follows:

- *Head*: Is it tucked in too tightly or pushed too far forwards, creating throat constriction?
- *Spine*: Is it slumped so that you cannot safely align the body to free the throat?
- *Shoulders*: Are they lifted and tense? Pulled back or rounded? Each of these positions restricts the breath and throat.
- *Breath*: Is it too shallow and insufficient to support the vocal challenge? Is it disconnected from the voice? Too irregular?
- *Voice*: Are you pushing or pulling too hard? Feeling abuse in the throat? Are you clamping down or holding it? Are you using too much glottal attack; experiencing a pronounced click or kick as you begin a sound? Are you shouting or screaming more than usual?
- *Jaw*: Is it tight or clenched, causing the throat to tighten?

Answering 'yes' to any of these questions may help you to diagnose a common vocal problem that will not require medical attention. Try to release the problem with an exercise. What I hope you will begin to realise is the need to break free of restrictive habits. Deep relaxation helps in many instances because it returns us to centre so we can rebuild the voice naturally. If you are resting from loss of voice, keep trying to reduce the tension with deep relaxation exercises, especially before going to sleep. Discomfort in vocal production makes all of us uneasy and anxious, especially when we have to produce sound daily. The problem may be superficial or deep. So follow the above guide for quick checks, but seek medical advice for persistent problems.

Vocal loss can also come from a host of other causes: fatigue, dieting, depression, recuperating from an illness, being silent for long periods. Look at your whole physical and mental well-being. Any weakening or shock to the system can be evidenced in the voice. Some women experience vocal problems during monthly menstruation when their body undergoes changes, and during menopause as well. Emotional stresses like loss or bereavement, sudden rages, fits, constant preoccupations with personal affairs, marital or professional strife, rejection, even the thought of oncoming stress and pure nervousness are likely to affect the voice. Look at the problems carefully. They may need sorting out by other qualified counsellors or therapists if any of these problems persist beyond your ability to control them.

The voice needs to rest between extreme challenges. It also needs as much relaxation as possible and the reminder to support fully.

C. Regular Prevention

The more you know about your voice and are able to exercise and finely tune it, the more likely your awareness will be if anything goes wrong. Regular vocal workouts of the kind provided in the exercises throughout this part of the book will keep the voice tuned and healthy. Remember to always warm up the voice for any challenge or difficult circumstance. Be aware of how the voice must perform and gear the warm-up accordingly. Never take this process for granted or ignore it. The voice needs this massaging and care. Remember that throughout the day the voice warms up naturally. It is more oiled by late afternoon and evening. A morning voice needs more concentrated work to get it going.

Dental care is of vital importance in maintaining good placing speech. Dental work will affect your speech and if you have major bracing you will need to replace the positions of your consonants and vowels after the braces are removed. This is always a difficulty for young people which should not be underestimated. Dentures and capping also create speech problems, sometimes requiring new speech technique. Infected teeth and nasal infections can lead to throat infections and give the voice trouble. Ear infections can also affect the voice.

Any physical injury or surgery (particularly around the face, neck, shoulders, sternum, ribcage, spine, abdomen or knees) can lead to the domino cause and effect that eventually reaches the voice. Take every injury you have ever had to heart and examine whether or not it might have influenced your voice and the way you speak. After you have recuperated from a new injury, begin to work the area and reconnect it to the whole working of the voice. Do this gently and with patience.

Finally, you will be the one who best gets to know your own voice and will sound the alarm when necessary. Let the bell sound sooner rather than later if your voice suffers trouble which you know you cannot cope with and cure through exercise alone. The most alarming problems I have encountered have always been suffered by professional performers who have *no* basic knowledge of how their voices operate or how they can manipulate them to prevent injury. They have lost their voices through helplessness and sheer blunders. I know singers who can no longer speak, speakers who can only croak and actors whose lack of training causes them to inject their throats with pain-killing drugs before taking the stage, all because they have suffered irreparable damage through neglect and ignorance. Please, don't join their ranks. Trained speakers acquire the right to speak because they have learned through diligent practice how to work with their voice and keep themselves healthy and safe from harm.

Professional Voice Training

The final words of this section are really intended for extended professional voice users and for students and teachers preparing for a career in voice work. All other speakers can be effective and efficient with their voices without going further into these more athletic areas of training. Any voice, I believe, can be rapidly changed and improved within weeks for the average range of vocal tasks. It takes longer, however, to train and mould a first-class professional voice for acting, singing and public speaking. It is even harder, I think, to train good teachers of the voice.

Having never encountered a 'normal' voice or a 'normal' process of training I am wondering why I am writing this section at all. I think I am doing it to throw out a few ideas and answer the sort of questions I am most frequently asked like: 'How long does it take to train a voice?'; 'How do you become a classical speaker?'; 'What are the formats and phases of training like?'

I am constantly shifting points of view about how to answer these questions. What makes voice work and working with voices so thrilling is its 'unknown' and changing character. It is crucially linked to individuals and their voices. It is very much a one-on-one process. Progress is variable and sometimes sudden. The fact of the matter is that there is *no* normal development or phase of training. Any individual works according to his or her own separate will and desire. I find that a constant stimulation and challenge. For the educationalist, however, structures are a must so I have listed some personal thoughts that will remain open to change and may be hotly disputed by others:

- There is no such animal as a bad or untrainable voice or ear. It is very possible that I or someone else may not be the teacher for certain individuals, yet if someone is willing to improve they can improve. Nothing about voice work excludes anyone apart from their own restrictive habits.
- It is generally agreed that it takes three to four years to train a voice to cope with professional demands (varying spaces, performance conditions and texts) and to instil professional attitudes. Having said that, I have worked with voice 'virgins' (i.e. those never previously subjected to any sort of voice work) who have grasped principles so quickly and worked at them so concentratedly that they have achieved in three months what it normally takes people three years to accomplish. (Six of these students have been trained dancers so were presumably in touch with their bodies and knew how to connect physically through self-discipline.) Conversely, I have felt enormous failures after three years' work with people who showed marvellous potential and who were still locked and blocked vocally after all that time. I have even worked over fourteen years with some people who after that long a period of training finally make connections that click in their bodies. It sometimes takes time for the work to gain

the right perspective. A previous experience with a voice teacher may disrupt a person's progress and take time to sort out.

- Some students can understand and accomplish an exercise on the first try, others take years to get it right. I can give the same note again and again but it still does not activate that crucial link between energy and spirit. This is why the work must ultimately become personalised and be understood from the individual's point of view.

- I adamantly believe that certain areas of technical work must be covered before long-lasting results show in a voice. Work on the body, breath, vocal freedom and placing must take its course and become second nature through practice. Being specific I would say that eighty per cent of students take a full year to grasp the basics that I outline in this book before turning them into organic habits. So I do see vocal improvement as being a result of constant work done over a period of time. You have to allow for the occasional lapses and slips and then the recoveries.

- The abandonment of restrictive habits, likewise, takes about a year. Again, this depends on the habit, where it is located in the body and how long it has remained embedded. Is it physical or psychological? It also depends on the willingness of an individual to surrender it or live with it through choice. An individual needs to be monitored so that his or her body takes on organic shape through centring, freeing and natural positioning. This is a different process for everyone and may require allied work with other sorts of teachers and therapies.

- *Repetition of exercises and techniques is the only way to change a voice permanently.* I don't believe in resorting to tricks as a teacher or to quick 'band-aid' fixes. The exercises that work best have to be done again and again to keep the instrument oiled and ready for work. The voice is like a high performance vehicle that needs tuning. Remember that a slip in routine can take the voice two weeks to restore to prime rhythm. I wish I could suggest an easier or a more imaginative alternative but the hard repetition of work has to be done like any athletic routine in order for the benefit to show. Emphasis of work has to be geared to each individual's need, so place it where it is needed most. Progress through a phase can vary from person to person. Generally more work tends to be done on articulation and freeing.

- I think it can be depressing and ultimately negative either to impose too demanding a text too early in training or place a voice novice on the stage of a huge auditorium before they have developed enough technique and the capacity to cope. In both instances individuals usually react by pushing and retreating into restrictive habits. We easily forget what we have patiently learned if we panic. There is always a danger of pushing progress past its threshold. I never give a student a heightened text to work on or allow them into a large theatre until the second year of training.

- There is always a moment as you 'open' a voice during training when the instrument is frailer and more prone to damage than it was before the start of training. This is because muscles are readjusting and coordinating throughout the body. This phase usually occurs about three months into training and can last a further three months. It is a sensitive period that the voice teacher must monitor carefully. Students who have sung in a rock band before training, for instance, must be cautioned not to do so during this phase of training.

- Five to seven hours of organised voice classes per week seem to be the minimal requirement for student professionals who ought to then supplement that with their own work each day.

- Ten solid minutes of voice work each day is a better regime than two hours once a week. The regular nature of the work disperses habits more uniformly than one massive assault on them. By all means try extended work provided that you stick to one regular routine. Improvements will come within weeks.

- During the second year of training it gets progressively more difficult to reach and help someone unless a student is prepared to take ownership of their voice, using and sounding it as they should by this point. The initial year is much more one-sided as a student digests, exercises and uses practical and technical information. After that point the burden falls more and more on the individual to set the pace.

- The first year of work is about articulating, grasping and putting into practice good principles of voice. The second year is about applying them widely to your own language and to texts of various sorts. The third year

298 The Right to Speak

consolidates all areas of work plus 'forgetting' the work as the individual voice emerges on its own. You should only need to return to the work when a problem arises.

- I was trained with the notion that some speakers are destined to be better classical performers than others, that some have better voices for verse speaking than others. I don't believe this any more. I have seen too many so-called 'unpromising' individuals make huge creative leaps and end up as excellent classical speakers. In voice work pigeon-holing can be as dangerous as prejudging.

- I know now that if I am really listening and responding to a student or class in action I might have to abandon a preplanned lesson in order to do something more immediate. I may enter a class to work on 'range' but end up dealing with 'support' because the student or class is not ready yet for range exercises. I generally do not take a class into screaming until the second year but have done it in the first year when groups have shown readiness to venture in this direction.

- Although there are objective criteria guidelines you can work from, I don't believe in the end that I can teach someone to 'teach voice' because the work is so very personal and subjective. You pick and choose what works best for you. There are wonderful voice exercises which I cannot teach or use because they are outside my experience, knowledge and personality. I rarely resort to jargon when I work although voice classes can be full of it. The lesson to derive from this is to teach what you know and have experienced yourself. Your job is to comfort and connect with someone. Never trust the purely theoretical when doing your own practical work. You can easily mislead others at their peril.

- I don't think there would have been a need for voice coaches in the time of Shakespeare. I think his culture was far more oral and naturally took the right to speak as given. The voice then may have been under far less stress, competing with far fewer sounds than those of our modern, overpopulated, industrialised planet. Today, however, actors and professional speakers need constant work on their voices to keep all sorts of pressures and negative forces at bay. Even with the right to speak the modern voice can never veer too far from the right kind of work.

Some Final Thoughts

As you do all the thinking and work I have outlined in both parts of this book, the main things to always keep foremost in your mind are: how your voice works naturally; how habits prevent it from working; where habits have taken root both inside and out and how these habits can be brought under control.

Voice work requires vigilance and a ceaseless desire to explore yourself and your physical make-up. It also takes courage.

Index